The Case for
SAME-SEX MARRIAGE

ALSO BY THE AUTHOR

Dynamic Statutory Interpretation

The Case for
SAME-SEX MARRIAGE

From Sexual Liberty to Civilized Commitment

WILLIAM N. ESKRIDGE, JR.

THE FREE PRESS

New York   London   Toronto   Sydney   Tokyo   Singapore

THE FREE PRESS
A Division of Simon & Schuster Inc.
1230 Avenue of the Americas
New York, NY 10020

THE FREE PRESS and colophon are trademarks
of Simon & Schuster Inc.

Designed by Carla Bolte

Manufactured in the United States of America

10 9 8 7 6 5 4 3 2 1

Library of Congress Cataloging-in-Publication Data

Eskridge, William N.
    The case for same-sex marriage: from sexual liberty to civilized
  commitment / William N. Eskridge, Jr.
        p.   cm.
    Includes bibliographical references (p.   ) and index.
    ISBN 0-684-82404-3
    1. Gay marriage—United States.   2. Gay couples—Legal status.
  laws, etc.—United States.   I. Title.
HQ76.3.U5E85   1996
306.84—dc20   95-51540
                                                                  CIP

For Pedie

CONTENTS

1

CIVILIZING GAYS,
CIVILIZING STRAIGHTS

Americans are romantics. We fantasize about finding our "one true love." For most of us, that fantasy culminates in a proposal of marriage, a religious ceremony, and a honeymoon. In the fairy-tale romance the couple live happily ever after, sharing mutual love, perhaps creating a larger family, and parting only at death. Reality is seldom as good as fantasy, but the attractions of marriage maintain a powerful hold on our imagination and aspirations.

Ninia Baehr shares that American dream. She is engagingly intellectual, a woman of personal as well as physical beauty. Fawnlike, she has brown eyes that engulf you with understanding and alert sympathy. Slight of build, Ninia is anything but frail. She is enthusiastically engaged with life. Spiritually, she is something of a romantic. Now thirty-four years old, she wants to be able to look back on her life and know that there was someone she loved so much that she was willing to pledge lifelong fidelity to that person. Although Ninia had dated ardently in her twenties, she never found the right person. Then her mother introduced her to Genora Dancel in June 1990.

Genora has happy, dancing brown eyes. Her broad, dimpled smile and friendly, easygoing disposition belie her serious work ethic. For much of her adulthood she has held down more than one job. In 1990 one of her jobs was as a technical engineer for KHET, the PBS television station in Honolulu. There she met C. J. Baehr (Ninia's mother), who worked in another department. They liked one another, and C. J. told Genora about her wonderful daughter Ninia, a lesbian (Genora made a mental note of that). One day Genora was waiting outside the station when Ninia came to pick her mother up. Upon seeing Ninia in the car, Genora was impressed with her beauty. When Ninia saw Genora, she thought, "Oh my God, this woman is perfect!" On the ride home Ninia asked her mother about the woman she had just seen. C. J. explained, "Oh that's my wonderful friend Genora; I hear she's a lesbian. I'd be happy if she were your friend, too. Why don't you meet her?" Ninia was interested.

Several days later Ninia came calling at KHET. Both she and Genora were exceedingly nervous, but mutual friends say that sparks were flying from both sides. The two women went out for drinks. That night Genora called C. J. for advice about how to proceed, but Ninia herself happened to answer the phone. They spoke for hours, indicating to each that this was a relationship that needed to be explored. In the course of dating for several months Ninia and Genora developed a warm friendship and found they had many interests in common. Mainly they were delighted just to be with one another. Each thought of the other when they were apart, looked forward to their time together, and realized that it was becoming increasingly hard to imagine life without the other.

When Genora traveled to San Diego for a technical training course in September, the pain of separation for each woman was intense. Ninia called every day. During one call Genora said, "When I get back, you'll know that I love you." She was referring to an engagement ring she had purchased, a stunning arrangement of three rubies and two diamonds set in gold. Genora paused and then popped the question, "Will you marry me?" A microsecond later Ninia answered, "Yes!"

At this point most couples would announce their engagement to their families, friends, and coworkers. Most couples would set a date for the ceremony and obtain a marriage license. These steps were not possible for Ninia and Genora. Lesbian and gay couples are not allowed to marry in the United States.

Still, Genora Dancel and Ninia Baehr were prepared to consider themselves committed to each other. They began to plan their life together. As one step in that plan they decided to change their life insurance policies to name one another as beneficiaries. To their surprise, the insurance companies refused to make the change, allowing only legal spouses, not unmarried partners, to be named as beneficiaries. The couple sought advice about this policy from Bill Woods, a lawyer and longtime gay activist in Honolulu. Woods mentioned that Hawaii's discrimination against same-sex couples might be vulnerable to constitutional challenge and asked if Baehr and Dancel were interested in such a challenge. He suggested that other couples might be interested, too.

This was a tough decision for Baehr and Dancel. The couple strongly support domestic partnership laws, through which same-sex couples can register their partnership and obtain some of the legal benefits of marriage. The question was, should they work for Honolulu or the state of Hawaii to adopt a domestic partnership law, or should they leapfrog domestic partnership and seek full marriage rights? As a feminist scholar and historian, Baehr was aware that many women consider marriage to be an oppressive institution that has traditionally bound women to subordinate roles. Her own parents' marriage had ended in divorce, and the motive of a relative who was about to enter into a marriage had more to do with an unexpected pregnancy than lifelong love and commitment. Baehr had no illusions about marriage, but it galled her that so much fuss is made over the most ill-fated different-sex marriage while the most committed same-sex couple is typically ignored. "Why shouldn't Genora and I have the same right as everyone else?" she asked.

For Dancel it was less the feminist criticisms of marriage than the publicity from a lawsuit that presented a problem. In the closet to her family and most of her coworkers, Dancel was apprehensive about coming out. Would her parents still love her? Would her coworkers treat her differently, even shun her? Would she lose her job? Would she suffer public harassment? These were not hypothetical concerns. Dancel had occasionally heard vicious antihomosexual remarks from her coworkers. In light of Dancel's delicate situation, Baehr was perfectly willing to forgo the opportunity to mount a challenge against discrimination. Dancel, in turn, agreed with Baehr's view that their relationship stood on an equal footing with any heterosexual one and that they should not be ashamed of their sexuality or hide their union. "When you're told you can't get married, you feel like a second-class citizen," Dancel noted. After much soul searching, the couple notified Woods that they would be interested in participating in a constitutional challenge to Hawaii's discrimination against same-sex couples.

On December 17, 1990, Baehr and Dancel filed an application for a marriage license with the Hawaii Department of Health. They were joined by two other couples: Tammy Rodrigues and Antoinette Pregil, and Pat Lagon and Joseph Melilio. All three couples met the requirements for a marriage license except for the requirement that the applicants be of different sexes. Their view was that this discriminatory requirement is invalid and in conflict with both the Hawaii and United States Constitutions. John C. Lewin, the state's director of health, requested an opinion from the state attorney general as to the legality of denying same-sex couples state marriage licenses.

On December 27, the attorney general opined that the state's discrimination was lawful. Admitting that "the right to marry is considered to be a fundamental one" under the United States Constitution, the attorney general insisted that this fundamental right is not available to same-sex couples. Under his view, constitutional rights in this arena are limited to decisions "to marry and raise [a] child in a traditional family setting."[1] The attorney general followed the approach of the Kentucky Supreme Court, which had said in 1973, "Marriage has always been considered as the union of a man and a woman."[2]

In accord with this legal opinion, the Hawaii Department of Health wrote Baehr and Dancel on April 12, 1991, denying their application "since you are both of the same sex and for this reason are not capable of forming a valid marriage contract within the meaning of [the marriage statute]. Even if we did issue a marriage license to you, it would not be a valid marriage under Hawaii law."[3] On May 1, Baehr and Dancel, together with Rodrigues and Pregil and with Lagon and Melilio, filed their complaint seeking a declaration that the statutory exclusion of same-sex couples is invalid under either the United States Constitution or the Hawaii Constituion. The couple moved in together on the same day they initiated their lawsuit.

The trial judge upheld the exclusion, and the plaintiffs appealed to the Hawaii Supreme Court. At oral argument on September 13, 1992, some justices seemed open to their position, Baehr recalls. One justice asked the state: Isn't your policy a discrimination against gay and lesbian couples? The state admitted as much but defended the exclusion as "permissible" discrimination. The oral argument got Baehr and Dancel's hopes up, but their attorney, Dan Foley, warned them not to be too optimistic. The good news came on May 5, 1993; Foley called Baehr and Dancel to tell them that the Hawaii Supreme Court had found the exclusion discriminatory under the Hawaii Constitution.[4]

For the first time in American history a court had, even if tentatively, suggested that legally recognized marriage need not necessarily be a union between a man and a woman. The court remanded the case for a trial to determine whether the discrimination is in fact "permissible" because it is supported by a "compelling" state interest. If the trial proceeds as scheduled (later in 1996), an appeal to the Hawaii Supreme Court will likely follow.[5] If they win at trial or on appeal, Baehr and Dancel plan to get married in a joyous ceremony. Dancel's fantasy is to pledge herself atop the volcano Haleakala.

Baehr and Dancel's lawsuit is a political as well as legal event. Even if they prevail in the Hawaii courts, there will be political efforts to deprive them and other same-sex couples of their legal rights. Some groups in Hawaii want to amend the state constitution to deny lesbian, gay, and bisexual people the right to marry one another. Groups in other states want to amend their state marriage laws to ensure that same-sex marriages in Hawaii are not recognized in their states. Some members of Congress desire to negate or limit the consequences of any validation of same-sex marriages in Hawaii.

Whatever the ultimate resolution of Ninia Baehr and Genora Dancel's lawsuit, it has had the effect of putting same-sex marriage on the front burner of American public life. Steadily (sometimes stealthily, sometimes not), gay marriage is emerging as an important issue—not just in the United States but around the world. Opponents react in horror. The idea of gay marriage is itself unsettling, for it is both radical and conservative; people objecting to the legal recognition of same-sex marriages speak from both perspectives. For some, gay marriage is unnatural or abominable. For others, it is an assimilative sellout. For me—and I hope for you after you read this book—same-sex marriage is natural and just.

The initial response of many people to same-sex marriage is based on their feelings that it is unprecedented. "This just can't be! It's never been done and therefore never should be done." When all is said and done—that is, in spite of all the other arguments that can be offered (and that I intend to address)—this is the most common objection. The Hawaii attorney general relied on it, arguing that marriage has not included and, for that reason, cannot include same-sex couples. But, as I shall show early on in this book, this is a belief contradicted by history. Historical, anthropological, and ethnographic evidence of same-sex marriage in other times and other cultures is overwhelming (see chapter 2). Ancient myths are replete with same-sex unions, and same-sex intimacy was widely practiced in the cultures for which we have records. According to Judaic scripture, same-sex unions in ancient Egypt were recognized as marriages. Same-sex unions were an integral part of the cultures of classical Greece and republican Rome, and imperial Rome recognized same-sex marriages.

During the Middle Ages the Greek Orthodox and Roman Catholic Churches celebrated same-sex unions, as did imperial China (the most sophisticated culture of the time). Spanish explorers and missionaries discovered that the native cultures of the Americas valued same-sex marriages and treated them as marriages similar to different-sex ones. Marriages in the so-called *berdache* tradition of gender-crossing effeminate men and "amazon" women have been documented for dozens of other cultures in Africa, Australia, and Asia. Many African tribes have recognized what anthropologists call "woman marriage," in which a woman becomes the "female husband" to another woman. Conversely, some societies in Africa and Asia have recognized male military unions, in which "boy wives" were joined to senior warriors. Modern Western culture has been less open to same-sex unions, but American law is no stranger to same-sex marriages. Same-sex couples have been given marriage licenses throughout our history, and Native American same-sex marriages are legally valid marriages of United States citizens.

Evidence from other cultures and other times demonstrates that same-sex marriages are neither unprecedented nor unnatural. This is not to deny the modern West's hostility to same-sex unions but merely to situate that hostility in a broader perspective. To say that same-sex marriage is a novelty is true from the point of view of a twentieth-century American but is false from the point of view of a nineteenth-century Native American or African, a seventeenth-century Chinese merchant or Japanese samurai, a first-century Roman or Greek citizen, or an ancient Egyptian. Novelty, in short, is in the eye of the beholder.

Moreover, the fact that an idea is new does not mean that it is bad. This book will show the many ways in which same-sex marriage is a good institution. History suggests that same-sex marriages have served the same functions that are claimed, exclusively, for different-sex marriages. Throughout human history people have entered into same-sex unions because they loved one another and desired the intimacy that close companionship offers. Two of the most popular saints in the Middle Ages, Sergius and Bacchus, were a bonded male couple who exemplified *agape*, or Christian brotherly love. Throughout human history people have formed same-sex households for economic as well as personal reasons; nineteenth-century Chinese sisterhood households enabled women to be economically independent of men and also satisfied the women's emotional (and, sometimes, erotic) needs. Throughout human history people have raised children in same-sex households; well-to-do women in Africa became female husbands precisely for this purpose; the progeny of their female wives and male donors were considered children of the female husband.

Oddly enough, the lack of novelty is a problem some people have with same-sex marriage. For some thoughtful lesbian and gay theorists the historical evidence provides the basis for arguments against same-sex marriage: it is not new (or revolutionary) enough. Such theorists either view marriage as too rotten an institution to be acceptable for gay men and lesbians or understand the marriage option as a move toward assimilation into a culture that we should be changing (chapter 3). Such a left-wing antiassimilation argument is mirrored by a right-wing argument against assimilation. From the point of view of some straight Americans, state recognition of same-sex marriage would represent a stamp of approval for homosexual relationships, which these objectors believe should be discouraged (chapter 4). These mirror-image arguments exemplify my thesis that same-sex marriage is both conservative and radical.

My further thesis is that same-sex marriage is good for gay people and good for America, and for the same reason: it civilizes gays and it civilizes America.[a] Start with the former. For most of the twentieth century, lesbians, gay men, and bisexuals have been outlaws. The law relevant to us was the criminal code—not just sodomy prohibitions, which virtually defined us, but also disorderly conduct, lewdness, and vagrancy statutes, infractions of which led to employment and licensing penalties. The law relevant to us today is found in the civil code, most prominently in antidiscrimination statutes but increasingly in family law as well. Virtually no one in the gay and lesbian community would deny that this "civilizing" shift in the law reflects enormous progress and that such progress is incomplete until gay people enjoy the same rights and responsibilities as straight people. Marriage is the most important right the state has to offer, in part because being married entails dozens of associated rights, benefits, and obligations under state and federal law (chapter 3). As a formal matter, law's civilizing movement will not be complete until the same-sex married couple replaces the outlawed sodomite as the paradigmatic application of law to gay people.

Law's gradual decriminalization of homosexuality finds a parallel in gay lives. As we shed our outlaw status, we are increasingly integrated into (as opposed to being closeted from) the larger society and its spheres of business, religion, recreation, and education. Recognizing same-sex marriages would contribute to the integration of gay lives and the larger culture, to a nonlegal form of civilizing gays. Marriage would contribute to this integration because same-sex

---

[a]My discussion in this and the next two paragraphs exploits the different meanings of *civilize* (all of which are found in unabridged dictionaries). As a law professor I naturally start with the strict legal meaning of *civilize*, namely, "changes from the criminal law to the civil law." This should be the least controversial (and admittedly pedantic) use of the term. The discussion immediately progresses to broader and more interesting meanings: "integrate into the law and customs of society" or simply "educate." I also use *civilize* in its most provocative sense: "tame" or "domesticate." The remainder of this chapter continues to play upon these ambiguities.

couples would be able to participate openly in this long-standing cultural institution. Such participation would establish another common tie between gay people and straight people. We are already coworkers, teachers, students, public officials, fellow worshippers, and parents; we share institutions of employment, religion, and education with the rest of the population. Once we are permitted to marry, we should also share the aspirations, joys, anxieties, and disappointments that straight couples find in matrimony. In time, moreover, same-sex marriage will likely contribute to the public acceptability of homosexual relationships. The interpersonal commitments entailed by same-sex marriages ought to help break down the stereotypes straights have about gays, especially about gay and bisexual men.

Lesbian and gay skeptics fear that civilizing gays would domesticate and tame us. This sort of fear is usually overstated, for same-sex couples do not simply ape the mores of traditional marriage. Indeed, the old-fashioned marriage of breadwinner husband and housekeeper wife cannot be replicated by same-sex couples; at least one of the husbands will be a housekeeper, and at least one of the wives will be a breadwinner. More important, a greater degree of domestication should not be rejected out of hand. Human history repeatedly testifies to the attractiveness of domestication born of interpersonal commitment, a signature of married life. It should not have required the AIDS epidemic to alert us to the problems of sexual promiscuity and to the advantages of committed relationships. In part because of their greater tendency toward bonding in committed pairs, lesbians have been the group least infected by the virus that leads to AIDS and have emerged in the 1990s as an unusually vital group. To the extent that males in our culture have been more sexually venturesome (more in need of civilizing), same-sex marriage could be a particularly useful commitment device for gay and bisexual men.

Since at least the nineteenth century, gay men have been known for their promiscuous subcultures. Promiscuity may be a consequence of biology (men may be naturally more promiscuous than women; if so, all-male couples would exaggerate this trait), or it may be the result of acculturation (the peculiar way Western society defines virility). In the world of the closet, furtive behavior that is not only practically necessary but also addictively erotic may increase the likelihood of promiscuity. Whatever its source, sexual variety has not been liberating to gay men. In addition to the disease costs, promiscuity has encouraged a cult of youth worship and has contributed to the stereotype of homosexuals as people who lack a serious approach to life. (Indeed, a culture centered around nightclubs and bars is not one that can fundamentally satisfy the needs for connection and commitment that become more important as one grows older.) A self-reflective gay community ought to embrace marriage for its potentially civilizing effect on young and old alike.

Same-sex marriage would also civilize Americans. Ours is a "creole" culture, created out of many constituent groups, each of which blends into the larger culture only after adding its own distinctive flavor. American society today is a synergy of Chinese, English, Mexican, Native American, Puerto Rican, African, Jewish, Japanese, Irish, Italian, Filipino, and *Gay* influences. Yet some segments of our society have at times militantly opposed some of these groups; witness our history of anti-Semitism, nativist sentiment against new immigrants, and interracial prejudice. Time after time, group hatred has been replaced by group acceptance and cooperation. Cooperating with others, people learn and grow. Our country has profited from the heterogeneity of the populace. The history we Americans point to with pride is a history of accommodation and inclusion. The history we Americans would rather forget, and should try to correct, is our history of prejudice and exclusion.

Gay people are neither an ethnic nor a racial group, but we are a group that has been traditionally excluded from equal rights in the United States. Our contributions have until recently been actively suppressed by laws that require or encourage us to remain closeted. This country would be edified—civilized, if you will—if it would end all vestiges of legal discrimination against its homosexual population. Essential to this project is the adoption of laws guaranteeing equal rights for lesbian and gay couples.

Bisexuals, gay men, and lesbians are citizens of the United States. Notwithstanding our ill treatment in the past, we love this country and have contributed in every way to its flourishing. A civilized polity assures equality for all its citizens. There can be no equality for lesbians, gay men, and bisexuals in the United States without same-sex marriage. This equality point has constitutional bite (chapters 5 and 6). The United States Supreme Court has repeatedly held that a civilized polity can only restrict the fundamental right to marry if there is a compelling reason to do so. The state cannot restrict the right to marry on the basis of punitive grounds or prejudice. For example, the Warren Court in 1967 struck down Virginia's law prohibiting people of different races from marrying.[6] The Court did not dispute Virginia's claims that its citizens considered different-race marriages repulsive, contrary to their religious beliefs, and a threat to human genetic flourishing. The Court merely held that these beliefs do not justify limiting the fundamental right to marry. The Court's decision is in the best "live and let live" tradition of American law. The arguments rejected by the Court are eerily similar to those advanced by traditionalist opponents of same-sex marriage.

The Warren Court was not alone in protecting the right to marry. The Burger Court required states to permit remarriage of "deadbeat dads" in 1978.[7] The Rehnquist Court in 1987 struck down a state's restrictions on marriage by prison inmates.[8] The Court reasoned that prisoners have the same right to marry, to achieve the emotional, religious, and economic benefits of the institution, that other citizens have. The Court further held that restrictions on that right must be justified by something more than dislike of prisoners or generalized concerns about prison discipline. This unanimous decision reflects broader features of marriage law and suggests the civilizing consequences of recognizing same-sex marriage. In today's society the importance of marriage is relational and not procreational. Although Ninia Baehr and Genora Dancel might decide to have children (through artificial insemination, for example), their desire to marry is based foremost on their commitment to one another, a commitment in the face of social hostility. Each love story is a different tale. The stories of lesbian and gay couples, some of which are told in this book, are illuminating stories, often distinct from those of straight couples who enjoy greater support for their relationships. Such stories would enrich the institution of marriage.

When the state recognizes a couple's right to marry, it offers a recognition of the couple's citizenship, not a seal of approval for their lifestyle. Citizenship in a heterogeneous polity entails state tolerance of a variety of marriages, and states are not a bit choosy about who receives a marriage license. Convicted felons, divorced parents who refuse to pay child support, delinquent taxpayers, fascists, and communists—all receive marriage licenses from the state. The Supreme Court stands ready to discipline any state that denies these citizens their right to marry, yet no one believes that the license constitutes state approval of felony, default on support obligations, tax delinquency, communism, or fascism. People considered sexually deviant also routinely get marriage licenses. Pedophiles, transvestites, transsexuals, sadists, masochists, sodomites, and hermaphrodites can get marriage licenses in every state—so long as they can persuade the state that they are heterosexual pedophiles, transvestites, transsexuals, sadists, masochists, sodomites, and hermaphrodites (sometimes this is a pretty scholastic exercise). Gay people constitute virtually the only group in America whose members are not permitted to marry the partner they love. This is intolerable.

The state justifications for prohibiting same-sex marriage ultimately boil down to one negative reason and one positive reason. The negative reason is prejudice against lesbians, gay men, and bisexuals. As a matter of politics, homophobia is not a productive state policy, for it engenders a competition of spite and vengeance, the antithesis of a civilized polity. Civilizing America means taking homophobia off the national agenda—by constitutional decision making, if necessary. The positive reason for the prohibition is to foster family values in the state by reserving marriage for those who want to procreate and raise a family. This is a much more attractive value than homophobia, but *it does not support existing state bars to same-sex marriage*. Families are as heterogeneous as they are wonderful: they include couples with children, single mothers with children, grandparents with their grandchildren and a niece or nephew, and just couples. Families need not be heterosexual, and they need not procreate. The state has always allowed couples to marry even though they do not desire children or are physically incapable of procreation. Would anyone deny a marriage license to an octogenarian couple? Marriage in an urbanized society serves companionate, economic, and interpersonal goals that are independent of procreation, and the Supreme Court's most recent marriage decision (involving prisoners) reflects that reality. Civilizing America does not require that all couples have children.

Moreover many same-sex couples do have and raise children. Some bring children from prior marriages and relationships into the same-sex household. Lesbians have children through artificial insemination, and gay men have children through surrogacy and other arrangements. Same-sex couples can now adopt children in most states, and many take advantage of this opportunity. Every study that has been done of children raised in lesbian or gay households has found that the children have been raised well. Some studies have found that children of lesbian couples are better adjusted than children of single heterosexual mothers, presumably because there are two parents in the household. If this finding can be generalized, it yields the ironic point that state prohibitions against same-sex marriages may be antifamily and antichildren. The civilizing influence of family values, with or without children, may ultimately be the best argument for same-sex marriage.

Ninia Baehr and Genora Dancel are waiting for a marriage license before the wedding bells will ring for them. In the interest of civilizing gays and civilizing America, people of good will should support them.

2

A HISTORY OF
SAME-SEX MARRIAGE

We'wha was an important cultural and political leader in the Zuni community in the late nineteenth century. At one point he served as an emissary from that southwestern Native American nation to Washington, D.C.[1] He was the strongest, wisest, and most esteemed member of his community. And he was a *berdache*, a male who dressed in female garb. Such men were revered in Zuni culture for their supposed connection to the supernatural. The most gifted *berdache* were *lhamana*, spiritual leaders. We'wha was the most celebrated Zuni *lhamana* of the nineteenth century. He was married to a man.

Ifeyinwa Olinke lived in the nineteenth century as well.[2] She was a member of the Igbo tribe, situated in what is now eastern Nigeria. She was an industrious and wealthy woman in a community where most of the entrepreneurial opportunities were seized by women. Ifeyinwa socially overshadowed her less prosperous male husband. As a sign of her prosperity and social standing, she herself became a female husband to other women. Indeed, the epithet *Olinke* refers to the fact that she had nine wives.

Sergius and Bacchus were Roman soldiers who lived in the late third and early fourth centuries.[3] They were male lovers, but it was for their Christian faith that they were persecuted by the Romans.

This chapter is a revised and expanded version of William N. Eskridge, Jr., "A History of Same-Sex Marriage," 79 *Virginia Law Review* 1419 (1993).

15

Ultimately, Bacchus was tortured to death by the intolerant Romans. According to Christian tradition, Sergius's faith faltered with the death of his lover only to return when Bacchus appeared to him in a vision and said, "I am still with you in the bond of union." Sergius kept faith and, like his friend, died a martyr to the new religion. During the Middle Ages, the relationship of Sergius and Bacchus was considered an exemplar of companionate union, and possibly even marriage, based on *agape* (brotherly love) and mutual respect.

The stories of We'wha, Ifeyinwa Olinke, and Sergius and Bacchus resonate strangely in modern American minds. Most twentieth-century Americans consider marriage to be an institution that intrinsically involves different- rather than same-sex partners. While numerous Americans are willing to tolerate same-sex relationships, and even to sanction them to some extent, few consider them to be marriages. In contrast, historians, social anthropologists, and scholars of comparative literature have been writing about same-sex unions and marriages for most of this century, with a boomlet in the last two decades. Though few critics like to admit it, same-sex marriages are a commonplace in human history and have served civilizing functions, providing couples with social support and integrating them into the larger culture.

This chapter presents a minihistory of same-sex unions. To the modern Western mind it is surprising how common same-sex unions and even marriages have been in other times and other cultures. While there has been plenty of anxiety about these unions as well, they have at least been tolerated in most societies—except in Western society since the thirteenth century. I shall leave it to others to argue why the West became and remained intolerant for so long. Instead, I only wish to put to rest the argument that same-sex marriage is somehow so unnatural or dysfunctional as to be unheard of. Hear of it now.

Several points should be made at the outset. The story I am going to tell is episodic and fragmentary. A thorough history of human relationships in general may never be written because the records of everyday lives of the past no longer exist or exist in hard-to-decipher form. A history of same-sex unions will be even more fragmentary. Moreover, it is perilous to generalize about institutions across cultures as well as time periods. I shall use the phrase *same-sex union* to refer to any kind of culturally or legally tolerated institution whereby individuals of the same sex are bonded together in relationships for reasons of affinity, economy, or society. Included within the general category of same-sex unions are same-sex relationships, which are culturally but not legally recognized in the society, and same-sex marriages, which have sanction or consequences under the society's legal regime.

I am not using the term *marriage* casually. Although some of the same-sex relationships described in this chapter have marriage-like features, I do not always deem them same-sex marriages. The term is used only when it appears that the same-sex union was treated by contemporaries and legal authorities as about the same as different-sex marriage *and* met one or more of the civilizing functions of marriage, namely, long-term emotional support and bonding between the couple; economic security and division of labor in the household; or legitimacy and support of a family, including children. In cases of ambiguous evidence, I shall indicate the ambiguities, albeit sometimes in the notes.

For narrative convenience this history of same-sex unions will unfold in three segments: the premodern antecedents of Western (European) culture; Native American, African, and Asian cultures, with a focus on the treatment of same-sex unions prior to Westernization; and the modern period, in which Western culture has dominated the world. The first two segments reveal that many communities, including premodern Western society, recognized same-sex unions, including marriages. In the modern period same-sex marriage has been suppressed, forced into a closet from which it has recently emerged.

PREMODERN WESTERN CULTURES

The early Egyptian and Mesopotamian societies that are considered important antecedents for Western culture apparently tolerated same-sex relationships in their culture, literature, and mythology. Evidence that these societies recognized same-sex marriage is speculative. Later, however, one finds more tangible evidence of same-sex marriage in classical Greece, imperial Rome, and medieval Europe. Same-sex relations were met in the later cultures with a mix of tolerance and anxiety.

Ancient Civilizations (Egypt and Mesopotamia)

Because there are so few surviving records pertaining to family and sexual matters, we know little of the specific practices of the most ancient cultures, namely, those of Egypt, Mesopotamia, and their environs. At the very least, one can say that the leading ancient cultures sometimes treated same-sex relationships similarly to marriages involving different-sex partners.

Information about Egyptian unions, whether partners were different or same sex, is indirect but suggestive. Some artifacts have depicted same-sex couples in intimate poses, suggesting that Egyptian society at some points in its history was accepting of same-sex relationships. For example, a tomb for two male courtiers of the Fifth Dynasty (about 2600 B.C.) includes bas-reliefs of the two men holding hands and embracing, with noses touching, poses that are strikingly more erotic than those seen in the depictions in Egyptian tombs of different-sex couples. Social historian David Greenberg argues that the men were lovers whose same-sex relationship was apparently accepted by the state, since the pharaoh provided their tomb.[4] Indeed, the tomb of at least one pharaoh, the renowned Akhenaton (Ikhnaton), contains figures of the pharaoh and his male consort posed even more intimately.

The most interesting evidence of same-sex unions in ancient Egypt is fascinatingly indirect. After living for several generations in Egypt, the Israelites (according to biblical tradition) fled that land, ultimately settling in Canaan near the end of the second millennium B.C. Their religion rejected many Egyptian mores. Chapter 18, verse 3 of the Old Testament Book of Leviticus admonished the Israelites to avoid the "doings of the land of Egypt, wherein ye dwelt . . . neither shall ye walk in their ordinances." Verses 24 and 27 referred to those "doings" as "abominations" that defiled "the nations," apparently Egypt and perhaps also Canaan. Verse 22 is more specific: "Thou shalt not lie with mankind, as with womankind: it *is* abomination."

The implication that same-sex intimacy was common in Egypt and Canaan is elaborated by the Sifra, a midrashic exegesis of Leviticus. The Sifra says of chapter 18:[5]

A. If "You shall not copy the practices of the land of Egypt . . . or of the land of Canaan,"

B. might one think that they are not to build their buildings or plant vineyards as they did?

C. Scripture says, "nor shall you follow their laws":

D. "I have referred only to the rules that were made for them and for their father and their fathers' fathers."

E. And what would they do?

F. A man would marry a man, and a woman would marry a woman, a man would marry a woman and her daughter, a woman would be married to two men.

G. That is why it is said, "nor shall you follow their laws."

Given the parallel references to marriage by a man to a woman and her daughter and by a woman with two men, the author of this midrash was using the term *marry* in its juridical sense. This evidence would suggest that same-sex unions at least functionally similar to marriages were accepted in Egypt and Canaan but not by the Israelites. Sifra is not, however, conclusive evidence of same-sex marriage in Egypt, because it was a biased account of Egyptian culture and was written long after the practices it describes. (Some scholars even doubt the accuracy of the Bible's account of the escape to Egypt.)

Mesopotamian mores pertaining to same-sex relationships are illustrated in the most celebrated of the Near Eastern myths, the Epic of Gilgamesh. Written through a collective process over several generations, the epic describes the relationship between Gilgamesh, the great powerful ruler of Uruk, and Enkidu, a male created by the gods to divert Gilgamesh from wreaking havoc in the world.[6] Gilgamesh and Enkidu become comrades, friends, and lovers before Enkidu dies at the hands of the fates. Enkidu is often called Gilgamesh's "brother" (*ahu*), a term connoting family-like intimacy. Significantly, Gilgamesh's feeling for Enkidu is modeled on sexual attraction. In the two dreams that presage the arrival of Enkidu, Gilgamesh takes pleasure in his vision of Enkidu as in a woman. The Assyrian version of the myth refers to Enkidu, "[I loved it, and like] a wife I caressed it."[7]

When Enkidu dies, Gilgamesh mourns for him as a widow (literally, "a wailing woman") would have mourned and veils his corpse as if it were a bride. Because the Epic of Gilgamesh was a collective project and achieved great popularity in ancient times, one might infer that same-sex relationships had some resonance in the cultures of ancient Babylonia and Assyria. This inference is supported by evidence that several Mesopotamian monarchs (notably Hammurabi, the great Babylonian lawgiver) openly enjoyed male lovers. Moreover, the Almanac of Incantations contained prayers favoring, on an equal basis, the love of a man for a woman, a woman for a man, and a man for a man.[8]

Consider also Mesopotamian statutes, which, unlike Egyptian laws, have been preserved. None of Mesopotamia's early legal codes—the Laws of Urukagina (2375 B.C.), the Laws of Ur-Nammu (2100 B.C.), the Laws of Eshnunna (1750 B.C.), the Laws of Hammurabi (1726 B.C.) and the Hittite Laws (around 800 B.C.)—prohibited or disapproved of same-sex relationships, even though sex and marriage were otherwise heavily regulated.[9] On the other hand, the legal codes contained no provision sanctioning same-sex marriages, with one possible exception. Table 1 of the Hittite Laws regulated marriage, specifically the husband's payment of a bride-price to the wife. While it was assumed that this regulation applied to the advantage of free Hittite citizens, special provisions in Table 1 afforded explicit legal authority for slaves to obtain brides in this way; otherwise, slaves apparently could not marry. For example, section 34 stated: "If a slave gives the bride-price to a woman and takes her as his wife, no-one shall [make him] surrender her."[10] According to one translation, section 36 then stated: "If a slave gives the bride-price to a free youth and takes him to dwell in his household as spouse, no-one shall [make him] surrender him."[11] There has for generations been legitimate controversy over the correct reading of section 36. If the quoted reading were correct, a male slave with money (the bride-price) to pay for a male spouse could acquire one and could expect that the transaction would be enforceable at law. If a slave were allowed to do this, it went without saying that a free Hittite citizen could do the same.

Classical Greece and Pre-Christian Rome

Classical Greek culture was keenly interested in and developed rich cultural norms for same-sex relationships, some of which were close to marriages. Plato's *Symposium* is the first recorded essay in "the praise of Love" (line 177E), with love and relationships between men being its primary focus.[12] One of the speakers, Pausanias, delivers an impassioned defense of companionate same-sex relationships:

> Those who are inspired by . . . Love are attracted to the male: they find pleasure in what is by nature stronger and more intelligent. But, even within the group that is attracted to handsome boys, some are not moved purely by this heavenly Love; those who do not fall in love with little boys; they prefer older ones whose cheeks are showing the first traces of a beard—a sign that they have begun to form minds of their own. I am convinced that a man who falls in love with a young man of this age is generally prepared to share everything with the one he loves— he is eager, in fact, to spend the rest of his own life with him. (Lines 181C–D)

Likewise, Phaedrus praises unselfish love (*agape*), citing as examples Alcestis' willingness to die for her husband Admetus (lines 179B–C) and Achilles' willingness to die for his lover Patroclus (lines 181C–D). This analogy suggests both the companionate feature of same-sex relationships and the formal distinction drawn by the author between same-sex relationships and different-sex marriage.

Historians of classical Greece and its romantic institutions consider the *Symposium* a reflection of the attitudes toward same-sex relationships prevailing in at least some of the Greek city-states. In Athens and, it appears, other major city states, no law prohibited same-sex relationships. They were, in fact, institutionalized for free male citizens, who were expected to court and have a relationship with a boy in their early adulthood. While historians have not ventured to consider these relationships to be marriages, they have demonstrated that they often followed the same courtship rituals as marriages.[13] A closer link between same-sex relationships and marriage was a ritualized same-sex courtship in Crete. The ancient geographer Strabo described the "peculiar laws regarding love" followed on that island, whereby two men would become "partners" (or "companions") after the abduction of one by the other, followed by a feast where the partners announced their mutual intentions before witnesses.[14] Several historians have characterized these Cretan abduction ceremonies as same-sex "marriages."[15] Another Greek island, Lesbos, gave the Western world the concept of female same-sex relationships, which probably had broader currency. Eva Cantarella believes that some of the lesbian relationships arising out of female collectives (*thiasoi*) were "initiation marriages" similar to the male same-sex unions common in the city states.[16]

The consensus among historians is that republican Rome, like classical Greece, was tolerant of same-sex relationships.[17] Imperial Rome considered some of them marriages. The best documented are the same-sex marriages of Rome's emperors. Roman historian Suetonius reported, disapprovingly, that the first-century emperor Nero "went through a wedding ceremony with [Sporus]—dowry, bridal veil and all—which the whole Court attended; then brought him home and treated him as a wife. He dressed Sporus in fine clothes normally worn by an Empress and took him in his own litter not only to every Greek assize and fair, but actually through the Street of Images at Rome, kissing him amorously now and then." Later, a freedman, Pythagorus, "married [Nero]—just as he himself had married Sporus—and on his wedding night he imitated the screams and moans of a girl being deflowered."[18] Dio Cassius, a historian and contemporary of Suetonius, confirmed Nero's marriages to these men[19] and also provided a reliable account of the same-sex and opposite-sex marriages of third-century emperor Elagabalus.[20] Indeed, it was said that men seeking advancement in Elagabalus's imperial court rushed to marry other men to curry favor with the emperor.[21] Second-century emperor Hadrian was renowned throughout the ancient world for his wise and moderate reign and for his love of the tragic youth Antinoüs. Though not Hadrian's spouse, Antinoüs attained the status of legend and was commemorated for generations through sculpture, architecture, painting, and literature.[22]

Other evidence indicates that same-sex marriages were not limited to Rome's emperors. The satirists Martial and Juvenal sarcastically

noted the casual way in which men married other men by the end of
the first century. "I have a ceremony to attend tomorrow morning in
the Quirinial valley," says the interlocutor in Juvenal's *Satires*. "What
sort of ceremony?" he is asked. The reply: "Nothing special: a friend
is marrying another man and a small group is attending."[23] Martial described the marriage of "bearded Callistratus" to the "brawny Afer,"
complete with torches, wedding veil, songs, and dower.[24] The novel
Babylonica, an early exemplar of the pulp romance, has a subplot involving the passion of Egypt's Queen Berenice for the beautiful
Mesopotamia, who was snatched from her. After one of the queen's
servants rescued Mesopotamia from her abductors, "Berenice married
Mesopotamia, and there was war between [the abductor] and Berenice
on account of Mesopotamia."[25] These and other references do not
exclude the possibility that same-sex marriages were culturally or
legally distinct from different-sex marriages, but they confirm the
acceptance of same-sex unions in imperial Rome. The marriages of
emperors such as Nero stand as examples of publicly celebrated same-
sex marriages in the same period.

Christian Rome and the Middle Ages

The late Roman Empire grew less tolerant of same-sex unions than
either the republic or the earlier empire had been. In 342 A.D.,
Rome adopted a statute that seemingly—but perhaps facetiously—
prohibited same-sex marriages:[26]

> When a man "marries" in the manner of a woman, a "woman" about
> to renounce men, what does he wish, when sex has lost its significance;
> when the crime is one which it is not profitable to know; when Venus
> is changed into another form; when love is sought and not found? We
> order the statutes to arise, the laws to be armed with an avenging sword,
> that those infamous persons who are now, or who hereafter may be,
> guilty may be subjected to exquisite punishment.

While the statute reinforces the impression that same-sex marriages
were not uncommon in the Roman Empire, it also evidences an
anxiety about same-sex unions that antedated the fourth century. For
example, Plutarch's *Moralia*, written in the second century, includes

a heated dialogue filled with comments both for and against same-sex relationships, which suggests that their propriety was a matter of controversy. A subsequent anonymous dialogue entitled *Affairs of the Heart* was sympathetic to same-sex relationships but sharply distinguished them from marriage.[27]

Imperial Rome's anxiety about same-sex relations was related to the institutionalization of companionate marriage, in which husband and wife were friends and marital partners in the creation of the family unit. The rise of companionate marriage also involved the linkage of procreation with sexual partnership. There might also be a connection between the aforementioned statute of 342 A.D. and the increasing influence of Christianity during the late Roman Empire. Inspired in part by its Judaic heritage (recall Leviticus, quoted earlier), the early Christian tradition advocated companionate different-sex marriage that served procreative purposes, and was correspondingly ambivalent about same-sex relationships.[28] The major philosophical traditions of the Late Empire—Stoicism, Neo-Platonism, and Manichaeanism, all of which influenced Christianity—were intolerant of most forms of sexual pleasure and equivocal about the merits of same-sex relationships. Some of the Manichaeans, for example, thought homosexual pleasures worse than heterosexual ones since they did not reproduce the race, though others viewed same-sex relations more leniently.

The collapsing Roman Empire grew increasingly inhospitable to same-sex unions, and after Rome's fall in 476 A.D. state attitudes toward such unions became more hostile. In the surviving Eastern Empire, the Justinian Code of 533 A.D. flatly outlawed same-sex intimacy, placing it in the same category as adultery, both of which violated the then entrenched ideal of companionate different-sex marriage. In the remains of the Western Empire, the Visigoth state in Spain criminalized same-sex intimacy around 650 A.D.,[29] though most of the other Germanic states showed little interest in either advocating or decrying same-sex relationships. At first glance, it appears that the same-sex unions of the earlier Roman Empire had all but died out during the early Middle Ages. A closer look reveals the story to be more complicated.

The complication owes much to the Roman Catholic and Greek Orthodox Churches' ambivalent responses to same-sex unions. During the early and high Middle Ages, the Church was doctrinally critical of same-sex erotic intimacy because it could not result in procreation and constituted sex outside of marriage. On the other hand, the Church favored same-sex companionate intimacy; *agape* between brothers, such as the love of Sergius and Bacchus, was the Christian ideal. Church practice thrust the faithful into "homosocial" environments (schools, monasteries, nunneries) that were sure to engender what we would today deem sexual responses. Erotic feelings repeatedly arose between teachers and students, clerics and their fellows and acolytes, yearnings that are documented in a proliferation of love letters, poems, and stories written in the Middle Ages.[30]

In the early Middle Ages the Church developed institutions, memorialized in liturgies included in its formal collections, that combined the Church's spiritual commitment to companionate relationships with its members' desire to bond with people of the same sex. The existence of Roman Catholic and Greek Orthodox rituals of "brother-making" or "enfraternization" has been known in the academic literature for decades and was brought to my attention by the Reverend Alexei Michalenko.[31] Ceremonies creating these brotherhoods were performed for same-sex couples (often male missionary pairs) from the fifth century onward. According to Church archives, these early liturgies were typically structured as follows:[32]

- The couple stand in front of the lectern, on which are placed the Gospel and a cross. The older of the brothers stands to the right.
- The ceremony starts off with prayers and litanies celebrating earlier examples of same-sex couples or friends in the early Church. Sergius and Bacchus were the most frequently invoked precedent.
- The couple is girded with a single belt, signifying their union as one, and they place their hands on the Gospel and receive lit candles.
- The priest reads from one of Paul's epistles (1 Cor 12:27 ff.) and the Gospel (John 17:18–16), which are followed by more prayers.
- The assembled are led in the Lord's Prayer, followed by Holy Communion, the Eucharist, for the couple.

- The priest leads the couple, who are holding hands, around the lectern while the assembled sing a hymn.
- The couple exchange a kiss, and the service concludes with the singing of Psalm 132:1 ("Behold how good and sweet it is for brothers to live as one").

Significantly, this early brotherhood liturgy was acted out in formal terms very similar to the liturgy later developed by the Church for the purpose of performing different-sex marriages.

The main difference between the brotherhood liturgy and the one originally used to wed different-sex couples is that the former emphasizes the companionate (see Psalm 132) rather than the pro-creative (see Psalm 127) nature of the relationship. Hence, rather than orating on procreation, one version of the enfraternization liturgy read as follows:[33]

> O Almighty Lord, you have given to man to be made from the first in Your Image and Likeness by the gift of immortal life. You have willed to bind as brothers not only by nature but by bonds of the spirit Your most celebrated Apostles Peter, the Chief of them all, and Andrew; James and John the Sons of Zebedee; Philip and Batholomew. You made as very brothers Your Holy Martyrs Sergius and Bacchus, Cosmas and Damien, Cyrus and John. Bless Your Servants united also that, not bound by nature, [they be] joined with bonds of love. Grant them a love mutual and without offense and a brotherhood upset by naught of hatred all the days of their lives, through the might of Your All-Holy Spirit and through the intercession of our All-Holy spotless ever-Virgin Lady. . . .

The precise significance of these enfraternization liturgies remains mysterious. They may have simply been friendship ceremonies or send-offs for missionaries. Medieval historian John Boswell argues for a broader reading, however.[34]

Expanding on earlier academic examinations of enfraternization liturgies and suggestions from Reverend Michalenko, Boswell un-covered a large variety of manuscript versions of Christian same-sex union liturgies in libraries and ecclesiastical collections throughout Europe. Although his earlier claim that these liturgies are identical to same-sex marriages[35] was overstated, he has argued that there are tangible connections between the liturgies of same-sex unions and different-sex marriages. The same-sex union ceremonies are usually located right after different-sex marriage ceremonies in the liturgical collections Boswell consulted. As previous scholarship had established, the same-sex ceremonies are structurally and thematically similar to the different-sex ones, but Boswell insists on a more ambitious connection. "[I]n the case of the same-sex ceremony, standing together at the altar with their right hands joined (the traditional symbol of marriage), being blessed by the priest, sharing Communion, and holding a banquet for family and friends afterward—all parts of same-sex union in the Middle Ages—most likely signified a marriage in the eyes of ordinary Christians."[36] Critics contest this claim and find much of Boswell's argumentation "tendentious."[37] Notwithstanding these criticisms, which strike me as fair but not conclusive, it seems likely that the Church did sanction these brotherhood ceremonies and that there is some likelihood that the brothers so joined enjoyed relationships of affinity and erotic possibilities.

NON-WESTERN CULTURES

There is strong evidence demonstrating the existence of same-sex unions, including legally recognized marriages, in Native American, African, and Asian cultures. I shall not attempt to survey all the cultures here and shall instead introduce three recurring patterns: same-sex marriages with gender-bending *berdaches;* same-sex unions serving social, economic, and companionate needs; and female same-sex marriages for purposes of maintaining a family lineage.

Same-Sex Marriages with Berdaches

Accounts by stunned Spanish explorers, missionaries, and bureaucrats provide early evidence of same-sex relationships and marriages in the Americas. Francisco López de Gómara's *History of the Indies* (1552), one of many examples, reported that "the men marry other men who are impotent or castrated and go around like women, perform their duties and are used as such and who cannot carry or use the bow."[38] Same-sex unions between women were also reported: Pedro de Magálhaes's *The Histories of Brazil* (1576) described Native American women in northeastern Brazil who "give up all the duties of women and imitate men, and follow men's pursuits as if they were not women. . . . [E]ach has a woman to serve her, to whom she says she is married, and they treat each other and speak with each other as man and wife."

What these accounts describe is the *berdache* tradition, which was institutionalized in the West Indies and throughout what is now the United States, as well as in the Aztec, Mayan, and Incan civilizations. The Native American *berdache* is a person who deviates from his or her traditional gender role, taking on some of the characteristics and perceived responsibilities of the opposite sex. The *berdache* does not, however, cross gender lines so much as mix them. Indeed, many Native American cultures considered *berdaches* to be a third sex.[39] Most important for the present study, *berdaches* (like We'wha) married individuals of the same sex, and those marriages were recognized by Native American laws and cultures.

Outsiders' depictions of the Native American *berdache* have often been colored by their antihomosexual attitudes. The accounts of Spanish authors such as those quoted above usually expressed shock and offered Native American same-sex unions as evidence of these cultures' barbarism, which they sought to correct. Until the twentieth century, accounts by Western anthropologists suppressed the tradition. The first detailed academic study focusing on Native American same-sex unions was George Devereux's article on the Mohave *berdaches*.[40] Devereux reported that gender-crossing men (*alyha*) and women (*hwame*) had long been tolerated by the Mohave and that their same-sex marriages were institutionalized and socially accepted. Thus, under tribal custom and law *alyha* married (and divorced) men and *hwame* married (and divorced) women.

Ethnographers and anthropologists studying the culture and evolution of various Native American tribes throughout this century discovered similar *berdache* institutions.[41] In *The Spirit and the Flesh* Walter Williams draws from earlier accounts as well as his own field work and synthesizes existing scholarship probing the Native American *berdache* tradition.[42] Williams concludes that *berdaches* have been an accepted and in fact valued part of culture and law in a large majority of Native American tribes. Most academic attention has been focused on male *berdaches*, like We'wha, who frequently became revered leaders in their communities. Often, a male child was consciously raised to be a *berdache* who would assume a special role in the community, mediating between the spiritual and physical worlds. Marriages between men and male *berdaches* were widespread among Native American cultures. As a general matter, same-sex marriages tended to conform to traditional Native American marriage patterns, in which labor was divided between the wife, who kept house, and the husband, who hunted and directed the household. The men who married male *berdaches* were usually attracted to women as well as to men and were not themselves considered *berdaches*. Many such men preferred *berdache* wives for economic reasons, as *berdaches* would not only do the housework but also help with hunting and other traditionally male activities. While some men believed that marrying a *berdache* guaranteed greater marital stability, others pursued male *berdaches* on the basis of simple sexual attraction.

Although they have received less academic attention, female *berdaches* represented an important cultural institution in most Native American communities. Like her male counterpart, the female *berdache* assumed many of the responsibilities traditionally performed by the opposite sex, including hunting and heading a household. And she would commonly marry another woman.[43] Female *berdaches* and woman–woman marriages were integral to women's ability to achieve a higher status in most Native American cultures. Thus, a female *berdache* would marry a non-*berdache* woman and would assume a position as head of the household, accepting responsibility for hunting and other traditionally "male" jobs.

Most American scholarship about *berdaches* draws from Native American cultures, but the phenomenon is worldwide. According to an authoritative survey of sexual practices around the world in 1951:[44]

> In 49 (64 percent) of the 76 societies other than our own for which information is available, homosexual activities of one sort or another are considered normal and socially acceptable for certain members of the community. . . .
>   . . . In many cases this [same-sex] behavior occurs within the framework of courtship and marriage, the man who takes the part of the

female being recognized as a *berdache* and treated as a woman. In other words, a genuine mateship is involved.

Anthropological fieldwork since 1951 has not only confirmed but deeply elaborated on this observation. Particular attention has been paid to the *mugawe* of the Kenyan Meru, the Siberian Chuckchee, Tahitian *mahus*, and the Indian *hijras*.[45] With the exception of the *hijras*, the unions of these *berdaches* to people of the same sex have been treated by their indigenous cultures as culturally and legally recognized marriages.

Functional Same-Sex Unions

Same-sex unions in non-Western cultures have typically served companionate, economic, or cultural functions. This section will sample several prominent examples of same-sex unions that display different kinds of functions. Often arising in homosocial situations, the following examples involve bonding between two people of the same sex. The bonding may be sexual, but its main functions transcend the partners' intimacy. The unions serve important functions for the partners: economic, professional, or social in nature. The unions may be temporary and are not necessarily legal marriages, though they usually involve marriage-like features and even terminology.

Military "Wives." The most common functional union in history involves pair bonding in military settings. Many societies have institutionalized same-sex relationships, akin to the Achilles–Patroclus and Gilgamesh–Enkidu relationships of ancient myth, among warriors or soldiers. The samurai warriors of feudal and Tokugawa Japan went to battle accompanied by apprentice warrior-lovers.[46] Literary sources, such as *The Great Mirror of Male Love* by Ihara Saikaku, depict these relationships as highly choreographed and romantic, with strong loyalty on each side.[47] The beginning of a relationship between an apprentice (*wakashu*) and a samurai involved a formal exchange of written and spoken vows, giving the relationship a marriage-like status. Each participant promised to love the other in this life and the next—one step beyond our "till death do us part." As in marriage, sex was only one element of the samurai relationship. The samurai was supposed to provide social backing, emotional support, and a model of manliness for the apprentice. In exchange, the latter was expected to be worthy of his lover by being a good student of samurai manhood.

The warrior tradition epitomized by the samurai can be illustrated in African cultures even more vividly. E. E. Evans-Pritchard documented the institution of "boy wives" for military men among the Azande in what is now Sudan.[48] The Azande considered the relationship a marriage both legally and culturally. The warrior paid bride-price (some five spears or more) to the parents of his boy and performed services for them as he would have done had he married their daughter (if he proved to be a good son-in-law they might later replace the son by a daughter). Also, if another man had relations with his boy, he could sue him at court for adultery. The warrior addressed the boy as *diare* (wife), and the boy addressed the warrior as *kumbami* (husband). The relationship was both sexual (the warrior would have intercourse with the boy between his thighs) and functional (the boy performed traditional wifely duties such as housekeeping). Anthropologists have reported finding similar institutions in other African societies.[49]

Companionate Unions. Marriage-like same-sex unions have been documented in China during the Yuan and Ming dynasties (1264–1644).[50] Useful evidence comes from the widely read seventeenth-century stories of Li Yu. Many of his stories speak openly and approvingly of companionate love affairs between men, a practice particularly associated with Fujian and other provinces in southern China. In at least one story Li Yu relates the tragic romance of two men (Jifang and Ruiji) who become "husband and wife." In describing the couple's wedding, Li Yu goes out of his way to emphasize that the couple adhered to the formal requisites of marriage (bride-price, the various wedding rituals), giving some indication that similar same-sex marriages were common in southern China and perhaps elsewhere in the region. It has been inferred from Li Yu's work and other evidence that there were "institutionalized relationships between males in some areas, and that these relationships were often expressed in terms of marriage and carried out in [the same] social forms connected with 'regular' marriage."[51] Same-sex relationships elsewhere were celebrated as "brotherly" unions, "sworn friendships," and even adoptions, that is, as close but platonic relationships reminiscent of those solemnized in the early Christian Church's enfraternization ceremonies. Although the Manchus of the Qing dynasty sought to discourage same-sex relationships, outlawing same-sex eroticism in 1740, these alliances continued for generations after peaking in the seventeenth century.

Less is known of female same-sex unions in China. While some historians credit accounts of woman–woman unions during the Qing dynasty as evidence of marriage-like institutions, the first well-documented unions were those associated with the "marriage resistance movement" in southern China in the nineteenth and early twentieth centuries. The development of China's international silk industry during this period helped many women attain their economic independence from men. After acquiring this newfound freedom, thousands of women renounced marriage and became *sou hei* (literally, "self-combers"). Upon deciding to become *sou hei*, a woman took a formal ceremonial vow to remain unwed at least for a time, moved out of her parents' house, and built "spinster houses" with other *sou hei*. These women formed sisterhoods in which small groups of women (typically five to seven) would bond together for mutual support and affection. Andrea Sankar reports that physical as well as emotional bonds often developed between two or three of the sisters.[52] Other scholars believe that sisterhood relationships shared many attributes of marriage, including a ceremony with witnesses and a division of labor within the family unit.[53]

Initiatory Unions. Same-sex relationships have also frequently served as social or even sexual initiations prefatory to marriage. An interesting example is the "mummy–baby" games among Basotho girls in Lesotho.[54] In contrast to women in many other African societies, those in Lesotho are particularly vulnerable, both economically and socially, because they are dependent on males who tend to be employed as migrant workers. For these women, relationships outside of marriage serve as important support networks, and young girls are initiated into such relationships beginning with mummy–baby games played in their grade school years. In a mummy–baby relationship, an

older girl, acting as "mummy," develops an intimate, maternal association with a younger one, the baby. Typically, the mummy presents
gifts to the baby, who reciprocates by obeying and respecting the
mummy. The two share emotional and informational exchanges and
are physically, and sometimes sexually, intimate. Rather than displacing marriage, these relationships help to prepare younger girls for
marriage, including its rockier moments. Scholars have documented
similar female–female friendships in other African societies.[55]

The most interesting example of same-sex initiation relationship is
the "ritualized homosexuality" developed by aboriginal populations
of Australia and the islands of Melanesia. This is the term anthropologist Gilbert Herdt uses to describe the events whereby a boy
entering manhood would engage in a short-term sexual relationship
with an older man.[56] By implanting his semen within the boy, the
older man is thought to empower his younger partner, helping him
to complete the journey to virility and manhood. According to
Herdt, about fifty Melanesian societies practice some form of ritualized homosexuality. In some communities the ritualized man–boy
relationship serves as a prelude to a traditional different-sex marriage.
"A most striking aspect of social organization in societies with ritualized male homosexuality concerns the overlap between marriage
and homosexual relationships." That is, by inseminating a boy the
older male is believed not only to facilitate the boy's passage into
manhood but also to prepare him for his marriage to a woman. Many
of the Melanesian societies institutionalizing this ritual treat marriage
not as an exchange relationship involving the payment of bride-price
but as a complex method of bonding two families. In keeping with
this notion, some of these cultures require a boy seeking to enter into
marriage with a woman to submit sexually to the woman's brother.
"Thus, life force (as semen) flows between same-sex and different-
sex partners, linking individuals and groups in complex chains of
mutual dependency and obligation."[57]

Woman Marriage and Female Husbands

A form of same-sex union that may be unique to African cultures is
the institution of "woman marriage." Noted as a curiosity by earlier

researchers, the institution was not given serious attention until anthropologists Eileen Jensen Krige and Melville Herskovits publicized it in the 1930s.[58] The following is an early description of woman marriage among the Nuer of Sudan:[59]

> What seems to us, but not at all to the Nuer, a somewhat strange union is that in which a woman marries another woman and counts as the pater [father] of the children born of the wife. Such marriages are by no means uncommon in Nuerland, and they must be regarded as a form of simple legal marriage, for the woman-husband marries her wife in exactly the same way as a man marries a woman. . . . We may perhaps refer to this kind of union as woman-marriage.
>
> A woman who marries in this way is generally barren, and for this reason counts in some respects as a man. . . . [I]f she is rich she may marry several wives. She is their legal husband and can demand damages if they have relations with men without her consent. She is the pater [father] of their children, and on the marriages of their daughters she receives the cattle which go to the father's side in the distribution of bridewealth. Her children are called after her, as though she were a man, and I was told that they address her as "father."

Krige describes woman marriage as "the institution by which it is possible for a woman to give bridewealth for, and marry, a woman, over whom and whose offspring she has full control, delegating to a male genitor the duties of procreation." She suggests that woman marriage is "closely bound up with rights and duties arising from the social structure" of the culture, a "flexible institution that can be utilized in a number of different ways to meet a number of different situations."[60] For example, in African cultures where women occupy a high position and can acquire property or other forms of wealth, woman marriage is one way that a woman may strengthen her economic position and establish her household. Ifeyinwa Olinke, whose tale was recounted in the beginning of this chapter, was a powerful and prosperous woman in the Igbo society who advanced her position by taking many wives.

Woman marriages were common in Africa. "The term female husband . . . refers to a woman who takes on the legal and social roles of husband and father by marrying another woman according to the approved rules and ceremonies of her society . . . [and] she may belong to any one of over 30 African populations," writes Denise

O'Brien.[61] She reports that the institution is most popular in three parts of Africa: (1) West Africa, especially Nigeria and Dahomey; (2) South Africa, including the Southern Bantu, on whom O'Brien reported; and (3) East Africa and the Sudan (the Nuer).[62] In contrast to Krige's view that woman marriage empowers women, O'Brien's belief is that the institution helps keep women in their subordinate place. Woman marriage, she argues, is usually a social adaptation by which a male-dominated society allows powerful wealthy women to take a leadership role only if they assume the social role of a man, acting as husband and father. This debate resonates with similar discussions in the feminist, lesbian, and gay communities today. Is same-sex marriage liberating? Or does it ape attitudes that suppress women?

Contrast African woman marriage with the Native American *berdache* marriage, the Azande boy wife, and the Chinese sisterhood described earlier. The aforementioned same-sex unions involved companionate emotional bonds between the partners as well as traditional divisions of labor within the household. Although a woman marriage might occur for those reasons, it more typically occurs so that a woman can have children (heirs) through a surrogate.

THE MODERN WEST

Notwithstanding acceptance of same-sex unions in Greece, Rome, and even the medieval Church, modern Western culture is peculiarly hostile toward same-sex unions. The most critical point in the West's attitudes toward same-sex unions or marriages can be located in the thirteenth century.[63] It was then that many secular governments enacted their first laws prohibiting "crimes against nature" and that prior ecclesiastical laws came to be more stringently enforced. The Church took a stronger stand against same-sex intimacy. Leading scholastic thinkers Albertus Magnus and Thomas Aquinas systematized theological arguments against such behavior. In contrast to the relatively open and tolerant attitudes expressed during the eleventh and twelfth centuries, Europe after 1200 acted in an increasingly persecutory manner toward any kind of behavior that transgressed established gender lines, including not just same-sex intimacy but also aggressive, independent behavior by women such as cross–dressing.[64]

Huon of Bordeaux, a thirteenth-century version of an older French romance,[65] illustrates this point. Ide, the work's female protagonist, dressed in men's garb and surreptitiously employed her skill as a warrior with such proficiency as to earn not only a knighthood but also the hand of the emperor's daughter in marriage. Ide went through with the marriage ceremony but later revealed her biological sex to her bride, who snitched to her imperial father. Condemning the possibility of "buggery" between the two women, the emperor decreed that Ide be burned to death. Though Ide was saved at the last minute by metamorphosing into a man, the drastic punishment imposed for her predicament was consistent with the harshened thirteenth-century attitude toward same-sex intimacy and cross-dressing.

Why this shift in attitude occurred is not clear. It can be said that more punitive attitudes coincided with the quickening of a culture in the West that was urban, bourgeois, and statist. The aborning urban culture created more occasions for people to find, pursue, and enjoy same-sex partners. Increasing economic opportunities available to the bourgeoisie gave substantial numbers of men more freedom to choose and diversify the nature of their sexual liaisons. Urbanization, on the other hand, rendered such activity more prominent or widespread, and perhaps more troubling. At the same time, powerful nation- and city-states were emerging in the West. The political powers taking this new form flexed their muscles against nonconforming people of many stripes; state aggression directed against Jews, heretics, and witches stands out as an important theme in European history after 1200.[66]

During the early modern period (about 1400–1700), Western society's obsession with certain categories of people became more pronounced. Isolated persecutions of individuals engaging in sinful conduct (heresy, witchcraft, sodomy) gave way to hysterical persecutory crazes that swept up throngs of people (heretics, witches, sodomites) in popular, ecclesiastical, and official dragnets. Thus, same-sex unions, which had been viewed as merely problematic during the Middle Ages, were believed in the early modern period to constitute a severe threat to the social order and the now powerful state. For example, even as Montaigne was reporting that same-sex marriages were performed by Catholic priests in Rome's Church of St. John during the 1570s, other observers reported that some of the male couples married in St. John's were later burned in the city square.[67] The Church and its rival and ally, the state, were becoming officially unambivalent about same-sex unions.

The West's hostility to same-sex unions and its state-sanctioned suppression of them affected other cultures' attitudes toward such unions. As Western nation-states in the early modern period conquered the New World, colonized and enslaved Africa, and cartelized and evangelized Asian cultures, they aggressively suppressed these cultures' indigenous attitudes and institutions concerning same-sex unions. Thus, the Spanish persecuted the *berdache* tradition in what is now Latin America, and the United States supported a less concerted campaign against such relationships as it stripped Native Americans of their land and culture.[68] Slave traders and colonial administrators broke up family institutions (including same-sex family institutions) in Africa and sometimes disrupted the economic patterns that gave women standing and authority to command female marriages. Missionaries in Africa, China, Japan, Melanesia, and other cultures imposed an increasingly rigid, official Christian view of sexuality and marriage on "converted" peoples, discouraging and sometimes persecuting traditional practices, including same-sex unions.[69]

The Survival of Same-Sex Unions in the Modern West

While the modern turn in Western attitudes and their ascendancy in the world surely threatened same-sex unions, they survived nonetheless. Because the modern West has been almost uniquely intolerant of unions that depart from its norm of different-sex companionate marriage, same-sex unions have occurred primarily in the interstices and at the fringes of society. The following pages present three fascinating contexts within which same-sex unions flourished.

Women Passing as Men. Countless female couples married in the modern era. This was accomplished by marriage of one woman to another woman who was passing as a man. While hundreds of women are known to have "passed" during the early modern era, the story of Elena de Cespedes (1545–1588) is mysterious and unusually interesting.[70] Raised as a girl, Elena escaped from the traditional women's work of weaving by dressing and passing as a man; she became a soldier and then a tailor, adopting the name Eleno. Eventually, Eleno fell in love with a peasant woman and obtained a license to marry her after passing a physical inspection designed to establish manhood. Unhappily, Eleno's former lover challenged the forthcoming marriage on grounds of fraud, asserting that the first inspection was inaccurate and that Eleno was really a woman. In response to this challenge, the Madrid authority ordered a more thorough inspection to be conducted by physicians and surgeons, who once again pronounced Eleno a man. Following the marriage, Eleno was inspected for yet a third time, and on this occasion the examiners determined that Eleno, the husband, was a woman.[a] After the damning verdict was rendered, Elena was referred to the Inquisition, where she was convicted of devilry and promptly immolated.

Elena/Eleno's case was far from unusual in the early modern period. Records kept by the Dutch East India Company reveal hundreds of women who were caught passing as men. The leading study of cross-dressing women concludes that they did so for both economic and personal reasons. Many women not only passed as men in the workforce but enjoyed intimate relationships with and even married other women.[71] Women passed as men just as easily in the United States as they did in Europe, and for a similar mix of economic, social, and personal reasons. As many as four hundred women passed as men in order to serve in the Union Army during the Civil War, for example. Of the women who passed as men a substantial number sought female relationships, and hundreds of passing women

---

[a]It is a mystery as to why the doctors were fooled. One possibility is that Elena was a hermaphrodite, a person whose genitals are ambiguous. Hermaphrodism is legendary in human history, but modern sexologists have documented it as a medical phenomenon. See John Money and Anke A. Ehrhardt, *Man & Woman, Boy & Girl: The Differentiation and Dimorphism of Gender Identity from Conception to Maturity* (Baltimore: Johns Hopkins University Press, 1972), and Anne Fausto-Sterling, "The Five Sexes: Why Male and Female Are Not Enough," *The Sciences*, March/April 1993, pp. 20–24.

legally married other women.[72] For example, Mary Anderson, who died in 1901, passed as Murray Hall in New York City for thirty years.[73] Hall made boatloads of money; was active in Tammany Hall politics; gained a reputation as a man about town; and married twice, the first marriage ending in separation and the second cut short by her wife's death.

An even more interesting history is that of Nicholai de Raylan, a woman who passed as a man named Nicholas de Raylan; the masquerade proved a success apparently for most of her days. According to one doctor's account of her life:[74]

> She was born in Russia and was in many respects very feminine, small and slight in build, but was regarded as a man, and even as very "manly," by both men and women who knew her intimately. She was always very neat in dress, fastidious in regard to shirts and ties, and wore a long-waisted coat to disguise the lines of her figure. She was married twice in America, being divorced by the first wife, after a union lasting ten years, on the ground of cruelty and misconduct with chorus girls[!]. The second wife, a chorus girl who had been previously married and had a child, was devoted to her "husband." Both wives were firmly convinced that their husband was a man and ridiculed the idea that "he" could be a woman. I am informed that De Raylan wore a very elaborately constructed artificial penis. In her will she made careful arrangements to prevent detection of sex after death, but these were frustrated, as she died in a hospital.

According to another account of de Raylan's life, the two wives were incredulous that their husband had been a woman and expressed no regrets about their marriage.[75]

Female Friendships and Boston Marriages. Women did not have to pass as men in order to enjoy intimate relationships with other women. Historian Lillian Faderman has documented dozens of examples of intense, marriage–like friendships between pairs of women from the Renaissance to the twentieth century.[76] Such passionate friendships became a social phenomenon in the eighteenth century, when a greatly increased number of women had the economic means to be independent of men (without passing as men). For many, these same-sex relationships generated a great deal more emotional intensity than they could find in marriage. For example, the celebrated "Ladies of

Llangollen," Sarah Pononsby and Eleanor Butler, disguised themselves as men and eloped together in 1778. They settled down in
Llangollen Vale in 1780 and shared every moment together for the
next 53 years.[77] Their "Davidean friendship" (as poet Anna Steward
termed it) became a celebrated romantic ideal, and their friend
William Wordsworth, described them in this way:

> Sisters in love, a love allowed to climb
> Ev'n on this earth, above the reach of time.

The ladies' union is the best documented of this period, but Faderman has found evidence of many other romantic female relationships
occurring throughout the late eighteenth century.

These relationships proliferated in the nineteenth century as expanded economic opportunities gave some women greater freedom
to marry or not and to fashion their own personal relationships. This
era even came up with a name for a long-term monogamous relationship between two otherwise unmarried women: a "Boston
marriage."[78] These relationships were so called because they were
similar to the lives of a female couple in Henry James's 1885 novel,
The Bostonians. Boston marriages were very popular among well-
educated, professional women in particular.

The Love of Comrades. The emotional, and surely sometimes sexual,
needs that Boston marriages filled for women were similarly gratified
in male "buddy" relationships during the eighteenth and nineteenth
centuries. Men in frontier communities without women tended to
form personal and often sexual partnerships with other men. Such
intimate buddy or sidekick relationships have been documented for
communities of pirates, hoboes, cowboys, and miners. The accounts
are striking in the parallels between these informal same-sex relationships and the customs of different-sex marriage.[79] Even in mainstream
contexts male relationships were not uncommon in nineteenth-
century America. For example, Thomas Wentworth Higginson
wrote of his Harvard classmate William Henry Hurlbut: "I never
loved but one male friend with passion—and for him my love had no
bounds—all that my natural fastidiousness and cautious reserve kept
from others I poured on him; to say that I would have died for him

was nothing. I lived for him."[80] Notwithstanding this passionate language, it is not clear that Higginson and Hurlbut engaged in sexual activities, but there is such evidence for other male-bonded friends of that era.[81]

The poet Walt Whitman sought to describe this "manly love," what he called the "love of comrades," in the forty-five *Calamus* poems published in the 1860 edition of *Leaves of Grass*.[82] Although closeted by today's standards, Whitman glorified male companionate relationships:

> Clear to me now, standards not yet published—clear to me that my
>   Soul,
> That the Soul of the man I speak for, feeds, rejoices only in comrades:
> Here, by myself, away from the clank of the world,
> Tallying and talked to here by tongues aromatic,
> No longer abashed—for in this secluded spot I can respond as I would
>   not dare elsewhere,
> Strong upon me the life that does not exhibit itself, yet contains all the
>   rest,
> Resolved to sing no songs to-day but those of manly attachment,
> Projecting them along that substantial life,
> Bequeathing, hence, types of athletic love,
> Afternoon, this delicious Ninth Month, in my forty-first year,
> I proceed, for all who are, or have been, young men,
> To tell the secrets of my nights and days,
> To celebrate the needs of comrades.

Whitman was the century's master of a male eroticism barely concealed beneath the language of comradeship.

In 1869, German psychiatrist Carl von Westphal published a case study of a woman who cross-dressed and was attracted to other women sexually. While such preferences presented nothing new, Westphal's prognosis did: the woman, he concluded, was a "congenital invert" whose abnormality was not an adaptation to the boring lot women faced day in and day out but was instead a result of physical degeneration and mental neurosis. Westphal's study and subsequent ones conducted by Richard von Krafft-Ebing and Havelock Ellis contributed to a popular as well as medical sensation. Once the category of the "true invert" (soon popularized as the homosexual) gained currency among the American middle class, same-sex relationships became newly problematic. Same-sex intimacy, once stigmatized as sodomy, was now evidence of "inversion" or "homo-sexuality." Everyone now had a sexual identity, some healthily normal, others abominably "perverted." In this context Whitman's *Calamus* poems took on a different kind of meaning. Whereas his late-nineteenth-century contemporaries were alternately impressed, mystified, and scandalized by Whitman's erotic romanticism, early-twentieth-century medical critics used it to expose Whitman's homosexuality, his passive inversion, and his "thorough consciousness of abnormality."[83] Just as male comradeship grew problematic, so too did intimate female friendships; Boston marriages had become objects of suspicion by 1920.[84] After World War I, the phenomenon of same-sex unions became joined with America's increasing hysteria about homosexuality.

Homosexual Marriages

The West's obsession with sexual identity yielded results that the new inquisitors did not desire. In the face of (and perhaps even because of) increased scrutiny of sexual practices, more and more people attracted to those of their own sex gravitated to underground communities inhabited by like-feeling residents, namely, subcultures of inverts in urban areas. Such subcultures existed in London; Paris; most major Dutch cities, including Amsterdam; most major Italian cities, including Venice; and elsewhere by the early eighteenth century.[85] Same-sex relationships were not uncommon once these subcultures became established. On occasion such couples were legally married. Same-sex male and female couples repeatedly sought legal marriages in the Netherlands in the sixteenth and seventeenth centuries. At least one female couple obtained a marriage authorization, and other couples entered into marriage contracts that might have been binding.[86]

In the United States discernible subcultures of inverts were well established in New York City, Chicago, San Francisco, Washington, D.C., and other cities before World War I.[87] The subcultures were built around gathering places for people who recognized themselves as inverted: YMCAs, tenements, bars and pool halls, private bathhouses, and public streets and parks. Socializing beyond the margins of society and united primarily by sexual interests, these early denizens of "the life" did not create many lasting relationships. For men in particular, the characteristic activity was "cruising" for sex partners, and the common enemy was the vice squad and its decoy cops. Apart from the fun of sex, these men often reveled in the cat-and-mouse games they had to play with potential partners ("Is he one of us?"), family ("What excuse can I give tonight?"), and cops ("Is this a trap?"). Strong social disapproval of inversion and uneven legal surveillance contributed to a community of outlaws and lone rangers.

The culture of cruising did not satisfy the emotional needs of the aborning homosexual community, however. The feelings of many in that community were similar to those Washington's Jeb Alexander confessed to his diary in 1921: "I want love and affection. Damn it!"[88] Jeb was not able to hold on to his true love, C. C. Dasham, but some homosexuals were able to form lasting relationships, especially after World War I. Expatriates Gertrude Stein and Alice Toklas are probably the best-known example of an American same-sex couple in this era, but others less noted by history were able to come together within American borders. In Harlem's thriving subculture, butch–femme lesbian couples married each other in large wedding ceremonies replete with bridesmaids and attendants. "Real marriage licenses were obtained by masculinizing a first name or having a gay male surrogate apply for a license for the lesbian couple. Those licenses were actually placed on file in the New York City Marriage Bureau. The marriages were often common knowledge among Harlem heterosexuals."[89] Similar stories can be told for homosexual people in other cities. Lesbians in particular were able to combine same-sex socializing in bars and streets with the formation of companionate relationships.[90] Men attracted to other men were less successful even when, like Jeb Alexander, they strongly desired commitment from one other person.[91]

World War II stimulated a major expansion of homosexual subcultures. The growth of these communities made it easier to find partners, and with more support from friends these partnerships lasted longer. The upswing in same-sex partnering fueled interest in homosexual marriages (see chapter 3). As early as 1953 the Mattachine Society (the leading early homophile organization) was debating the issue.[92] Many same-sex couples engaged in what Donald

Webster Cory and John LeRoy described in 1963 as "mock weddings," events at which "all the formalities of an actually legally certified and religiously sanctioned ceremony are carefully copied." According to Cory and LeRoy:[93]

> Cases have been known of an all-male couple, one of whom will don an expensive bridal gown, or if they are both females, one of the women will wear a tuxedo. Engraved invitations are sent out, an elaborate cake is baked, and a banquet is prepared. If a "gay" (homosexual) religious official is known, his services may be sought. . . .
>
> With or without the aid of a religious official, however, some form of ceremony may take place in which the partners vow lifelong devotion to each other, and the wedding rings are put in place. The bridal march is played, while the guests follow the patterns of normal weddings.

In 1963 it went without saying that these "marriages" enjoyed neither legal recognition nor the prospect of legal recognition. Not only were homosexuals still socially marginal, but they were politically despised. At the same time homosexuals were congregating together in greater numbers, mainstream culture was seeking to reaffirm traditional gender and family values. The predictable result was a political era of panicked reaction. The craze of the McCarthy persecution of political "subversives" focused equally on sexual "deviates." Far from tolerating open homosexual relationships, this era sought out homosexuals simply to persecute them. It was a period where employer investigations (especially in the public sector) rooted out homosexual employees, police dragnets emptied lesbian and gay bars, and military witch-hunts purged thousands of homosexuals from the armed services.[94]

The Gay Marriage Movement

The June 1969 riots triggered by a police raid of the Stonewall Bar in Greenwich Village did for homosexual citizens what lunch counter sit-ins did for African Americans: they galvanized an excluded community and alerted mainstream society that the excluded were prepared to resist oppressive social practices. People came out of the closet in droves and organized in hundreds of social and legal action groups. The homophile movement of the 1950s and early 1960s became, literally overnight, "gay liberation," with an ambitious agenda of social and legal demands. The ramifications of "gay lib" are deep and complex. Three are relevant to the history of same-sex marriage.

A Demand for Gay Marriage. As lesbians, gay men, and bisexuals became more open about their sexuality, more long-term same-sex relationships than ever before in human history were established. Empirical and other surveys in the decade after Stonewall found that lesbian, gay, and bisexual people coupled in a range of patterns, with a strong trend toward close-coupled unions. The partners in such unions overwhelmingly considered themselves committed, and many considered themselves "married."[95] In spite of continued social prejudice, legal disadvantages, and economic discrimination, more and more lesbians, gay men, and bisexuals were openly coupled with partners of their own sex. Studies in the 1980s and 1990s have found an even more pronounced tendency for the unions of lesbian and gay couples to involve long-term commitment. For just one example, Overlooked Opinions, a company that surveys several thousand lesbians and gay men periodically, found in 1990 that 75 percent of the lesbians and 60 percent of the gay men were in an "on-going intimate" relationship.[96] The 1990 Census reported that 157,400 same-sex couples identified themselves. In short, more same-sex couples have been openly bonding in patterns resembling different-sex marriage. This is wholly unsurprising. Lesbians and gay men are a cross section of America. With their relationships more open, one would expect them to resemble more closely those of other Americans.

As this chapter has tried to show, the foregoing development is not new in human history. The gay and lesbian marriages of today bear resemblance to the same-sex unions associated with classical Lesbos and Crete, the same-sex marriages of imperial Rome, the brotherhood unions of the early Church, Native Americans' *berdache* marriages, woman marriage in Africa, and Chinese male marriages and sisterhoods. What is similar about all these unions is that they are a response to the human desire for companionate relationship. What is new is that a community defined solely by its members' "sexual orientation" (a concept that is uniquely Western) is seeking recognition of their unions by the larger community that for centuries persecuted them. Also distinctive is the way in which same-sex marriage is a barometer of the "cross-civilization" of gay and straight culture.[b] Few gay people aspired toward lifetime commitment when they were social and political outlaws. Now that being lesbian, bisexual, or gay is better tolerated, gays view marriage not only as more conceivable but more desirable.

The Religious Debate. Richard John Baker and James Michael McConnell fell dead in love with one another while they were graduate students. When Baker matriculated as a law student at the University of Minnesota in 1970, they moved to Minneapolis; McConnell got a job as a cataloguer at the university. They attended religious services at the university's Newman Center Chapel. One Sunday, Baker asked the priest, "Do you feel that if two people give themselves in love to each other and want to grow together with mutual understanding, that Jesus would be open to such a union if the people were of the same sex?"[97] After thinking for a moment, the priest reportedly said, "Yes, in my opinion, Christ would be open." Baker and McConnell purchased wedding rings and were married in a religious ceremony. Since then, thousands of lesbian and gay couples have similarly petitioned for religious blessing of their unions. Perhaps surprisingly, their marriages have been sanctified by representatives of virtually all of America's leading religions. The appendix to this book includes letters in support of same-sex marriages by a variety of religious figures in the United States.

Many of the gay marriages have been performed by religious groups formed specifically for the gay, lesbian, and bisexual faithful. One such group, the Universal Fellowship of Metropolitan Community Churches (MCC), has been conducting Holy Union ceremonies for same-sex couples since 1968. The MCC estimates that its ministers perform more than two thousand gay marriages each year.[98] Temple Beth Chayim Chadashim in Los Angeles (founded 1972),

---

[b]Recall my insistence in chapter 1 that same-sex marriage serves to "civilize" straights as well as gays. Cross-civilization, therefore, is a phenomenon by which each group is illuminated, educated, and even domesticated by values the other group has to offer.

Congregation Bet Mishpachah in Washington, D.C. (founded 1975), and other lesbian and gay synagogues have regularly performed ceremonies of *kiddushin* (sanctified holy union, usually translated as marriage) for same-sex couples within the Judaic tradition.

The situation is more complicated among mainstream religious denominations. A few are openly supportive of gay marriages or unions. Following a vote on the matter in 1984, the Unitarian Universalist Association now "affirms the growing practice of some of its ministers of conducting services of union of gay and lesbian couples and urges member societies to support their ministers" in this practice.[99] The Society of Friends leaves all issues to congregational decision, and thousands of same-sex marriages have been sanctified in Quaker ceremonies since the 1970s (see the representative Quaker letters in the appendix). The General Assembly of the Union of American Hebrew Congregations (Reform Jewish synagogues) adopted a resolution in 1993 advocating legal recognition of same-sex unions.

Other denominations are still studying the issue. The validity of same-sex marriage has been debated at the national level by the Presbyterian, Episcopal, Lutheran, and Methodist Churches. A committee of Episcopal bishops proposed in 1994 that "[homosexual] relationships need and should receive the pastoral care of the church," but the church diluted and downgraded the report.[100] After intense debate, also in 1994, the General Assembly of the Presbyterian Church (U.S.A.) adopted a resolution that its ministers are "not permitted" to bless same-sex unions.[101] The Lutheran Church in 1993 debated but did not adopt a report advocating the blessing and legal recognition of same-sex unions.[102] The Methodists followed a similar path in 1992.[103] The pattern in these denominations has been the following: An individual church will bless a same-sex union or marriage, and the ministers and theologians then call for study of the issue. A report is written that is open to the idea. The report ignites a firestorm of protest from traditionalists in the denomination. The issue is suppressed or rejected at the denomination level. Local churches and theologians again press the issue some years later, and the cycle begins again. My guess is that one or more of the foregoing denominations will tilt toward same-sex unions or marriages in the next five to ten years.

Even the religions that are most prominently opposed to gay marriages have clergy who perform gay marriage ceremonies. The Roman Catholic Church firmly opposes gay marriage,[104] but its celebrated priest John J. McNeill says that he and many other Catholic clergy have performed same-sex commitment services.[105] Although Father McNeill's position is marginalized within the Catholic Church, it reflects the views of many devout Catholics. Support for same-sex marriage is probably most scarce among Baptists in the South. When the Pullen Memorial Church of Raleigh, North Carolina, blessed a same-sex union, the Southern Baptist Convention expelled the church.[106]

In short, most religious groups in the United States have confronted the issue of same-sex marriage or union in the last twenty-five years. The religious leaders who have been most engaged in ministering to areas with sizable gay and lesbian populations have been the most accepting of same-sex unions and marriages. Their view is that same-sex marriage is a wonderful (civilizing) link between the gay community and the church. By sanctifying gay unions, the church is civilizing gays into the deep emotional and spiritual traditions of religion. By going to a church for celebration of their unions, lesbian and gay couples are civilizing straights as to the heterogeneity of marriage's companionate bonds.

The Legal Debate. With the blessing of their minister, Jack Baker and Mike McConnell applied for a state marriage license on May 18, 1970. The clerk of the Hennepin County District Court, Gerald Nelson, denied their request on May 22, after obtaining an opinion from the district attorney that same-sex couples were not allowed such licenses under Minnesota law. Baker and McConnell sued Nelson on the ground that denying them a marriage license is unconstitutional. They lost. The Minnesota Supreme Court's 1971 decision in *Baker v. Nelson,* affirming the state's refusal, was the first appellate decision in the United States on the issue of same-sex marriage.[107] Since 1971, lawsuits by other same-sex couples in other states have steadily pressed constitutional objections to the law's exclusion of gay and lesbian couples from the institution of marriage. The plaintiffs lost in all the cases[108]—until the Hawaii Supreme Court told the state that it was required to demonstrate a compelling reason to deny Ninia Baehr and Genora Dancel a marriage license.[109] Chapter 3 will introduce you to more of the plaintiffs in these cases. Chapters 4 through 6 will analyze the arguments pressed in those cases and will suggest reasons why the state must recognize same-sex marriages under the United States Constitution or under state constitutions.

The legal debate over same-sex marriages has also been conducted in legislatures. In connection with a bill revamping the District of Columbia marriage laws in 1975, Councilman Arrington Dixon included a provision authorizing same-sex marriages in the District. Gay activist groups supported the Dixon bill, but the Catholic Archdiocese of Washington and other opponents raised such a fuss that Dixon withdrew the proposal.[110] Bills to allow same-sex marriage have occasionally been introduced in state legislatures (e.g., California in 1991), but none has made any progress. On the other hand, some recognition of same-sex unions has been accorded by domestic partnership laws adopted in more than thirty cities, counties, and municipalities. These laws provide for same-sex couples to register their "domestic partnerships" and for a few legal benefits, mainly hospital visitation rights (see chapter 3). In July 1995, Mayor Benjamin Nichols and a unanimous Common Council of Ithaca, New York, fleetingly went on record in favor of same-sex marriage under New York law. Do the Hawaii Supreme Court's decision and the action of Ithaca demonstrate that legal resistance to same-sex marriage is weakening? Evidence from other parts of the world suggests that this might be the case.

Legal recognition of same-sex unions has made greater progress in Europe.[111] In 1987, Sweden adopted a nationwide law providing many legal benefits (fewer than those of marriage but more than those specified in American domestic partnership laws) for cohabiting couples. In 1989, Denmark enacted the Registered Partnership Act,[112] which provides same-sex couples with almost all the rights and obligations of different-sex marriages. The act applies only to same-sex couples (section 1), and at least one partner must have his or her permanent residence in Denmark and be a Danish citizen (section 2[2]). To obtain the benefits of the act, the partners must register according to rules laid down by the minister of justice (sections 1, 2[3]). Once registered, the partners have most of the rights, benefits, and obligations of married spouses (section 3). The main exception is that registered partners do not enjoy the same rights of adoption that married couples enjoy (section 4[1]). Danish divorce law generally governs the terms by which a registered partnership is dissolved (section 5). Norway adopted a similar statute in 1993, and Sweden expanded its cohabitation law to the same effect in 1994.

The Scandinavian laws come close to recognizing a same-sex union as marriage. Other European countries may take the final step. The European Parliament in February 1994 passed a resolution calling for study and, ultimately, adoption of a European Community recommendation to end "the barring of lesbians and homosexual couples from marriage or from an equivalent legal framework."[113] As this book goes to press, the Netherlands is debating the issue; among the options are simply extending Dutch marriage law to include same-sex couples or creating a Danish-style partnership registry extending most or all marital benefits and obligations to registered same-sex couples. Whatever the outcome of the Netherlands' deliberations, you can be assured that same-sex marriage is an issue that has arrived worldwide and that efforts to head it off will only be successful in the short term. Indeed, even laws such as the Danish statute, which uses a euphemism rather than the word *marriage* for the union of a same-sex couple, may be unstable solutions in the longer term. The argument of this book is that Western culture generally and the United States in particular ought to and must recognize same-sex *marriages*.

3

THE DEBATE WITHIN THE
LESBIAN AND GAY COMMUNITY

When Ninia Baehr and Genora Dancel go to court on behalf of marriage, they will be associating themselves with an institution under siege. Many heterosexuals cohabitate or remain single rather than marry, and half or more different-sex marriages end in divorce. Some feminists criticize marriage as oppressive to women. It should be no surprise, then, that for more than forty years gay rights leaders and thinkers have actively debated the following questions: Is same-sex marriage something the gay rights movement should seek? Should it be a priority? Is compromise (with the straight community) possible? Although straight readers may find this debate somewhat curious, it is relevant for all of us. Indeed, the discussions within the lesbian and gay communities illuminate the civilizing as well as problematic features of marriage that matter today—for both straights and gays.

Baehr and Dancel are on the right side. Marriage is not for everyone, but it should be an option for lesbians, gay men, bisexuals, and transgendered people. The heart of this chapter will be an exploration of the reasons why our community should seek this option. The most important is an argument of formal equality: Gay couples should have the same rights that straight couples have. Other arguments focus on functional reasons why marriage is useful for lesbians, gay men, bisexuals, and transgendered people. The rights and privileges provided by marriage laws afford tangible benefits to same-sex couples, and the duties and obligations imposed by marriage contribute to interpersonal commitment. In short, marriage is not so rotten as its detractors assert. The chapter concludes with an extended discussion of the most serious objections by gay men and lesbians to same-sex marriage, together with responses.

A HISTORY OF THE DEBATE

During the 1950s and 1960s the rights of gay people were vigorously pressed by the homophile movement, particularly the Mattachine Society (mainly gay men) and the Daughters of Bilitis (lesbians). These groups did not, however, stress marriage. E. W. Saunders wrote in 1953 that any serious effort to attain rights for homosexuals must advocate marriage rights, but he admitted that marriage was not then a prominent item in the homophile agenda.[1] During the period after World War II, homosexuals were fired right and left from federal and state government service, spied on and followed by the FBI, harassed and extorted by local police, beaten up and murdered by hustlers and hoodlums, excluded from entry into the country, and incarcerated and electroshocked pursuant to the "sexual psychopath" laws adopted by about half the states. Fighting these attacks had to come first. It was impractical for homophile groups to invest any of their scarce resources in a positive agenda such as marriage. Moreover, the antihomosexual hysteria of the 1950s assured that demands for homosexual marriage would not have been taken seriously and, if anything, would have been risky to make. An FBI investigation of "Mr. and Mrs. David Warren" turned up a lesbian couple (Thelma Jane Walker and Marieta Cook) who had obtained a marriage license in 1947. The couple were reportedly charged with criminal perjury.[2]

Although the foregoing are the obvious reasons why marriage would not have been a homophile priority, authors of that time emphasized an altogether different reason. Published in 1951, *The Homosexual in America* was the first major American book advocating homosexual rights by a homosexual, Donald Webster Cory (a pseudonym). Cory's chapter on relationships responds to the question, "Is it possible or desirable for two young people of the same sex to be in love with each other, just as a man is in love with a woman; to show the same affection and interest, to offer the same loyalty, to form a union as permanent?"[3] Cory's initial, agonized discussion, especially his belief that the homosexual's "deepgoing shame" precludes lasting unions,[4] was and still is sorely dated. Also open to some question is Cory's argument that male homosexual couples tend to be more unstable than heterosexual couples, because men tend to be promiscuous. Neo-Darwinian evolutionary biologists make the same argument today, but male promiscuity is as much a social phenomenon as a biological one. Gay monogamy has greatly increased in the last decade, both in response to AIDS and to some social acceptance of committed relationships.[5] Even Cory maintained that society and law bear much of the responsibility for the impermanence of homosexual relationships. Whereas society and law reinforce the commitment of the husband and wife, the antihomosexual attitudes of parents, friends, and law enforcement officials pry the homosexual couple apart and contribute to promiscuity and loneliness. This phenomenon, Cory noted, is a good reason why homosexuals ought to be able to participate in state-sanctioned marriage.

The homophile movement continued to focus on employment and police harassment issues through the 1960s. The years immediately after the Stonewall riots of June 1969 drastically expanded the agenda and number of people involved in "gay liberation," as the movement came to be called. The severity of antihomosexual police harassment and employment discrimination diminished in the big cities as gays became a political force to be reckoned with. Relief from much of the serious gay bashing freed up gay political energy for other issues. Would that energy be applied to gay marriage?

Much of the political energy freed up by Stonewall was radical. The Gay Liberation Front (GLF) was formed in New York within a month of the Stonewall riots. Nowhere was its radical philosophy more sharply expressed than in its attitude toward marriage: "We expose the institution of marriage as one of the most insidious and basic sustainers of the system. The family is the microcosm of oppression," said GLF's leaders in July 1969.[6] The radical critique gave a different spin to Cory's argument about promiscuity. By insisting on monogamy, marriage suppresses the sexual liberty that is a chief aim of gay liberation, the radicals maintained.[7] Drawing from Marxist theory, radicals also argued that marriage is an extension of the capitalist system, that through the customs of courtship and marriage, "[c]ompetition and exclusive possession, traits of the marketplace, are extended to erotic relations among persons."[8] The most important radical criticism of marriage drew from feminist and lesbian feminist theory.[9] Radicalesbians, another post-Stonewall liberation group, denounced marriage because it has traditionally been deployed to enslave and brutalize women. Women were enslaved by the role of housekeeper, rendering them dependent on the male breadwinner, and they were brutalized by the law's refusal to recognize a husband's rape of his wife as criminal or at least tortious.

Many gay activists did not subscribe to the ideas and rhetoric of the GLF and the Radicalesbians, however. The National Coalition of Gay Organizations drew up a comprehensive list of demands for law reform in February 1972. Reflecting the ideas of both gay marriage advocates and radical critics, the last demand was stated as follows: "Repeal of all legislative provisions that restrict the sex or number of persons entering into a marriage unit and extension of legal benefits of marriage to all persons who cohabit regardless of sex or numbers."[10] More important, lesbian and gay couples were voting with their feet, as they marched into clerks' offices to demand marriage licenses. Chapter 2 introduced Jack Baker and Mike McConnell, the first gay couple to file a lawsuit seeking recognition of their marriage. McConnell lost his job and the plaintiffs lost their lawsuit in *Baker v. Nelson*,[11] but they were followed by a steady stream of lesbian and gay couples seeking legal recognition for their unions.

Because the gay marriage issue was an unformed one in the early 1970s, marriage license clerks did not know exactly how to respond to these new kinds of applicants. When Tracy Knight, a dancer, and Marjorie Ruth Jones, a mother of three, applied to Jefferson County [Kentucky] Clerk of the Circuit Court James Hallahan, the clerk asked the district attorney for a legal opinion. District Attorney J. Bruce Miller opined that the application should be denied because it represented "the pure pursuit of hedonistic and sexual pleasure."[12] Hallahan denied the application. He later testified that such a marriage would "lead to a breakdown in the sanctity of government," would jeopardize the country's morality, and "could spread all over the world."[13]

Other clerks and district attorneys were more open-minded. In March 1975, Boulder County [Colorado] Clerk Cela Rorex issued marriage licenses to no fewer than six same-sex couples after District Attorney William C. Wise told her that Colorado's gender-neutral marriage law did not clearly forbid same-sex marriages.[14] "I don't profess to be knowledgeable about homosexuality or even understand it," said Rorex. "But it's not my business why people get married. No minority should be discriminated against."[15] Both Rorex and Wise received more than a hundred telephone calls, some of which threatened them with God's punishment or violence because of their understanding of the law. Responding to citizen complaints, the state attorney general put a stop to the Boulder County experiment in same-sex marriage. A series of lawsuits by the married couples followed.[16]

A few months later, the Montgomery County [Maryland] Clerk's Office issued a marriage license to Michelle Bush and Paulette Hall, even though Maryland had adopted a 1973 statute specifically prohibiting same-sex marriages.[17] The clerk grumbled that he had been misinformed as to the exact nature of the applicants, but a state attorney opined that the clerk could not revoke the license once he had issued it. In any event, the lesbian couple moved to the District of Columbia, where Councilman Arrington Dixon had introduced a bill to legalize gay marriage. The district's Gay Activists Alliance enthusiastically supported the bill, and longtime gay activist Frank Kameny proclaimed the bill necessary to assure lesbian and gay residents of first- rather than second-class citizenship. Alerted to the Dixon bill, however, the Roman Catholic Church and various Baptist churches mobilized in fervent opposition to the bill. Once the red flags were flying, Dixon withdrew his proposal.[18]

The difficulty of obtaining gay marriage rights from the political process was vividly illustrated by experiences in Wisconsin and California. In October 1971, Manomia Evans and Donna Burkett applied for a marriage license from Milwaukee County Clerk Thomas Zablocki.[19] Like other clerks, Zablocki obtained a legal opinion before acting; the county's lawyers told him not to issue the license.

Suing Zablocki, Evans and Burkett were the first African American couple to bring legal proceedings in pursuit of same-sex marriage. At the same time, Senate Bill 1410 was introduced in the Wisconsin legislature to amend the state's marriage law to include same-sex couples. Both the bill and the lawsuit went nowhere.

The California legislature, as part of a general review of domestic relations law in 1971, revised its authorization for marriage to include "[a]ny unmarried person,"[20] gender-neutral language that replaced the previous statutory language, "[a]ny man or woman." When the legislature repealed California's sodomy law, effective in 1976, gay activists interpreted California law to permit same-sex marriage and filed a lawsuit to that effect.[21] An alarmed County Clerks Association went to the legislature to fix the statute by changing *[a]ny person* back to *[a]ny man and woman*. After a gay-bashing debate over same-sex marriage, both chambers of the legislature voted by overwhelming margins to amend the marriage law precisely as requested.[22]

The stories of same-sex marriage petitions in Colorado, Maryland, the District of Columbia, Wisconsin, and California reveal some typical patterns of action and reaction. Lesbian and gay couples eagerly grasped for the right to marry after Stonewall and sometimes had initial success, but once the community at large was alerted to the possibility of "gay marriage," political opposition surfaced with a vengeance and crushed the effort. For two decades after the 1975 defeats, lesbian and gay couples continued to petition clerks, attorneys general, and (on rare occasion) legislators for recognition of their right to marry. For two decades, these officials said no.[23] Many of these petitions were accompanied by lawsuits alleging that state statutory or constitutional law assured gay people of same-sex marriage rights. The aspiration was that judges would be more farsighted and less attentive to popular attitudes. They were not. Starting with the Minnesota Supreme Court's decision in Jack Baker and Mike McConnell's case (1971) and continuing with the Kentucky Court of Appeals' decision in Tracy Knight and Marjorie Jones's case (1973), every judge who considered the issue before 1993 ruled that same-sex couples have neither a statutory nor a constitutional right to marry.[24] Even a New Jersey decision recognizing the marriage of a postoperative male-to-female transsexual and a biological male did so only because the judges were able to persuade themselves that the partners were different sexes.[25]

The issue of gay marriage was impaled on these failures to make any legal headway. Lacking success in the marriage forum, lawyers and activists concentrated their energies on issues for which there were tangible legal successes: repeal or nullification of state sodomy, vagrancy, and lewd conduct laws; challenges to state and some private discriminatory employment practices; partial nullification of the federal exclusions of gay people from immigration and citizenship; anticensorship campaigns; and official sanction of gay organizations on college and university campuses.

A further, and more curious, problem existed. In the late 1970s and early 1980s the gay marriage issue languished in a generational purgatory. Although there was a decided ebbing of sixties-style revolutionary radicalism, the new generation of "out" gay people was ambivalent about marriage. Older gay people were often the most enthusiastic about gay marriage and were typically the best exemplars of long-term same-sex relationships. Perhaps the most admired lesbian and gay couples in the 1970s were Phyllis Lyon and Del Martin, who founded the Daughters of Bilitis in 1955, and Harry Hay (who founded the Mattachine Society in 1951) and John Burnside.[26] These couples were exceptional—not for their longevity but for their openness. Most older lesbian and gay couples remained in the closet, even after Stonewall. As a group they played little role in post-1969 gay liberation.[a] The younger lesbians, gay men, bisexuals, and transgendered people who came out after Stonewall—the queer baby boomers—dominated the gay liberation movement after 1969. The more radical activists were disinclined to seek or even approve of gay marriage, for the reasons developed earlier.[27] Many of the less radical gay activists were discouraged from giving same-sex marriage a high priority because of the free-swinging sexuality of the gay subculture in particular, the many other issues that demanded attention, and the singular lack of success of gay marriage in the legal arena.

---

[a]As individuals, some of these first-generation lesbian and gay activists have continued to play prominent roles. Del Martin and Frank Kameny are the most obvious examples. Both have been strong advocates of same-sex marriage.

Nonetheless, the 1980s saw a stealthy revival of the gay marriage issue.[28] The revival was a product of several forces. One was the success of the gay rights movement in reducing discrimination against lesbian, gay, and bisexual employees, especially state and local government workers. Success in that arena bred dissatisfaction in another. Lesbian and gay employees with partners were being paid far less than similarly situated but married heterosexuals, because the latter had access to increasingly lucrative spousal health and insurance benefits. More important, gay men, lesbians, and bisexuals were themselves changing in the 1980s and changing in ways that made them more likely to settle down in a committed relationship. The "queer boomers" were aging, making more money than love, and settling down with partners. The guppie (gay urban professional) with a partner and a Porsche was replacing the free love advocate with a placard and a toke. The new Generation Xers were open to the diverse sexuality offered by gay liberation but more skeptical of its early barn-burning radicalism.[29]

The role of the AIDS epidemic is surely as complicated as it is significant. Its most apparent effect has been to scare gay and bisexual men into safer sex with fewer partners, but its deeper consequences are more important for the marriage issue. Commitment to another partner became a more attractive norm for those infected by the virus that leads to AIDS, as well as for those not infected. The need of people with AIDS for physical as well as emotional support brought many couples together and cemented more relationships than it tore apart. Most important, AIDS helped bring lesbians and gay men back together in a vigil of collective care for the suffering and dying. Whatever gravity gay life may have lacked in the disco seventies it acquired in the health crisis of the eighties. What it lost in youth and innocence it gained in dignity. Gay cruising and experimentation, noted by Cory as a permanent obstacle to gay marriage, gave way somewhat in the 1980s to a more lesbian-like interest in commitment. Since 1981 and probably earlier, gays were civilizing themselves. Part of our self-civilization has been an insistence on the right to marry.

One response of gay activists to these developments has been pragmatic and somewhat successful: the domestic partnership movement.[30] The first major domestic partnership bill was passed by the

San Francisco Board of Supervisors in 1982, but Mayor Diane Feinstein vetoed it on the ground that anything that even faintly "mimics a marriage license" was unacceptable to straight society.[31] Two years later, the Berkeley City Council adopted the first operative municipal domestic partnership policy, which ultimately allowed city employees to obtain health benefits for their registered domestic partners.[32] Local coalitions of gay activists and allies obtained similar or slightly broader domestic partnership ordinances, executive orders, or policies in West Hollywood (1985, implemented in 1989), Santa Cruz and Madison (1986), Los Angeles (1988), Seattle and New York City (1989), San Francisco (1990, after a referendum repealed a 1989 ordinance), Washington, D.C. (1991), Chicago and Baltimore (1993), New Orleans and San Diego (1994), and Denver (1995). The first county-wide domestic partnership policy was adopted in 1990 by Santa Cruz County. Vermont was the first state to offer domestic partnership benefits to its employees (1994). In the same year, the California legislature passed a domestic partnership bill; like Mayor Feinstein a dozen years earlier, Governor Pete Wilson vetoed the bill on the ground that it would be a "foot in the door" for same-sex marriage.[33]

A little toe, at best, Governor. Domestic partnership laws usually provide pitifully few benefits: registration as a "domestic partner," allowance for municipal employees to add their domestic partners to their health insurance (usually at market, not reduced, rates), and sometimes hospital visitation privileges. (Compare this svelte list with the ample array of benefits for married couples, detailed in the next part of this chapter.) In most jurisdictions only a handful of employees have registered, many or even most of them with different-sex partners. More economically meaningful have been domestic partnership policies adopted by hundreds of nonstate employers (AT&T and Stanford University were among the pioneers), for those policies typically allow the domestic partner to be added to their employees' fringe benefits package on the same terms as spouses. Unhappily, even this benefit is diluted by the federal government's position that the employer subsidy is taxable for domestic partners but not for spouses.

A further response of the gaylegal community has been piecemeal litigation to expand particular family benefits to same-sex partners.

In the most prominent example, the New York Court of Appeals held in *Braschi v. Stahl Associates*[34] that a long-term same-sex companion was a "family member" who could succeed his lover as a tenant in a rent-controlled New York City flat. Several states and numerous local governments accord government workers leave time to care for same-sex partners on similar or the same terms as for different-sex spouses or blood relatives. As of 1995, the gains have been modest in the United States. The New York Court of Appeals, for example, has declined to extend *Braschi* to any other statute dealing with family members.[35] In contrast, Canadian same-sex couples have been relatively successful in obtaining many of the benefits of marriage through benefit-by-benefit appeals or litigation.

In the last decade, the foregoing developments have suggested both the possibility of legal recognition for same-sex unions and the limitations of a piecemeal approach. As they had been through the 1970s and early 1980s, same-sex couples were still eager to assert their rights. In the late eighties, unlike the earlier period, a legally sophisticated "gayocracy" (Robert Raben's term) was in place that could champion such lawsuits. Nan Hunter established the American Civil Liberties Union's Gay and Lesbian Rights Project in 1984, and the Lambda Legal Defense and Education Fund was founded in 1973. Both organizations had top legal talent and could undertake constitutional impact litigation of the sort pioneered by the NAACP Legal Defense and Education Fund, Inc. As Hunter has suggested, 1989 was the critical year. It was a year of notable and publicized success for legal recognition of same-sex unions: New York City and San Francisco first adopted domestic partnership policies, the New York Court of Appeals decided *Braschi*, and Denmark amended its marriage laws to create "registered partnerships" as a virtual marriage for same-sex couples (recall the description in chapter 2 of the Danish law).[36]

The year 1989 is also when the internal organizational debates broke into the gay press. Thomas Stoddard, Lambda's executive director, argued in the pages of *OUT/LOOK* that "it is time to renew the effort to overturn the existing marriage laws [prohibiting same-sex marriages], with a commitment of money and energy."[37] The right to marry is practically useful to lesbian and gay couples and symbolically important for gay liberation. "[M]arriage is the political issue that most fully tests the dedication of people who are not gay to full equality for gay people, and it is also the issue most likely to lead ultimately to a world free from discrimination against lesbians and gay men," Stoddard claimed. Yet on the same pages of *OUT/LOOK*, Paula Ettelbrick, Lambda's legal director, countered that marriage is *not* a path to liberation. She feared that married lesbians and gay men would "force our assimilation into the mainstream" and defang the gay liberation movement.[38] Starting with the feminist critique that marriage is intrinsically limiting for women, Ettelbrick further maintained that gay marriage would squeeze out other forms of commitment such as domestic partnership. Because marriage is more attractive to middle-class gays, whose partners would be able to tap into substantial health care and other employee benefits, recognition of same-sex marriage might drive a decisive wedge between the more bourgeois gay population and the less privileged one, Ettelbrick warned. By emphasizing the sameness of lesbian and gay couples to straight spouses, a gay marriage movement would give up the dreams of transforming society held by the early gay libbers. It is no escape from Ozzie-and-Harriet sensibility to aspire to be Harriet-and-Harriet or Ozzie-and-Ozzie.

The Ettelbrick–Stoddard exchange set a high standard for debate. It has provoked considerable discussion and further commentary within gay communities all over the United States.[39] For example, Nan Hunter accepts Ettelbrick's concerns about marriage's patriarchal tradition but is nonetheless sympathetic to Stoddard's position. Her argument is that "legalizing lesbian and gay marriage would have enormous potential to destabilize the gendered definition of marriage."[40] In other words, old ideas that man is naturally the breadwinner-boss and woman is naturally the housekeeper-childrearer would be undermined by day-to-day examples of same-sex households where a woman is the breadwinner, a man is the housekeeper, or (best yet) the partners share the roles. By this logic, marriage for gays is not an end in and of itself so much as a means to impel a general redefinition of masculinity and femininity. Nancy Polikoff has responded to Hunter, arguing (from evidence I compiled!) that same-sex marriages in other cultures have aped rather than transformed traditional gender roles and thereby reinforced gender inequality.[41]

The gay marriage debate is now focused on Hawaii and the forth-coming trial in Ninia Baehr and Genora Dancel's case. Co-counsel for plaintiffs, Lambda Senior Staff Attorney Evan Wolfson, has emerged as a leading proponent of marriage within the gay, lesbian, bisexual, and transgendered community. While we await the outcome of the *Baehr* case and any future litigation, gays have time to ponder who is right: Stoddard, Hunter, and Wolfson, who say that gay mar-riage is an idea whose time has come, or Ettelbrick and Polikoff, who say that gay marriage will undermine gay liberation.

WHY THE GAY AND LESBIAN COMMUNITY SHOULD INSIST ON THE RIGHT TO MARRY

Nancy Polikoff and I are the District of Columbia touring company for the Ettelbrick–Stoddard debate. We have presented our view-points together or separately at several legal fora in and around the District. At such events no one (including Polikoff) disputes that lesbian, gay, transgendered, and bisexual Americans ought to have the same rights as everyone else. That is a decisive point in favor of in-sisting on legal recognition of same-sex marriage. The arguments remaining to the critics are that gay marriage should not be a high priority or that the drawbacks of gay marriage outweigh the argu-ment for formal equality. Yet the advantages of marriage rights and duties for gay couples who choose them are substantial enough to warrant this struggle as an important one that should be pursued.

Equal Citizenship for Gay Americans

The intuition of homophile authors, such as Cory and Saunders in the 1950s; litigants, such as Jack Baker and Mike McConnell in the 1970s; and activists, such as Hunter, Wolfson, and Stoddard in the 1990s, has been that lesbian, gay, and bisexual Americans will not enjoy the complete rights of citizenship until same-sex marriages are recognized by the state.[42] As a matter of political symbolism, we ought to be able to marry the persons we love. Without the right to marry,[b] gay Americans are second-class citizens. Stated another way, the United States will not be gay-civilized until its states include same-sex couples in the institution of marriage.

The states themselves advertise marriage as an institution fundamentally linked to political citizenship. Wisconsin's marriage statute codifies the understanding of marriage that recurs in the case law: "Marriage is the institution that is the foundation of the family and of society. Its stability is basic to morality and civilization, and of vital interest to society and the state."[43] Consistent with this philosophy, the states are not discriminating about who can partake of this institution. It is open to any consenting nonrelated couple—except any lesbian or gay couple.[c]

The state makes no moral judgment about whether the applicants for a marriage license are good people or will be good for one another. No state denies a marriage license to a couple on the ground that one of the partners is an abusive lover or that the couple is dysfunctional. Only a few states deny a marriage license to a couple on the ground that one of the partners carries an infectious agent, such as HIV, that might kill the other partner, and the federal Americans with Disabilities Act (ADA) nullifies those few laws that discriminate on this ground.[44] Most important, no state refuses to issue a marriage license to a couple on the ground that society disapproves of their erotic practices or their sexual orientation—unless they are homosexual. The state will issue a marriage license to sadists, masochists, transvestites, and fetishists so long as they are heterosexual sadists,

---

[b]An initial hurdle is the argument that gay, lesbian, and bisexual citizens are free to marry just like everyone else; a lesbian is free to marry a gay man (or any man!) and is only restrained from marrying another woman. This is a bad form of argument. If the state denied Jews the right to marry Jews, or Irish the right to marry Irish, anyone could see that this discriminates against Jewish or Irish citizens. Additionally, this is an argument that the Supreme Court rejected in *Loving v. Virginia*, 388 U.S. 1 (U.S. Supreme Court, 1967), which invalidated state prohibitions against different-race marriages. The state had argued that whites and blacks were equally free to marry but not to marry one another. Just as different-race couples were once denied the right to marry, so too are same-sex couples today denied a *meaningful* right to marry (see chapter 6).

[c]The statement in text is phrased to reflect that states disallow marriages where one party already has a legal spouse (bigamy), where the parties are closely related (incest), and where the parties have not meaningfully consented (force or fraud) or are not capable of meaningful consent (under age or mentally incapable). Chapter 5 of this book considers whether it follows from my arguments for same-sex marriage that the state should modify any of these other traditional restrictions.

masochists, transvestites, and fetishists. The state will issue a marriage license to a transsexual[d] only if the state can persuade itself that the transsexual is actually marrying someone of a different "sex"—a nice scholastic exercise.

In the course of surveying the state marriage laws, I was surprised to learn that the pedophile (someone who is sexually attracted to minors[e]) can also get a marriage license, so long as he or she is a heterosexual pedophile and is willing to go to some trouble (chapter 5). All fifty states plus the District of Columbia allow children under eighteen to marry (usually the consent of the child's parents is required). Forty-nine states (all but Oregon) allow sixteen-year-olds to marry under these circumstances. Forty states allow fourteen-year-olds to marry, and thirty-five states theoretically allow children under the age of fourteen to marry (usually a court order as well as the consent of the child's parents is required). Nine states allow children of any age to marry if the female is pregnant or has borne a child by the male (in these cases parental consent is usually *not* required). In a bizarre twist, it is statutory rape in Virginia for an adult male to have sex with a girl of fourteen, *unless* the man subsequently marries the girl.[45] Under this law, marriage not only tolerates heterosexual pedophilia but becomes the retrospective refuge of the heterosexual pedophile who has committed statutory rape.

The message of the foregoing pattern of statutes is that the state has made heterosexuality an essential criterion for full citizenship in the United States. If marriage is so "basic to morality and civilization" that it is open to all citizens of all sexual appetites and orientations, even those people who have transgressed other societal norms, then why should the institution not be open to lesbians and gay men? An indication of the respect Native American tribes have shown to *berdaches* as valued citizens of their communities is tribal recognition of same-sex *berdache* marriages. An indication of the dis-

---

[d]A transsexual is someone whose biological sex does not match his or her gender identification. Some transsexuals undergo hormone treatments or, ultimately, sex-change operations in an effort to match their sex with their gender. A transvestite is someone who enjoys dressing in the garb of the opposite sex. Most transvestites are not transsexual.

[e]I am not using the term *pedophile* in its traditional sense, namely, sex with a prepubescent child. My broader use, to include adolescents, is a popular use of the term.

respect American states have shown to gay men and lesbians is their refusal to recognize gay marriages. It is no defense for the states to claim that their laws only follow universal understandings of marriage and do not target homosexuals for exclusion. Chapter 2 demonstrates that there is nothing new about same-sex marriage in either human or American history. Many American churches are reconstructing marriage to accommodate lesbian and gay couples, and there is no reason the law cannot. Instead, in response to the gay marriage movement of the last twenty-five years, nine states[f] have amended their marriage laws specifically to exclude same-sex marriages. As Indiana's statute dogmatically puts it, "[o]nly a female may marry a male. Only a male may marry a female."[46]

State insistence on heterosexuality in marriage is a denial of formal equality for gay and lesbian citizens. Forty years ago there were many state policies that explicitly discriminated against homosexuals. Simply because of the sex of the person they loved, perfectly healthy, law-abiding people were excluded from government employment, denied security clearances, dishonorably discharged from the armed forces, refused professional licenses, arrested and harassed by police, and denied entry into this country or citizenship once here. Those policies were only possible in a culture in which homosexuals were considered subversive or psychopathic; that is, they were considered people who are not entitled to the full rights of citizenship. As those beliefs about homosexuals became discredited, the rigidly exclusionary policies dropped away, one by one.[47] Today, there is no government policy that explicitly and rigidly discriminates in this way except for the institution of marriage. Even the federal military exclusion, as currently formulated, allows for retention of lesbian, gay, and bisexual personnel who either "don't tell" or (possibly) who can show that they have not committed forbidden acts of sodomy.[48]

Marriage, in short, is the last legal bastion of *compulsory* heterosexuality (Adrienne Rich's term).[49] It is the most blatant evidence that gay and lesbian citizens must sit in the back of the law bus, paying for a first-class ticket and receiving second-class service. As E. W. Saunders observed in 1953, any serious agenda for homosexual

---

[f]California, Florida, Indiana, Kansas, Louisiana, Maryland, New Hampshire, Utah, and Virginia.

rights must presumptively include marriage. The remainder of this section of the chapter explains how both the benefits and obligations associated with marriage provide compelling functional reasons for gay people to insist upon this right.

The Practical Benefits of Marriage for Gay Couples

The state not only recognizes marriage, it encourages marriage.[50] Being married is a legal status that entails a broad range of associated rights and benefits for the couple. The following legal rights and benefits associated with marriage are provided by federal and state law in the District of Columbia, which is representative of other jurisdictions:[51]

- The right to receive, or the obligation to provide, spousal support and (in the event of separation or divorce) alimony and an equitable division of property[52]
- Preference in being appointed the personal representative of an intestate decedent, that is, someone who dies without a will[53]
- Priority in being appointed guardian of an incapacitated individual[54] or in being recognized as acting for an incapacitated person in making health care decisions[55]
- All manner of rights relating to the involuntary hospitalization of the spouse, including the right to petition,[56] the right to be notified,[57] and the right to initiate proceedings leading to release[58]
- The right to bring a lawsuit for the wrongful death of the spouse[59] and for the intentional infliction of emotional distress through harm to one's spouse
- The right to spousal benefits statutorily guaranteed to public employees, including health and life insurance[60] and disability payments,[61] plus similar contractual benefits for private sector employees
- The right to invoke special state protection for "intrafamily offenses"[62]
- The right to visit one's spouse on furlough while incarcerated in prison[63]
- The right to claim an evidentiary privilege for marital communications[64]

- A presumption of joint ownership of real estate as a tenancy in common[65] and a right not to be held to a mortgage or assignment of rights to creditors without the spouse's written permission[66]
- A right to priority in claiming human remains[67] and to make anatomical donations on behalf of the deceased spouse[68]
- Various inheritance rights, including priority in inheriting the property of an intestate decedent,[69] the right to a family allowance,[70] and the right to dower[71]
- The right for one's non-American spouse to qualify as an "immediate relative" (i.e., receive preferential immigration treatment)[72] and become an American citizen under federal law[73]
- The right to receive additional Social Security benefits based on the spouse's contribution[74]
- Survivor's benefits on the death of a veteran spouse[75]

An important right newly available to same-sex couples in the District of Columbia but not elsewhere is the right to adopt children. Add adoption rights to the list for most other jurisdictions.

There are serious implications of this list. An obvious implication is that when the state denies lesbian and gay couples a marriage license, it is not just denying them a simple, one-shot right to marry. Rather, the state is also denying those couples dozens of ongoing rights and privileges that are by law associated with marriage. More important, the listed rights and privileges of marriage are useful; they are good things to have. Some of the benefits are tangible economic advantages, especially employer spousal benefits and spousal rights to receive compensation for wrongful death and other injuries; the couple is economically better off with these benefits.

Many marital benefits are intangible but often just as valuable for the couple. Where they apply, these benefits contribute directly to the purposes of marriage. For most people, the overriding purpose of marriage is to be with the partner, physically and sexually. The couple can usually accomplish this without benefit of law. In exceptional circumstances—such as hospitalization, civil commitment, and incarceration—physical contact is mediated by third parties; the law often requires that the spouse, but not the friend or partner, be allowed physical visitation. Sometimes physical proximity is prevented by geopolitical factors; it is not uncommon to fall in love with a citizen of a different country. Under federal law a noncitizen is privileged to enter the United States and ultimately to become a citizen if she or he marries an American citizen. This is an enormous benefit of marriage in our transnational world. Same-sex couples denied this benefit often must go to great lengths just to be together.

Another typical goal of marriage is the creation of a single household. Two people become one, both metaphorically and legally. This is best exemplified in the support requirement but is also illustrated by the rule immunizing spousal communications. Such immunity both recognizes and contributes to the integrity of the couple's interpersonal sharing. The presumption that the spouse inherits and will administer the estate of a deceased has a dual role: it assures the integrity of the physical and economic household after the death of one spouse, and it creates a decision-making rule that probably reflects the actual preferences of the married couple. Similarly, when one spouse is incapacitated, the other is presumed to act in his or her stead and is first in line to be considered as a guardian.

The guardianship rule significantly contributes to a third goal of marriage: social insurance. Each spouse promises to marry the other "for better or for worse, for rich or for poor, in sickness and in health." So long as everything is for better, for rich, and in health, neither the law nor marriage has to do any heavy work. The work starts when something happens for worse, for poor, or in sickness. Marriage is a form of insurance against bad times; to the extent possible, the spouse is required to provide financial and emotional support when things are going badly. In the event of mental or physical breakdown (the nightmare people begin to have when they reach middle age), the unimpaired spouse is trusted to be both caretaker and surrogate decision maker.

Before turning to a final, and less obvious, benefit afforded by law to the married couple, I should note that some of the foregoing benefits can be created by the partners outside of marriage. Unmarried couples can create some features of marital union by drawing up wills setting forth inheritance and estate management rights, by directing care and responsibility in the event of incapacitation through living testaments, by setting up joint checking accounts, by agreeing to support the other spouse through explicit or implicit contracting, and by purchasing property in joint tenancy.[76] Numerous lesbian and gay couples have constructed do-it-yourself marriages, and such unions have the advantage of being tailor-made to the couples' specifications. Yet they have the disadvantage of requiring more planning and money than most couples are prepared to invest. A significant contribution that the law makes to married Americans is that it provides them with off-the-rack rules for a variety of occurrences (death, illness, poverty) that families often do not adequately plan for. Additionally, many of the advantages of marriage (such as hospital and prison visitation, employer fringe benefits) would otherwise have to be negotiated with third parties. Other advantages (spousal immunity, tort rights, citizenship for a non-American spouse) cannot be negotiated and are provided as a matter of law.

The insufficiency of self-help measures and a final benefit of marriage are revealed in the story of Karen Thompson and Sharon Kowalski.[77] Having exchanged rings and bought a house together, they were a committed couple living in Minnesota, the same state whence came the first gay marriage lawsuit by Baker and McConnell. In 1983, Kowalski was in an auto accident that left her mentally and physically disabled. Overruling Thompson's petition for joint guardianship, a judge appointed Kowalski's father, Donald, as her guardian. After a period of uneasy cooperation Donald Kowalski cut Thompson off from her partner, even though medical personnel testified that Sharon Kowalski responded best to therapy administered by the woman she loved. The father saw Thompson as an "animal" who was trying to corrupt his daughter, who he denied was a lesbian. After years of further litigation the Minnesota courts held that the father could not exclude Thompson. Very few couples plan for the sort of disaster that befell Sharon Kowalski and Karen Thompson. Heterosexual couples do not have to plan, for the law insulates the couple from avenging parents. Lesbian and gay couples alone suffer the consequences. That such couples are more likely to suffer from parental disapproval makes their need even greater, however.

The experience of Kowalski and Thompson suggests a subtle but important feature of the rights associated with marriage. Marital rights provide legally enforceable insulation protecting couples from outside interference. The powerful concept of marital privacy (reflected in the immunity for spousal communications, for one example) protects the married couple from state interference. Equally powerful is the law's empowerment of each spouse as presumptive guardian and representative of the other, for this protects the married couple from private interference. The law's protection of marital integrity is not always a boon, as the common law's discredited immunity for marital rape ought to remind us. In particular cases the spouse may not be the best decision maker, but in the general run of cases the law seems correct in presuming that their life partner should have priority in acting for those who are disabled.

Marital Duties and Interpersonal Commitment

Marriage is a bundle of rights, benefits, and *obligations*. No discussion can be complete without understanding the disadvantages of getting married. Again referring to the local and federal law applicable in the District of Columbia, the disadvantages or costs of getting married include the following (as of 1995):

- The obligation of sexual fidelity, enforced through criminal prohibition against adultery[78] and through the divorce law provision making adultery a ground for dissolving the marriage[79]
- The obligation to provide spousal support[80] and (in the event of separation or divorce) alimony and an equitable division of property[81]
- The emotional and financial expense of obtaining a divorce if the marriage does not work out
- The loss of some or all benefits pursuant to a range of federal welfare and social security programs[82]
- The modest "marriage penalty" for two-income families in paying federal and local income taxes
- Constriction of each spouse's economic opportunities because of conflict of interest and antinepotism rules in private as well as public workplaces[83]

The most significant implication of this list is that marriage is not a good idea for everyone. Its costs outweigh the benefits for many couples. Partners enjoying a sexually open relationship, for example, should consider the rules against adultery, even though they are virtually never enforced as a matter of criminal law. Moreover, for lesbian and gay couples there is a cost I have not listed: publicity. Marriage is a matter of public record. If one is still in the closet about one's sexual orientation (recall Kowalski and Thompson), marriage might risk unwelcome inquiries. This phenomenon reminds us of the complicated relationship between societal and legal homophobia.

Ironically, the biggest cost of marriage provides the best reason why gays and lesbians should seek legal recognition of their right to marry: marriage is easy to enter but hard to exit (domestic partnership, by contrast, is easy to exit as well as enter). That is a cost of marriage, but it also provides substantial advantages for the typical couple. One benefit is simply, but importantly, informational. When Ninia Baehr and Genora Dancel were dating, each shared her feelings of warmth and love for the other. Such verbal assurances are useful, but actions speak more loudly. An exclusive dating arrangement signals a certain level of love and commitment. Moving in together and setting up a joint household signals a different level of commitment, in part because each person knows that the partner would have to go to a fair amount of bother (finding a new place, moving out) if they were to break up. Getting married signals a significantly higher level of commitment, in part because the law imposes much greater obligations on the couple and makes it much more of a bother and expense to break up. Discussions about whether to move in together or to get married are an important way partners communicate with one another about the level of commitment they feel. The value of such discussions is diminished for gay couples because they do not have the option of legalized marriage. Thus, Dancel's proposal of marriage and Baehr's immediate acceptance signaled a higher level of commitment as a matter of words but not as a matter of action, because the two cannot yet be legally bound in matrimony.

Moreover, the duties and obligations of marriage directly contribute to interpersonal commitment. Any relationship has its ups and downs. Even the most ardent lovers regret their relationship at times. It is easier to walk out of a shared apartment than to walk out of a marriage. Hence, one function that marriage plays is to hold a union together during times of strife and disagreement and to force a sober second thought before a partner departs. To be sure, a large number of unions will not and should not last a lifetime; the costs of divorce often just forestall the inevitable and sometimes prevent breakups that should occur earlier. For the majority of married couples, however, the duties of the institution strengthen their lifelong commitment.

The foregoing argument assumes that interpersonal commitment is good. Is that proposition true in our individualistic society? The promise and the reasonable expectation of commitment are valuable for a variety of reasons, starting with the personal security that comes from knowing that one can depend on someone else for better or for worse (with an emphasis on the latter). Conversely, commitment provides an intense focal point for one to transcend the self and deepen one's identity through intimate interaction with another being. Consider this. We are all products of our relationships with our parents; the healthiest parent–child relationships are ones where children feel secure about the parent's commitment to them and their well-being. However complicated by biology, the mutual love between parent and child is as much a consequence as a cause of the mutual expectation that the relationship will be a lasting one. An analogous point can be made about partnership relations; they will be different, and deeper, if they are conducted within a mutual understanding of lasting commitment. As Professor Mitt Regan has argued,[84] the status of spousehood protects people's capacity for intimacy and thereby fosters a stable sense of self over time. The stable sense of self is at risk in a society that offers choice but not commitment, because such a world fractures self. Recall the parable of Buridan's ass: finding itself equidistant from two equally attractive haystacks, the animal starved because it could not choose between them. Buridan's ass may be a metaphor for the fractured postmodern personality, torn apart by too many choices.

In short, long-term commitment to another person is good. In the context of our culture there has been a special appeal to committing oneself to one special person, to "falling in love." Plato's *Symposium* offers a speech on the mythological origins of love. Humans were originally rotund giants with eight appendages (four arms and four legs) and two sets of sexual organs—either two male genitalia (male giants) or two female genitalia (female giants) or a combination of female and male genitalia (androgynous giants). Zeus cut them all in half, yielding gay, lesbian, and heterosexual humans, respectively. The speech concludes with a classic statement of the Western ideal of companionate love:[85]

> [W]hen one of them finds his other half, whether he is a lover of youth or a lover of another sort, the pair are lost in an amazement of love and friendship and intimacy, and one will not be out of the other's sight, as I may say, even for a moment: these are they who pass their lives with one another; yet they could not explain what they desire of one another. For the intense yearning which each of them has towards the other does not appear to be the desire of intercourse, but of something else which the soul desires and cannot tell, and of which she has only a dark and doubtful presentiment.

It may be excessively romantic to think that there is one and only one "other half" for each of us, but the idea of an "intense yearning" for that special person with whom one spends the rest of one's life has been robust in human history. It has been just as robust for same-sex pairs as for different-sex pairs.

This "intense yearning" has been particularly evident since Stonewall. The germinal study of gay male couples by Alan Bell and Martin Weinberg found that couples committed to an exclusive long-term relationship reported high self-acceptance and greater happiness than five years previously.[86] The authors contrasted that happiness with the greater tension in couples enjoying a sexually open, and therefore, less committed, relationship. Because this latter comparison has not been replicated by subsequent studies,[87] it cannot be considered anything but a hypothesis. What subsequent studies do confirm is Bell and Weinberg's initial conclusion, namely, that committed gay and lesbian unions generate a great deal of satisfaction for the participants and that commitment itself tends to increase satisfaction with the relationship.[88]

The last assertion might be surprising to readers who consider gay and bisexual men to be inherently (perhaps biologically) promiscuous and therefore incapable of commitment. It is true that before

Stonewall—and perhaps even more so during the heyday of gay liberation, when the message was that sexual and personal commitment
is an outdated bourgeois value—gay and bisexual men had more
sexual partners than heterosexual men, heterosexual women, and lesbians. In the late 1960s and early 1970s there was an existential appeal
to the promiscuous lifestyle, especially among bisexual and gay men.
That appeal is reflected in the gay literature of the period—boisterous
accounts of sexuality on a rampage. For example, Larry Kramer's
shocking novel *Faggots* both depicts and criticizes the pansexual world
of gay bars and baths in late seventies New York City.[89] Young men
saw themselves as sexual adventurers, with Norman Mailer appetites
and Gore Vidal orientations.[90] But recall that these young men were
carousing in a world that firmly denied the value of their relationships
and simultaneously offered them apparently riskless sex. Donald Webster Cory argued in 1951 that society's and the state's refusal to recognize same-sex relationships and marriages contributed to, rather than
reflected, gay promiscuity. Recent studies support Cory's commonsense insight.[91]

So does recent history. The existential self proved to be an unstable
self, and some of those carousing young men of the seventies wanted
to settle down in the eighties. Others died before their time. The
AIDS epidemic that ripped through the eighties not only cast a pall
over the sexual freedom of the seventies but, more important, illustrated the value of interpersonal commitment for gay people generally—and not just for safety's sake.[92] To the person with AIDS the
value of a committed partner is incalculable. Gay literature reflects
this shift. For example, both the fictional and autobiographical work
of Paul Monette emphasize how much enriched is the life of both
the dying and the surviving partner in a couple coping with AIDS.[93]
One of the great love stories of our time is Monette's devotion to
Roger Horwitz, around whom *Borrowed Time* is focused. Neither
Monette nor I would insist that everybody concerned with AIDS
should go out and get married, but Monette's work is powerful testimony to the value of a committed relationship for those dealing
with the disease. The social insurance feature of marriage has never
been so relevant as it has been for people with AIDS.

RESERVATIONS GAYS HAVE ABOUT MARRIAGE

Reasonable concerns about same-sex marriage continue to be voiced within the lesbian, gay, bisexual, and transgendered community. Most critics do not deny that same-sex couples should have the same rights as different-sex couples. They do not disagree so much with the particular arguments I have made as with the way I have framed the issue, as a matter of equal rights and as a matter of commitment. The most compelling critics, Ettelbrick and Polikoff, pose the issue from a different angle. What is at stake is not just a *static* one of rights and benefits. It is also a *dynamic* one of consequences and ramifications. Should gays and lesbians be buying into such a rotten institution as marriage? Might gay marriage not crowd out other opportunities for reform? What effect will same-sex marriage have on gay liberation generally?

The Marriage-Is-Rotten Argument

"Marriage is a great institution . . . if you like living in institutions," cracks Ettelbrick. "Steeped in a patriarchal system that looks to ownership, property, and dominance of men over women as its basis, the institution of marriage has long been the focus of radical feminist revulsion."[94] As constructed in the West, marriage involves hierarchies that have systematically subordinated certain people's personal, economic, and social interests. The Ozzie-and-Harriet marriage of 1950s bourgeois America—man as breadwinner, woman as housekeeper—forced women into constraining roles. Moreover, the legal structure of marriage has been the last haven for all sorts of malignant social attitudes, including racism (the longtime statutory prohibition of different-race marriages), contempt for the poor (filing fees and other bureaucratic requirements for marriage and divorce), and abuse of women (the common law rule that rape could not occur within marriage) and children (the reluctance of the social welfare system to intervene when children are abused by their parents). Marriage, in short, is rotten. Why should gay and lesbian couples hasten to join a club that has treated so many people so badly?

Consistent with Ettelbrick's argument, most of the examples of same-sex marriage in other times and other places seem to replicate gender hierarchies, as Polikoff points out.[95] The lives of the same-sex spouses of Roman emperors, the boy wives of the Japanese samurai and Azande warriors, the female husbands in Africa, and the unions formed by women passing as men (surveyed in chapter 2) not only replicated but aped the subordination of wife to husband in their respective cultures. Even the Native American *berdache* tradition, involving the so-called "third sex," appears to have yielded marriages in which the *berdache* generally fell into the stylized role of wife (for the male *berdache*) or husband (for the female *berdache*). The best examples of same-sex unions that escaped stereotyped gender roles appear to be those that were relationships and not legally recognized marriages, namely, the sisterhoods formed by women participating in the Chinese marriage resistance movement, Boston marriages of the eighteenth and nineteenth centuries, and the spiritual brotherhoods recognized by the early Christian Church. Yet those nonstereotyped unions had little or no discernible influence on their surrounding cultures, a reality at odds with Nan Hunter's thesis that same-sex marriage will trigger a broader shift in gender values.

A problem with Hunter's thesis, a classic "we can transform from within" argument, is that it attributes too much transformative power to law. Gender roles and attitudes toward women are deeply embedded in a society such as ours, and merely introducing a new legal institution (same-sex marriage) will not necessarily change those roles and attitudes, at least in the short and medium term. This problem also afflicts the critics' objection, however. Ettelbrick and Polikoff come close to essentializing marriage as an inherently regressive institution. That Western marriages have traditionally been the occasion by which women have been subordinated does not mean that marriage causes that subordination. Women's subordination may be more deeply related to social attitudes about gender differences than to the formal construct of marriage per se. If that is true, same-sex marriage is not buying into a rotten institution; it is only buying into an institution that is changing, as women's roles and status are changing in our society.

Consider some ways in which marriage has changed in the last two generations. After World War II, thirty-one states prohibited interracial marriages, and most Americans believed that a marriage between a black and a white person was literally not a marriage. The civil rights movement discredited that canard, and about half the thirty-one states had repealed or invalidated their own prohibitions by the time the Supreme Court invalidated such laws in *Loving v. Virginia*.[96] When *Loving* was decided in 1967, every state's statutory or common law exempted coerced intercourse within marriage from the criminal rape laws, and most male Americans believed that the marital rape exemption was required to preserve the integrity of marriage. The women's rights movement compelled a rethinking of this bit of mythology, and every state either repealed or curtailed its marital rape exemption by 1993.[97] In that year every state prohibited same-sex marriage, and most Americans believed that the prohibition was consistent with the essential nature and history of marriage. The gay rights movement is challenging this exclusion, and the Hawaii Supreme Court's decision in *Baehr* promises to do for lesbian and gay couples what *Loving* did for interracial couples and what the women's movement did for abused wives: provide formal equality. On the other hand, *Baehr* will not assure social acceptance of same-sex marriages any more than *Loving* assured social acceptance of different-race marriages. That project is left to the couples and society.

Marriage is one field on which we struggle for gay rights in part because marriage is so important to American culture that any group liberation movement is going to have to deal with it. The typical strategy followed by civil rights and women's rights groups was to reform the legal institution to reflect new social realities or power alignments, not to abandon it entirely. This chapter presents reasons why some lesbian and gay couples—for example, Ninia Baehr and Genora Dancel, Jack Baker and Mike McConnell, Manomia Evans and Donna Burkett, Sharon Kowalski and Karen Thompson, Paul Monette and Roger Horwitz—would benefit from having the right to marry.

The Alternatives-to-Marriage Argument

Marriage is not an intrinsically rotten institution, and if homosexuals can openly participate in it, all the better. Still, this does not fully respond to Ettelbrick's concern that "[m]arriage runs contrary to two of the primary goals of the lesbian and gay movement: the affirmation of gay identity and culture and the validation of many forms of relationships."[98] Her point relates to a larger phenomenon. For all Americans, the post–World War II period has witnessed a relative decline of marriage vis-à-vis other forms of relationships. Many couples never marry, many live together before marriage, and an unprecedented number marry and then divorce soon thereafter.

If some couples crave the commitment and legal benefits of marriage while other couples prefer a less formal arrangement, one possible response would be for the American legal system to offer couples a menu of choices for their unions. Couples could choose (1) to marry, with the accompanying benefits and obligations; (2) to register as domestic partners, entitled to spousal treatment with respect to some economic benefits (such as health care) and decision rules (such as presumption of guardianship) but not limited by the rules of divorce and sexual exclusivity; or (3) to order their relationships contractually or quasi-contractually, as through agreements to enter certain economic relationships (such as a lease) as a joint enterprise. Under a menu approach such as this one couples could better tailor their status to the particular needs of their relationship. A couple who wanted legal reinforcement for their lifelong commitment could choose marriage while a couple who wanted to ease into commitment could choose domestic partnership, with marriage as a possibility in the future.

Perhaps all couples should be offered this or a broader range of options. States could adopt domestic partnership laws, and employers could adapt their spousal benefits policies to cover domestic partners (or be required to do so by state law). States could also allow same-sex marriage. Families would flourish along different dimensions of interpersonal commitment. Yet this scenario is not a likely one. Ettelbrick and Polikoff fear that if lesbian and gay couples get same-sex marriage, they will lose interest in domestic partnership. They are probably right.[99] The reason is that most lesbians and gay men want something more than domestic partnership; they want to be in a committed relationship at some point in their lifetime. The most ambitious poll on the topic, conducted by *The Advocate* in 1994, found that almost two-thirds of the gay men polled wanted to marry someone of the same sex, with 85 percent open to the idea and only 15 percent uninterested.[100] *The Advocate*'s poll of lesbians, published in 1995, also revealed strong interest in getting married.

The apparent marriage preference of lesbians and gay men is well-grounded. They do not want to be just another pair of friends or lovers, nor do they want to be domestic partners whose relation can end at the drop of a termination statement. The large majority of us feel as Genora Dancel does, "I want to be able to say at the end of my life that I had loved someone really well for a long time."[101] Gay and lesbian partners want a level of commitment that domestic partnership does not provide. More deeply, lesbian and gay couples desire a link to the larger historical community, something marriage (in all its troubled richness) provides and the just-concocted domestic partnership does not. Marriage involves collective participation. Witnesses to the marriage—one's family, friends, and neighbors (even, implicitly, one's forebears)—commit themselves to supporting the union. Most interestingly, the very choreography of marriage imbues it with a significance that flat, boring domestic partnership cannot easily match. The pomp, gravity, and religiosity of marriage might appall the avant-garde, but they lend the institution an air of sanctification that is meaningful to its participants. Getting married, with all sorts of consequences, is a memorable event in the lives of most people, an operatic drama hard to match.

If choice must be made, the gayocracy should opt for marriage over domestic partnership. Still, it is not completely clear that the choice has to be made. Domestic partnership laws have a constituency that reaches beyond committed homosexual couples. In several major cities there are more different-sex than same-sex couples registered as domestic partners, sometimes by big margins. The demand for domestic partnership laws is fueled in large part by the health care benefits; for example, the Washington, D.C., domestic partnership law was enacted under the auspices of a health care protection act. So long as health care costs rise at a rapid clip and the nation fails to develop a comprehensive health care policy, there will be a demand for domestic partnership entitlements. Moreover, as straight couples have followed the nontraditional family paths of gay couples, domestic partnership as a middle ground between marriage and living together might be a viable political option, even if gay marriage diverts the interest of same-sex couples. The evolution of American family law will surely not stop with the recognition of same-sex marriage.

The Antiassimilation (or "New Insiders") Argument

What fuels Ettelbrick's opposition to same-sex marriage is a fear that it will declaw the radicalism of the gay liberation movement. "At this point in time, making legal marriage for lesbian and gay couples a priority would set an agenda of gaining rights for a few, but would do nothing to correct the power imbalances between those who are married (whether gay or straight) and those who are not. Thus, justice will not be gained."[102] Gay and lesbian couples would be assimilated into the great American middle class. Indeed, the process of seeking legally recognized same-sex marriage involves compromising gay radicalism, because advocates will invariably find themselves pressured to put forward as plaintiffs or as witnesses at legislative hearings gay and lesbian couples who most resemble Ozzie and Harriet. "The thought of emphasizing our sameness to married heterosexuals in order to obtain this 'right' terrifies me," concludes Ettelbrick.[103]

Where I see marriage as civilizing gays and assuring gay rights, Ettelbrick sees it as co-opting gays and declawing gay liberation. Here is her argument, as I understand it: Most lesbian or gay couples are white and middle-class. If they were not homosexual or if homosexuality did not produce near-hysterical reactions in other white middle-class Americans, these people would be part of mainstream America, living a comfortable, middle-class existence. It is American homophobia, and not our choice, that makes us gender rebels. Once America recognizes our relationships and treats us like first-class citizens, then the gay middle class will assimilate and melt back into the great mainstream, as "new insiders" who have come in from the cold outside. When this happens, we will have moved from in the closet to out in the streets to behind white picket fences in scarcely more than one generation. But still outside the system would be the true gender rebels who do not want to get married and lesbians and gays of color or of limited means who would remain marginalized even if married. Ettelbrick, imploring us not to leave the least empowered among us behind, insists that marriage should be shelved and alternate institutions devised.

Initially, it seems unlikely that married gay couples would be just like married straight couples. For example, same-sex couples are less likely to follow the traditional breadwinner–housekeeper division in their households.[104] Nor would the gay and lesbian culture cease to be distinctive. One feature of our experience has been an emphasis on "families we choose," anthropologist Kath Weston's felicitous phrase.[105] Such families are fluid alliances independent of the ties imposed by blood and by law. Often estranged from blood kin, openly gay people are more prone to rely on current as well as former lovers, close friends, and neighbors as their social and emotional support system. Include children in this fluid network and the complexity becomes more pronounced.[106] Because same-sex couples cannot have children through their own efforts, a third party must be involved: a former different-sex spouse, a sperm donor, a surrogate mother, a parent or agency offering a child for adoption. The family of choice can and often does include a relationship with this third party. Gay and lesbian couples are pioneering novel family configurations, and gay marriage would not seriously obstruct the creation of the larger families we choose.

Moreover, the gay and lesbian community needs to be realistic about the complicated consequences of recognizing gay marriage. The immediate consequence would not be social acceptance of homosexuals. The opposite is more likely: vociferous, even violent, resistance by homophobic heterosexuals. Justified fear of renewed gay bashing would discourage most same-sex couples from getting married immediately, and those couples who did get married would decidedly *not* be welcomed as "new insiders." Even sympathetic straights would consider them avant-garde. Over time, attitudes would change. If the initial antihomosexual reaction did not engulf newly recognized gay marriages, same-sex spouses would slowly blossom in our society, popping up like dandelions in springtime. The consequences of this flowering would be impossible to predict, but they certainly cannot be captured by charges that married homosexuals will become new insiders, leaving unmarried ones outside the system.

Instead, gay marriage would have civilizing effects on same-sex couples, heterosexuals, and gay adolescents. Same-sex couples would be faced with an option they do not now have. For the reasons developed above, the marriage option would lead more couples toward more explicit commitments. On the whole, more commitment would be good for the families we choose for ourselves. Heterosexuals would have the same options they have now, but they too would be civilized. Gay marriage would undermine social homophobia as well as traditional assumptions about gender roles within marriage. In the medium or long term, the antihomosexual person is most likely to change his opinion on the basis of actually knowing people who are openly gay or lesbian. Thus, to the extent that same-sex marriage might embolden some couples to be open, the institution might help all gay men, lesbians, and bisexuals. In this respect those who argue that gay people should "just keep it quiet and out of sight" are both more intolerant and more incorrect than they realize. Tolerance of homosexuality *increases* with openness over time, especially if openness occurs in settings of common effort and interest such as neighborhoods, parent–teacher associations, and city softball leagues.

Potentially, the most advantaged by the new dynamic could be gay youth. If societal homophobia were blunted, the lesbian, bisexual, or gay adolescent who is confused or threatened by her or his sexuality would feel less constrained about seeking guidance and would be more likely to know a gay authority figure who can provide initial support. A world of gay couples and same-sex spouses should offer more accessible role models for the youths trying to reconcile their sexuality with the family environment in which they were raised. Gay marriage would be a possible aspiration for these young people, and gay marrieds useful role models. In short, the greatest beneficiaries of gay spouses as a civilizing move ought to be the next generations of homosexual youth. For them, the insider–outsider issue would seem almost irrelevant.

Finally, I am somewhat baffled at the suggestion in Ettelbrick's argument that "more marginal members of the lesbian and gay community (women, people of color, working class, and poor) are less likely to see marriage as having relevance to our struggles for survival. After all, what good is the affirmation of our relationships . . . if we are rejected as women, people of color, or working class?"[107] I am baffled because there is no evidence—neither polls, surveys, nor theoretical models—suggesting that the marriage option would be disproportionately exercised by rich gay men as compared to people of color or lesbians or less affluent homosexuals. The majority of surveys taken in the last twenty years have found more lesbians than gay men in committed long-term relationships.[108] Why is it not reasonable to believe that just as many (or more) lesbians will benefit from same-sex marriage?[g] Lesbians (such as Ninia Baehr and Genora Dancel) are often the plaintiffs in same-sex marriage lawsuits. The great majority of same-sex couples who have actually obtained marriage licenses in the United States have been women, including women passing as men in the nineteenth century and lesbians of color in 1920s Harlem.

Mark the irony. While lesbians enjoy more long-term committed relationships than do gay men, they also contribute more than their share of marriage critics. This irony suggests the following hypothesis: In order to achieve committed relationships gay men need the discipline of marriage more than lesbians do. Gay men are like Ulysses, who directed that he be bound to the ship's mast as it passed the Sirens, sea creatures whose seductive voices enticed men to their deaths. Likewise, gay men realize that they tend to lose their balance and succumb to private sirens if they are not socially and even legally constrained. For reasons that may be either cultural or biological, lesbians have achieved a balance of sexual freedom and interpersonal commitment more easily. The moral of this speculation is not that

---

[g]Similarly, I do not see why working-class lesbians would be any less likely to seek and benefit from same-sex marriage than would middle-class gay men. Historically, working-class lesbian communities have involved long-term unions that were extremely satisfying to the women involved. See Elizabeth Lapovsky Kennedy and Madeline D. Davis, *Boots of Leather, Slippers of Gold: The History of a Lesbian Community* (New York: Penguin, 1994). Spousal benefits provided by employers would be at least as great a benefit to working-class couples as to middle-class couples. Even if the latter would receive a larger monetary boon (because middle-class benefits are higher), the comparative need for spousal coverage is often more urgent for working-class families. The other legal rights and benefits associated with marriage would surely be more useful to working-class families. Many professional-class gay and lesbian couples are able to create marriage-equivalent rights by drawing up wills, contracts, and trust instruments. Because these mechanisms are costly to develop, they are systematically less available to working-class couples. The off-the-rack benefits and rights created by marriage ought to be more useful to working-class couples.

lesbians do not need same-sex marriage (most of them favor it) but that this institution could bring gay men and lesbians closer together. Certainly, this hypothesis invites the conclusion that same-sex marriage civilizes gay men by making them more like lesbians.

Consider a final story of the intersection of life and law: the case of Sharon Lynne Bottoms.[109] Bottoms married Dennis Doustou in 1989 and became pregnant the next year. In 1991, before her child, Tyler Doustou, was born, Bottoms divorced Doustou and began dating women. She ultimately settled down with April Wade. In January 1993, Sharon Bottoms informed her mother, Pamela Kay Bottoms, that Tyler would spend less time at his grandmother's house because of the presence of Tommy Conley, whom Sharon Bottoms considered an undesirable influence on her son. Pamela Kay Bottoms retaliated by instituting proceedings to remove Tyler from Sharon's custody. The Virginia courts ultimately upheld Pamela Kay Bottoms's claim, tearing the child away from his biological mother and making him a trophy to compulsory heterosexuality.

The *Bottoms* case illustrates the vulnerability of lesbian and gay families to disruption when both private and public actors operate under antihomosexual prejudice. The case also illustrates the insulation provided by marriage. These two different perspectives are related. Under similar circumstances, virtually no judge in the United States would have transferred Tyler from Sharon and Dennis Doustou, a married couple, to a grandmother who objects to her daughter's lifestyle. Indeed, even if the grandmother were able to show that Sharon was having a lesbian affair and that Dennis was normally absent from the house, most judges would still have been reluctant to terminate *married* parental custody. Sharon was vulnerable because she was lesbian *and* working-class *and* unmarried. Any success the lesbian and gay community might have in obtaining recognition for same-sex marriages would have insulating ripple effects for working-class lesbians like Sharon Bottoms and April Wade.

A lot of lesbian, gay, bisexual, and transgendered Americans want the right to marry someone of their own sex. They want the right to marry for good reasons. The arguments of marriage critics are too speculative to overcome the presumption of equality that has since the 1950s been the public demand of the gay and lesbian community. We should seek the right to marry, and we are doing so, thanks to Ninia Baehr, Genora Dancel, their coplaintiffs, and their attorneys.

More vehemently opposed to gay marriage than critics of marriage are, of course, critics of gays. Most straight Americans believe that marriage is a worthwhile institution but that homosexuals should not share in it. Why is that? The next chapter examines the reasons usually presented to same-sex marriage from a mainstream or traditional perspective.

4

MAINSTREAM OBJECTIONS TO
SAME-SEX MARRIAGE

Much of the opposition to same-sex marriage in the culture at large is inspired by antihomosexual emotions. People who dislike homosexuals or their imagined conduct are likely to oppose same-sex marriage. There is little I can say to such people, for visceral distaste is not susceptible to argument based on reason and facts. Nor do I have anything of use for people who have made up their minds about the issue and are unwilling to consider additional facts and contentions. Nonetheless, the assumption of this book is that many people have good-faith reservations and are at least partly open-minded about same-sex marriage. Indeed, most of the arguments against same-sex marriage that appear in print are based on reasons that can be analyzed and disputed.

Drawing from the academic literature, articles and debates in the popular media, and conversations with skeptics, I have found three recurring objections to same-sex marriage. The initial one is, "It just can't be!" To some, marriage, by definition, has got to be different-sex. Throughout human history, according to religious tradition and as a matter of natural law, marriage has been tied to procreative sexuality, which is a monopoly held by different-sex couples. Under this definitional objection, the state cannot recognize something that is an impossibility. My history of same-sex marriage in chapter 2 begins to address this definitional concern, for the history shows that there have been many same-sex marriages in human history, including

87

early Western history. But neither the evidence of history nor the a priori assumptions of the present are sufficient to settle such an important issue. This chapter shows how society constructs the institution of marriage to satisfy functional needs of its citizens. The only persuasive arguments for or against same-sex marriage must be ones grounded in a normative vision of what functions are important to marriage as an institution.

Some scholars and religious leaders concede that the state can construct marriage along functional rather than metaphysical lines but maintain that same-sex marriage is a bad form of marriage. Their argument usually takes the following logical form: State recognition of same-sex marriage would constitute state approval of such marriages, or even of homosexuality in general. Homosexuality is shameful because it is sex divorced from procreative possibility. Not only are homosexual marriages shameful, but they demean the institutions of marriage and family. To protect procreative marriage and family values, the state should prohibit same-sex marriages. The premises of this argument are questionable and, indeed, backward. A marriage license in the United States neither denotes nor connotes collective approval or even encouragement of the specific relationship, and gay marriages are just as functional as straight marriages are. In an ironic twist, state prohibitions of same-sex marriage undermine the values that these opponents embrace: commitment, family (including children), and sexual fidelity.

The first two objections to same-sex marriage ultimately rest on a natural law understanding of philosophy, history, and religion that is unacceptable to the large majority of people. (This same understanding is hostile to contraception and abortion, for example.) A third kind of objection is purely conventional and appealingly pragmatic. "What's the hurry? Given popular attitudes and the longstanding assumption that marriage is different-sex, adoption of same-sex marriage would be costly and disruptive. Go slow, one step at a time, and make compromises if necessary." This rationale justifies domestic partnership as a necessary first step, with gay marriage perhaps following a generation or two later, once society has had time to adjust. Because pragmatic objections such as these are relatively generous and yielding, it is hard to respond to them in anything but a generous and yielding spirit. It does appear, though, that there are in fact few costs or collateral effects that would be occasioned by recognizing same-sex marriages. The one-step-at-a-time feature of the argument is most appealing and, indeed, is consistent with the strategy that gay activists such as Evan Wolfson (of the Lambda Legal Defense and Education Fund) have been pursuing. On the other hand, "one step at a time" too often means "not in my lifetime," a danger of pragmatic arguments.

DEFINITIONAL OBJECTIONS

Probably the most popular argument to deny a right of same-sex marriage is definitional: Marriage is necessarily different-sex, and same-sex marriage is therefore oxymoronic, a contradiction in terms. The definitional argument is sometimes made as a matter of pure word meaning and contemporary usage. Thus, standard dictionaries of all stripes define marriage as the "[l]egal union of one man and one woman as husband and wife,"[1] but some dictionaries also define marriage more generally as "an intimate or close union."[2] Within the lesbian and gay community the word *marriage* has long been used to include same-sex couples,[3] and this conventional usage has seeped into mainstream, professional, and even official use.[4] For example, when Congress codified the armed services' ban against gays in the military, it specifically excluded people who enter into "homosexual marriages."[5]

Because conventional meaning easily embraces same-sex marriage, the definitional argument has to reach beyond dictionaries. Accordingly, opponents of same-sex marriage have appealed to both tradition and natural law. In *Jones v. Hallahan* the Kentucky Court of Appeals rejected both constitutional and statutory claims advanced by Tracy Knight and Marjorie Jones for the legal recognition of their marriage. The court reasoned that "[m]arriage has always been considered as the union of a man and a woman and we have been presented with no authority to the contrary." Hence, the applicants were "prevented from marrying, not by the statutes of Kentucky or the refusal of the County Clerk of Jefferson County to issue them a license, but rather by their own incapability of entering into a marriage as that term is defined."[6] The Minnesota Supreme Court in *Baker v. Nelson* (the first legal challenge to the same-sex marriage bar) began its constitutional discussion with the premise that "[t]he institution of marriage as a union of man and woman, uniquely involving the procreation and rearing of children, is as old as the book of Genesis."[7] As *Baker*'s reference to Genesis reflects, judges rejecting same-sex marriage have also relied on the nation's religious heritage. The District of Columbia Superior Court's decision in *Dean v. District of Columbia* quoted passages from Genesis, Deuteronomy, Matthew, and Ephesians to support its holding that "societal recognition that it takes a man and a woman to form a marital relationship is older than Christianity itself."[8]

The religious traditions invoked by lawyers and judges are capable of speaking for themselves, and some religious thinkers have relied on natural law to reject same-sex marriage. Responding to the European Parliament's resolution seeking member state recognition of same-sex marriage in February 1994, Pope John Paul II issued a hundred-page letter to Roman Catholics explaining the Church's opposition to contraception, divorce, and same-sex marriage. "Marriage, which undergirds the institution of the family, is constituted by the covenant whereby 'a man and a woman establish between themselves a partnership for their whole life,' and which 'of its own very nature is ordered to the well-being of the spouses and to the procreation and upbringing of children,'" the Pope declared. "Only such a union can be recognized and ratified as a marriage in society. Other interpersonal unions which do not fulfill the above conditions cannot be recognized, despite growing trends which represent a serious threat to the future of family and society itself."[9] Consistent with earlier Church teaching, Pope John Paul II urged the view that only procreative sexuality can redeem a relationship into the sanctity that is marriage. Like contraceptive sex, sex between two women or two men is not procreative and therefore is immoral and cannot be the basis for marriage. "No human society can run the risk of permissiveness in fundamental issues regarding the nature of marriage and the family!"[10]

Natural law thinkers writing for secular as well as religious audiences have defended the Pope's position.[11] John Finnis, for example, maintains that the Judeo-Christian vision of marriage is consistent with the vision of marriage held by Plato, Aristotle, Plutarch, and other leading philosophers who viewed marriage as natural and viewed nonprocreative sexuality as antimarriage and unnatural.[12] Like the other "new natural lawyers,"[13] Finnis maintains that this consensus bespeaks an underlying human truth: marriage is a union for both procreative and spiritually unitive goals, and it is impossible for these goals to be fulfilled by a same-sex couple.

In thinking about the foregoing arguments, it is useful to separate the descriptive from the normative. Hence, this discussion will begin with the descriptive claim, "The world has never known same-sex marriage." This claim is easy to refute, as chapter 2 demonstrates, but the treatment in this chapter will more ambitiously argue that any effort to insist on sex difference as a criterion for marriage is doomed to incoherence. The more difficult claim to refute is the normative one, that marriage *ought* to be different-sex by definition. This claim involves thinking about both religious and philosophical goals of marriage. My normative argument will be that the dominant goal of marriage is and should be *unitive*, the spiritual and personal union of the committed couple, and not *procreative*, the production of children by the couple. Relatedly, procreation is not and should not be a necessary condition for marriage.

The Historical Tradition Objection

The Kentucky Court of Appeals rejected same-sex marriage because "[m]arriage has always been considered as the union of a man and a woman and we have been presented with no authority to the contrary." Logically, this is a circular argument: because such and such has not been done in the past, we shall never allow it. Circular arguments are no response to a normative claim, whose very point is that things ought to change. That the thing to be changed has existed for a long rather than a short time ought not to be decisive. Should its longevity have entrenched slavery in the United States? For most of American history different-race marriages were not acceptable, but that was no argument to perpetuate this discrimination once our society rejected the racist assumptions of that exclusion (see chapter 6).

Nor has marriage "always been considered as the union of a man and a woman." There is in fact plenty of "authority to the contrary," assembled in chapter 2. New authority to the contrary is being generated in Scandinavia, the Netherlands, and Canada. The lesson of history is not that marriage must be between husband and wife but, rather, that marriage is a socially and politically created institution that serves social and political functions. Another way of making the same point is to observe that even when marriage is conceived as a union of husband and wife, either role may be cross-gendered. Thus, different cultures have recognized as marriages relationships involving "boy wives" (as in classical Crete and the East African Nuer); "female husbands" (various African cultures); and the male wives and female husbands of the *berdache* tradition (pervasive in Native American tribes and in many Asian societies). Simply put, husband and wife, like male and female, are constructed categories that need not correspond to biological categories. As I shall demonstrate below, even American law in its current discriminatory form cannot avoid strange constructions in its effort to fit all couples into cookie-cutter figures of "husband and wife."

Such historical evidence requires opponents of same-sex marriage either to abandon their "marriage has always been different-sex" argument or to formulate it more narrowly. Perhaps the most that can be said is that, in the history of the United States, marriage has always been restricted to different-sex partners. This is also factually inaccurate, though. Native American cultures in the United States have long recognized same-sex *berdache* marriages. We'wha and his husband, introduced in chapter 2, were both American citizens, and their same-sex marriage was a valid marriage under tribal law. Some states have explicitly recognized tribal marriages as valid under their state law,[14] and such recognition implicitly validated some same-sex marriages under state law. (There are no cases testing this proposition, however.)

Moreover, women passing as men have frequently married other women in this country. Recall Nicholai de Raylan (chapter 2), who married two women in succession. In the eyes of some people today, her marriages were obtained under fraudulent pretenses, but I challenge that view. De Raylan's same-sex marriages were marriages just as genuine as different-sex marriages of that era, and probably more satisfying to the parties than most. When the doctors informed her widow and her former wife of de Raylan's biological sex after her death, neither wife accepted the doctors' verdict and both testified as to the satisfactory nature of their sexual as well as emotional relationship. Although de Raylan's gender- and marriage-bending case received enormous publicity, there was no recorded effort to nullify her same-sex marriage or to deny her widow her legal spousal inheritance. This pattern was repeated in other cases. Very few of the same-sex marriages described in my survey were ever nullified by the state after being exposed to public attention. If heterosexual society were being defrauded by these marriages, it rarely did anything about it.

Transgendered unions such as de Raylan's illustrate the constructed nature of both marriage and gender. More important, such unions press the state's fetish against same-sex marriage into ridiculous positions. In every state cross-dressing men can marry women, but it appears that cross-dressing women are not supposed to marry women (though they often have, of course). Thus, a self-identified cross-dressed (but biologically male) "wife" can marry another "wife," but a self-identified cross-dressed (but biologically female) "husband" cannot marry a "wife." As the parenthetical terms suggest, the state's justification is biological: the cross-dressed "wife" is *really* a man, because he (not she!) has male hormones and sexual organs. What if the cross-dressing man is a transsexual who takes female hormones and has sex-change surgery to replace his male sex organs with female ones? Can a postoperative male-to-female transsexual marry a man? Looking to gender identification and sexual equipment, New Jersey's intermediate appellate court has held that she can;[15] looking to chromosomes (men are supposed to have an XY pattern, women an XX pattern), other states have said she cannot.[16] At least one of these states has legally recognized a form of same-sex union. Which one?

Consider this further complication: Many people are born in an "intersexual" state, with chromosomes of one sex and genitals of the other sex or of both sexes. These people (sometimes termed "hermaphrodites") are usually raised according to their predominant genital manifestations and typically marry people of the same chromosomal sex. Although many such marriages have been known and reported,[17] I am aware of no instance in which the state or society condemned these marriages as bogus. In fact, no state requires chromosomal verification of gender. Moreover, any chromosomal policing by a gender gendarmerie would only compound regulatory difficulties. If the state looks to the chromosomes to determine whether it has a "true" husband and wife, it not only does violence to personal choice but also becomes mired in chromosomal indeterminacy. A small minority of the American population have unusual chromosomal patterns, including XO, XXY (Klinefelter's syndrome), XXXY, and XXYY. How should they be characterized? However one might characterize them metaphysically, people with these chromosomal abnormalities have routinely married. There is nothing in the many studies to suggest that their marriages were anything but satisfactory to the participants or the state.[18]

There is no way to draw the sex-and-gender line consistently enough to deny that states have repeatedly recognized same-sex marriages. If a male-to-female transsexual's marriage to a man is same-sex, then New Jersey has recognized a form of same-sex marriage, as have the various states that have given marriage licenses to people whose chromosomal pattern did not match their genitals at birth. If it is different-sex, then other states have recognized same-sex marriages between male-to-female transsexuals and women.[a] Whichever choice one makes, one is hard put to deny that it is a normative choice about how to construct gender. Surely, the only way the state can box in transsexuals is to invoke a chromosomal definition, but hermaphrodites challenge the determinacy of that strategy. Why should an XY person who has been socialized as a woman not be able to marry a man? If so, why should a male-to-female transsexual not be able to marry a man? If so, why should a male cross-dresser not be able to marry a man? If so, why should a gay male not be able to marry a man? Where can the state stop on the roller coaster of gender bending?

---

[a]Because the marriage "licensocracy" believes anything written in an official document, it accepts at face value gender representations on one's birth certificate. Thus a male-to-female transsexual identified as a man on her birth certificate will be able to get a license to marry another woman. This is probably so even if the transsexual is presenting herself as a woman when she submits the application. The British authorities insisted on granting a marriage license when just such a case was recently publicized. See *The People*, June 11, 1995, reporting on the authorized marriage of Tracie-Anne Scott, a male-to-female transsexual, and Tina-Louise Dixon.

The only argument left to those who use the historical tradition argument is that no state in the United States (Indian tribes excluded!) has ever adopted a marriage law that explicitly singles out same-sex marriage and approves it. This form of argument is tortured in the extreme. It is worse than the circular form of argument we started with, for it borders on the openly discriminatory. In light of the history of same-sex marriage presented in chapter 2, there must be something more than bad history to motivate people to resist same-sex marriage. Otherwise, a reconsideration is surely in order. Consider a parallel reconsideration from the field of anthropology.

The anthropology profession was impelled to reconsider its traditional definition of marriage when the community of social anthropologists came to notice the African custom of woman marriage.[19] One official publication, *Notes and Queries*, defined marriage in 1951 as "a union between a man and a woman such that children born to the woman are the recognized legitimate offspring of both partners."[20] This definition was obviously a cultural statement more than a professional yardstick, and anthropologists familiar with African same-sex marriage traditions in particular discredited the definition as parochial. Edmund Leach, a noted social anthropologist, suggested that marriage be defined more loosely as a bundle of rights that society associates with intimate relationships.[21] Some anthropologists objected, arguing that such a definition was too open-ended. To accommodate woman marriage but not other relationships, Kathleen Gough proposed to delineate marriage as "a relationship established between a woman and one or more other persons, which provides that a child born to the woman under circumstances not prohibited by the rules of the relationship, is accorded full birth-status rights."[22]

Leach responded that this definition was too restrictive in light of male–male marriages also documented in Africa. He argued that marriage could only be defined, in light of social practice, as one or more of the following: (1) the rights and duties inhering in spousehood, (2) the personal relationship between people considered spouses, and/or (3) relationships and alliances created or cemented by espousal.[23] Eileen Jensen Krige, author of the earliest work to focus on female husbands, maintained that "[m]arriage can take widely different forms, even sometimes within the same society, each involving different categories of rights and duties" and "may be entered upon by people of the same sex."[24] The Krige–Leach approach to marriage is now the more accepted among anthropologists, and there is no great metaphysical reason keeping the rest of us from following it as well.

The Procreation-and-Family Argument

Secular as well as religious critics of same-sex marriage maintain that people have a legal or moral claim to marry only insofar as the marriage can be linked with "the fundamental rights of procreation, childbirth, adoption, and child rearing," for marriage "is simply the logical predicate of the others."[25] Because this is an openly normative argument, this is a better objection than the ill-informed invocation of historical tradition we have just considered. Marriage is good because it is the traditional venue within which children are conceived and reared. Same-sex couples cannot conceive children. Why should they be allowed to marry?

But consider this. If there is a necessary link between marriage and procreation, strange consequences would follow. A state could and, to be consistent, should prohibit marriages in which one or both partners are sterile or impotent. If procreation is the essential goal of marriage, why should postmenopausal women be allowed to marry? Surely, discrimination against sterile, impotent, or aged couples would be unacceptable to citizens of many different perspectives. The rationale would be that marriage serves functions that are as important as, if not more important than, procreation, including interpersonal commitment, religious or moral expression, sexual satisfaction, and the legal entitlements associated with spousehood. If elderly, sterile, or impotent couples cannot be denied the right to marry because of a traditional link between marriage and procreation, neither can lesbian or gay couples be denied the right for that type of reason.

There is a way of using the concept of natural law to make as well as respond to the foregoing argument. St. Augustine's *De Bono Conjugali* posited procreation as the goal of marriage but also considered the special case of sterile marriages. Perhaps surprisingly, St. Augustine approved the latter, on the argument that the communion and companionship of the spouses is a further goal of marriage.[26] St. Augustine's recognition of two goals of marriage, the unitive goal of communion and companionship as well as the procreative goal, ought to impel Catholic-inspired natural law thinkers to reconsider the issue of same-sex marriage. Indeed, the emphasis on the unitive instead of the procreative goal is one way of understanding the same-sex unions blessed by the Greek Orthodox and Roman Catholic Churches during the Middle Ages (chapter 2). Such an understanding is equally applicable to lesbian and gay couples today. The overriding reason Ninia Baehr and Genora Dancel want to get married is their complete devotion to one another, their desire to unite in love and mutual dignity. They are more obvious exemplars of the unitive goal of marriage than are most straight couples because they have made sacrifices (endured publicity about their minority sexual orientation) for their desire to be united.

John Finnis has posed an Augustinian response to this argument. He says that the unitive and procreative features of marriage are not separate goals but are, instead, common elements of the single goal of marriage. "Parenthood and children and family are the intrinsic fulfillment of a communion which . . . can exist and fulfill the spouses even if procreation happens to be impossible for them."[27] Finnis believes this solves the conundrum of the sterile couple. To the contrary, how can parenthood and children fulfill a couple's interpersonal communion if procreation remains impossible for them? This effort at synthesis is incoherent without a theory that explains how male-penis-in-female-vagina intercourse per se contributes to communion. Even if Finnis had such a theory, it is unclear how he would deal with the proposed marriage of a postoperative male-to-female transsexual and a man. From the tenor of his writing, I would expect Finnis to be hostile to such a marriage, but he has no principled way to distinguish such a couple from a sterile couple (who can marry under his understanding of the natural law of marriage).

Further conundrums are presented by different-sex couples who decide to divorce and marry other people and by fertile, different-sex couples who by means of contraception or abortion choose not to procreate. If marriage renders the partners a unity, surely divorce is a disunity that should be invalid under a natural law perspective. Some

of the new natural law advocates openly take this position and condemn divorce laws that essentially allow serial polygamy, but are silent
about this anomaly. All of the new natural law advocates I have read
condemn contraception and abortion, practices that are regularly engaged in by different-sex couples.[28] It would seem that these couples
are less worthy of marriage, under a natural law view, than either
sterile or gay couples. Sterile or gay couples cannot procreate because
of circumstances beyond their control, but fertile different-sex
couples practicing contraception or abortion are capable of procreation but *deny* its role in their union. This would seem to be a more
willful violation of Finnis's procreative ideal, yet neither he nor his
colleagues denounce marriages where fertile different-sex partners
assure their childlessness by disapproved means.

The extreme procreation-oriented position taken by the new natural law advocates is unacceptable (as well as exceedingly musty) in
modern society. It is several hundred years too late to deny that marriage serves unitive functions, and it is a century too late to maintain
that procreation is the overriding goal of marriage. Post-Freudian society understands sexual expression as an important goal of personhood,[29] the modern liberal state guarantees its citizens substantial liberty
to make choices about their own sexuality,[30] and an earth that struggles
to feed its existing population is not an earth that should overemphasize
procreation. Procreation is good and important, but procreation is no
longer central to either relationships or to social welfare.

The Religious Tradition Argument

The new natural law advocates are essentially dressing up a sectarian
religious argument in philosophical garb. They are hardly alone in
this enterprise. Secular officials regularly justify denying same-sex
marriage on the ground of religious tradition. For example, the trial
judge in the *Dean* case invoked passages from the Bible's Old and
New Testaments to justify the District of Columbia's implicit prohibition of same-sex marriage.[31] The judge in *Adams v. Howerton* prem-
ised his refusal to recognize same-sex marriages on the "combination
of scriptural and canonical teaching under which a 'marriage' be-

tween persons of the same sex was unthinkable and, by definition, impossible."[32] In making such arguments, these judges disserve both law and religion, however.

The rules of the Bible and canonical church traditions are not supposed to dictate the rules of the secular law. Even from a religious perspective, there should be a separation of church and state. The best reason for such a separation is that each religion should be free to practice its faith, without interference from other religions that see matters differently. They, in turn, ought to be free to practice their faiths without interference from the government. This reason relies in part on the sanctity of the individual religious conscience and in part on the heterogeneity of religious viewpoints. State espousal of one religion's beliefs risks state supression of another religion's beliefs. Freedom of religion is one of the most cherished liberties in American history. Religions ought to be free to take positions on issues like same-sex marriage, and the state cannot require religions to approve of or conduct such ceremonies. But neither can one religion force its position on other religions or on citizens following no organized religion. Everyone ought to be free to practice his or her faith. Traditional religious opposition to same-sex marriage is not a good reason for the state to prohibit it entirely—especially in light of an increasing toleration and acceptance of same-sex marriage on the part of some churches and many religious thinkers.

There is no univocal Judeo-Christian tradition against same-sex marriage. It appears that the Israelites fleeing Egypt were opposed to the same-sex marriages they witnessed in Egypt and that opposition is reflected in the admonitions in Leviticus against same-sex male intimacy.[33] At no point, by the way, does Leviticus condemn same-sex female intimacy or marriage. Nothing else in the Old Testament is telling on the issue of same-sex marriage. The story in Genesis of the destruction of Sodom is a complicated one. Some believe God was punishing Sodom for male intimacy ("sodomy") practiced within its walls (again, there is no condemnation of female intimacy). Others maintain that God punished Sodom for more general wickedness and inhospitality to visitors. Neither account speaks directly to same-sex marriage.

Christ's teachings, recorded in the Gospel books of the New Testament, contain no condemnation of same-sex unions or intimacy. Instead, Christ's message relentlessly emphasizes charity to others, compassion for those different from oneself, and God's equal love for every human being. Some early Christian authors, notably St. Paul and St. Augustine, were anxious about sexuality in general and male intimacy in particular, but scholars are in hopeless dispute over the precise meaning of their writings on the topic of same-sex intimacy.[34] Others did not share this anxiety, and early Church practice was relatively tolerant.[35] Like the Bible, Church fathers are almost completely silent about female relationships. Throughout the Middle Ages, the Roman Catholic and Greek Orthodox Churches performed same-sex enfraternization rituals, glorified the same-sex intimacy of Sergius and Bacchus, and developed same-sex union liturgies, which were later published in official church collections. That much has long been known as historical fact.[36] John Boswell's claim that some of these rituals were functional equivalents to same-sex marriage ceremonies[37] is a contested theory. All scholars agree that after 1300 Roman Catholic practice and theology sought to discourage same-sex unions.

In their legal challenge to the District of Columbia's prohibition of same-sex marriage, plaintiffs Craig Dean and Patrick Gill sought out the opinions of religious leaders on the issue. These leaders responded generously, and the specific letters referred to here are reprinted as an appendix to this book.[38] I was co-counsel, with Dean, for the plaintiffs. We presented to the court more than a hundred letters from priests, rabbis, ministers, and lay leaders, all of whom favored religious as well as secular recognition of same-sex marriage. This was not intended to be a representative sample of religious leaders, but the thoughtfulness of the responses from different religious perspectives makes these letters worth reading and pondering. Themes from these letters are presented in the following paragraphs.

To begin with, the priests, ministers, rabbis, and lay leaders who responded to our request have struggled with the issue of same-sex marriage from within the Judeo-Christian tradition and have concluded that same-sex marriages are consistent with its foundations. Some, such as the congregation of Synagogue Bet Mishpachah of the District of Columbia, believe that the scriptural admonitions against same-sex intimacy in Leviticus must be interpreted in light of modern understandings. As Rabbi Yoel Kahn puts it, "Jewish tradition has evolved over the centuries and millennia to meet our people's changing needs."[39] When you actually read Leviticus, you see why this must be so. Leviticus includes as the Lord's "statutes" to the Israelites commands that death be meted out to adulterers, men who commit incest, women or men who lie with beasts, or men who lie with men (book 20, verses 10–16); that the religious community offer animal sacrifices to the Lord, to be prepared according to highly specific directions (books 3–4, 8); that specified "unclean" or "abominable" animals, such as swine, not be eaten (book 11); that women who are "unclean" because of menstruation or childbearing cleanse themselves through specified animal sacrifices (book 12); and that since men who discharge semen and women who discharge blood are "unclean," they must cleanse themselves by thorough washing of self, clothing, bed, and anything else that comes into contact with the uncleanliness (book 15). Many of the specific admonitions in Leviticus were appropriate for a nomadic culture but not for an urban one, and both Jews and Christians recognize that they cannot all be followed today. Even the most observant of Orthodox Jews and fundamentalist Christians do not believe that adulterers must be put to death.

How do the faithful determine which Levitical traditions ought to be compromised? If specific passages from the Bible do not clearly guide our consciences on the issue of same-sex unions, what should? Reverend John Mack of the United Congregational Church of Christ looks to the general purpose of biblical teachings: God's love for us as inspiration for us to love our fellow humans. On the marriage issue he says the following:[40]

> In my opinion, it is extremely easy to interpret the profound teachings of our religious scripture to apply to same-sex relationships. It is extremely difficult to find clear condemnation of them within the religious literature. And the systematic persecution of those who would find romantic love with a person of the same sex violates virtually every major law and teaching of both Judaism and Christianity.

Reverend William Carey of the fundamentalist Pentecostal Church, who has studied the Bible in its original languages, concludes that the antihomosexual gloss placed on some passages when translated into English is not faithful to the original text. Believing that the prophet Daniel and the Babylonian eunuch Ashpenaz were joined in a same-sex marriage, Carey argues that same-sex marriages are faithful to the biblical concepts of commitment and love.[41]

Interestingly, clerical sympathy for same-sex marriage exists in denominations that have most fervently opposed same-sex unions. Reverend Carey, a Protestant fundamentalist, is an example. Same-sex marriages are frequently performed by ordained priests representing the Roman Catholic Church. One such priest, Father James Mallon of Philadelphia, views the Church's thinking concerning matrimony since Vatican II as retreating from the Church's long-standing demand that marriage be linked to procreation and endorses marriage as a loving covenant between two people, an evolution that Father Mallon believes validates same-sex unions, which he has performed.[42] Pro-gay clerics in religions that have long been antihomosexual reflect earlier, more tolerant, traditions in their faiths. Father John McNeill, an acclaimed Catholic scholar, justifies his favorable view of same-sex marriage by invoking the Christian Church's early liturgies sanctioning same-sex marriage, and he himself celebrates commitment services for same-sex couples.[43] Antonio Feliz, former bishop of the Church of the Latter Day Saints, argues from evidence in the Mormon archives that Joseph Smith, the founder of the Mormon religion, "sealed" (i.e., married) men to men and blessed male unions.[44] Although the Catholic and Mormon Churches will not soon abandon their hostility to same-sex marriages, it is notable that the faithful are divided on this issue.

Consistent with the above, the letters we received indicate that some churches and many religious leaders are seeking to withdraw religious tradition as a justification for secular discrimination against lesbians, gay men, and bisexuals (see also chapter 2). These leaders see the opportunity to assess same-sex marriage favorably as one way by which to reinterpret that tradition in light of established religious themes such as loving commitment, equality, and nondiscrimination. In this vein, we received a number of letters from various Quaker meetings that had considered whether to perform Quaker marriage ceremonies for same-sex couples. The prevailing theme of these letters was that it is unjust to treat loving and committed same-sex couples differently from heterosexual couples. As Ms. Peggy Monroe put it for her congregation, "it is in keeping with the Quaker testimony of equality that loving relationships between two people be acknowledged, accepted, and cared for without distinction to sexual orientation."[45] Presbyterian Reverend Carla Gorrell's letter asks, "When will our civil and religious systems take the lead to overcome unreasoned prejudice, as was necessary in earlier movements for African-American and women's rights?"[46]

Finally, these letters suggest that the decision to recognize same-sex marriage should be embraced as a civilizing opportunity for Christians and Jews, not feared as an evil thing. Methodist Reverend Richard Stetler put it most eloquently:[47]

> Should society allow two men or two women to marry? From my perspective, I believe the opportunity is here for the court to set a valuable precedent. . . .
>
> Permit one example which is all too commonplace. A year ago, a colleague of mine watched two people's lives become torn apart by our legal system. One was dying of AIDS while the other—the caregiver—remained helpless to make any decisions on his lover's behalf because he was not considered "family." The caregiver struggled with agency after agency all to no avail. Finally, when the partner with AIDS died, his mate stood by while all the funeral arrangements were made by the biological family, arrangements which were against the deceased's desires. The family proceeded to take all of the deceased's belongings. All the caregiver wanted were mementos of their lives together, but the family, living out its denial, left him with nothing but memories.

Catholic layperson Joan Sexton wrote a similarly eloquent epistle to *Commonweal*, the Roman Catholic weekly:[48]

> [I]t seems to me, as wife and mother, that it may be the most committed of hearts that would enter and stay in a marriage as a one-to-one relationship. I admire the courage of the homosexual person giving him/her self to one person, one body, one heart and to a lifelong struggle to understand and support that other. It's a promise that draws, from me, at least, respect and awe.

And I suspect that such marriages could teach us a lot in terms of realizing the ideal of true friendship. It's interesting that the challenge of women on ordination has brought forth a fresh look at what priesthood means; so the challenge of gay couples to be included in the institution of marriage promises a new look at what marriage means.

Sexton's letter epitomizes the theme of this book: Same-sex marriage will civilize both gays and straights, teaching each something about the unitive features of marriage.

These letters are a testament to an understanding that religious tradition is situated in a history of compassion and not etched in unyielding stone. The fluidity of religious beliefs underlines the responsibility of the faithful to interpret them in ways that are productive and not hurtful. Such an opportunity has been presented in the 1990s, and leaders such as Ms. Sexton, Reverend Stetler, Ms. Monroe, Reverend Gorrell, Reverend Carey, former Bishop Feliz, Father McNeill, Father Mallon, Reverend Mack, and Rabbi Kahn are interpreting their faith in ways that inspire. The Judeo-Christian "tradition" does not support *Howerton's* holding that "'marriage' between persons of the same sex [is] unthinkable and, by definition, impossible."

THE STAMP-OF-APPROVAL OBJECTION

The new natural law advocates do not rest their case against same-sex marriage simply on historical or definitional (procreation-based) objections. They also contend that same-sex marriage is bad and that the state should not sanction badness. Such thinkers start with the proposition that homosexual relationships are an "open challenge to society's sense of shame, as the gays recognize quite well. For if the practices of homosexuals are not shameful, what is?"[49] Some natural law thinkers are willing to leave homosexuals alone, but all of them adamantly oppose any state "sanction" of such "shameful" relationships. For these thinkers, marriage is a good, even blessed, form of life. To allow homosexual marriages would be to taint this good and send a signal that the state is somehow approving such relationships.[50] As one natural law enthusiast put it, gay marriage "would appear almost as a mocking burlesque" of marriage.[51]

This objection is hardly limited to adherents of natural law theories. Explaining why he thinks that sodomy law repeal is an easier issue than same-sex marriage, Judge Richard Posner cautions that "permitting homosexual marriage would be widely interpreted as placing a stamp of approval on homosexuality."[52] According to opinion polls, a substantial majority of Americans do not want legally recognized gay marriages.[53] Their reasons are various, often boiling down to simple dislike of gay people, but a significant number express their opposition in more neutral terms, believing that recognition of same-sex marriage would be a signal from the state that homosexuality, and perhaps also sodomy, is acceptable or even good. For citizens who view marriage as the embodiment of antihomosexual family values, this is disturbing.[54]

There are several problems with this line of argument, and they start with its premises. It is fanciful to think that the state's issuance of a marriage license is a signal of anything beyond the couple's ability to fill out a form. A church's decision to bless a marriage typically has normative significance as to the particular marriage, but the state's decision to issue a license does not. By privileging spouses with many benefits and entitlements, the state gives its stamp of approval to the institution of marriage. By issuing marriage licenses, the state is not conveying a stamp of approval to particular couples. Recall that transvestites, bisexuals, and other gender benders can obtain marriage licenses, usually without any fuss. Even if there were such a stamp, lesbian and gay relationships are good. They should be approved by the state and by religions. They are not shameful. What is shameful is a state policy that discriminates against same-sex couples, for such a policy is not only antihomosexual, but also antifamily and antichildren. One reason that marriage is an institution under siege is that its defenders are unwittingly sabotaging it by their inflexibility.

A Marriage License Is Not a Particularized Stamp of Approval

Opponents of same-sex marriage fear that state endorsement of it will demean the institution of marriage. But state endorsement of marriage in general does not connote state endorsement of particular marriages. In fact, the state is not a bit choosy about who can marry. There are few statutory prerequisites for obtaining a marriage license.[b] Many former prerequisites have been pruned away by Supreme Court decisions enforcing the right to marry (see chapter 5) and by the Americans with Disabilities Act, which prohibits state discrimination against people with disabilities. Virtually any man and woman of any persuasion or perversion can qualify nowadays, and even if they do not technically qualify, they can still get a license if they are brazen enough. The application process for a license is simple. You are not asked anything about your sexuality, the quality of your relationship, your moral background, or your future plans. You fill out the form and hand it over to a clerk. The clerk gives your application and any supporting documentation the most superficial scrutiny. If the couple wants to break the rules and sticks together on their rule breaking, they can be legally married all their lives. Women using men's names have married women throughout American history, and lesbians openly obtained licenses from gay-friendly clerks in Harlem during the 1920s.

In the District of Columbia, where I live, it is harder to get a driver's license than it is to get a marriage license. Not only are the lines longer for a driver's license, but the driver's licensocracy tests you. You can get a driver's license only if you more or less know how to drive a car, can guess 70 percent of the rules they ask you about on the written multiple-guess test, and can read the third line of eye charts (with glasses, if need be) and if your prior driving record is free of wild drinking sprees and other automotive atrocities. You can get a marriage license without any demonstrated or actual skill at social or sexual intercourse, without knowledge about or concern for the rules of sex or companionship, without good vision or a well-functioning body, and without a scintilla of moral scruple (you can even be in jail!). However evil, perverted, or incompetent you might be, the clerk will

---

[b]States prohibit marriage between people who are already married (bigamy) and between closely related people (incest). Parental consent or other requirements are imposed on individuals under the age of eighteen. (These prerequisites are discussed in some detail in chapter 5.) In almost all the states these are the only requirements that the state will enforce. Other disabilities can be invoked by one of the spouses as a justification for nullifying the marriage.

still give you the marriage license, because the clerk and the state do not care about your character, morality, or competence. As a matter of law (rather than religion), that license is your ticket to the legal benefits and obligations that marriage entails. Your church or the rabbi, priest, or minister you ask to perform your wedding service may impose more demanding prerequisites, but the state will not. The state is sending more of a normative signal about the particular applicant(s) when it issues a driver's license (this character can see, drive, and usually guess the rules of the road) than when it issues a marriage license (these people have filled out the form correctly).

Given the above description, it is unsurprising that marriage law is not a vehicle for conveying moral approval or disapproval of any particular form of marriage. Although every state freely gives marriage licenses to people convicted of rape, no one regards this state tolerance as a stamp of approval for rape. Although every state freely gives marriage licenses to people convicted of child molestation, no one regards this state tolerance as a stamp of approval for child molestation. No other category of despised people is subject to the marriage ban that gay people are.[c] Deadbeat dads are justifiably condemned for defaulting on important personal and social responsibilities owed to vulnerable persons, yet the state allows them to remarry and incur new obligations that will undermine any chance they will fulfill their old ones—and the Supreme Court requires the states to do so.[55] Gay people are condemned and denied the right to marry even though we fulfill our personal and social responsibilities. Although convicted murderers, drug dealers, spouse abusers, and the like are justifiably condemned for hurting other people, the state allows them to marry, and the Supreme Court requires the state to do so even while they are imprisoned.[56] Gay people are condemned and denied the right to marry even though we have done nothing to hurt others. I know of no moral system or religion that condemns homosexuality more severely than it condemns murder, rape, and hurting children, yet on the

---

[c] As noted in chapters 3 and 5, pedophiles can marry, so long as they are heterosexual. Polygamists can marry several spouses, but only seriatim (through easy divorce and remarriage) and not simultaneously (as they would prefer). Only incestophiles cannot marry. To the extent they are a despised group (I am insufficiently well informed), they should be read as a qualification of the statement in text.

issue of marriage we are treated worse than murderers, rapists, and child molesters.

The foregoing examples may make the stamp-of-approval argument seem more spiteful than it is. If the issue of "rapist marriage" had to be confronted de novo by our culture, more people would oppose it. Rapist marriage has been engulfed by the tradition of latitude in our marriage law, and its assimilation into history has rendered it politically invisible. Same-sex marriage has been ostensibly left out of our particular marriage law as it has developed, and its exclusion from the marital tradition has rendered it politically controversial. In short, it is harder to kick bad old couples out of legally constructed marriage than it is to bring good new couples in. This is an understandable impulse, but it is not a good argument for denying equality of opportunity to same-sex couples. Moreover, even this rehabilitated version of the stamp-of-approval argument is subject to deeper descriptive and normative difficulties.

As a descriptive matter, the state has already sacrificed heterosexual norms because of its uncritical license-issuing rules and process. It may be surprising to know that the state already places its stamp of approval on gender bending and even homosexuality. The state allows a male transvestite wearing a wedding dress to marry a woman wearing a wedding dress. By recognizing "transvestite marriage" does the state thereby convey approval of cross-dressing? Unless it is New Jersey, the state allows a male-to-female transsexual wearing a wedding dress to marry a woman wearing a wedding dress. By recognizing "transsexual marriage" does the state thereby convey approval of transsexualism and sex reassignment through hormones and surgery? The state allows the just-described transsexual marriage even though the transsexual considers herself a lesbian, her wife considers herself a lesbian, and everyone else in the community considers them a lesbian couple. By recognizing "lesbian marriage" of this sort, does the state thereby convey approval of lesbianism? Oops.

The stamp-of-approval argument, as a normative matter, should not affect legal rights. This form of argument, now so popular against same-sex marriage, was last sighted in opposition to different-race marriage. Virginians in 1967 overwhelmingly opposed different-race marriages, which had never been allowed in the South and were only recently sanctioned in other parts of the United States. Virginians feared that allowing different-race marriage would constitute state encouragement of racial intermixing. The Supreme Court unanimously rejected these arguments in *Loving v. Virginia*. Although most Americans still disapprove of different-race marriage and although white Americans overwhelmingly oppose it for close relatives, only one American in five believes different-race marriage should be illegal.[57] The Supreme Court recognized in *Loving* that popular desires to limit the marriage right to traditional criteria are inconsistent with the rule of law. No respectable scholar disputes the correctness of *Loving*, and the stamp-of-approval argument is a political as well as constitutional dead end.

Same-Sex Marriages Are Good

Loving suggests a deeper normative objection to the stamp-of-approval argument. People revolted by different-race marriage were wrong. Likewise, people revolted by same-sex marriage are wrong. These are marriages that would be as good and worthy as different-sex marriages.[d] The unitive features of marriage are just as potentially enriching to lesbian and gay couples as to straight couples, as dozens of studies of American relationships have demonstrated.[58]

Representative is the UCLA study by Letitia Anne Peplau and Susan D. Cochran.[59] The researchers selected matched samples of fifty lesbians, fifty gay men, fifty straight women, and fifty straight men, all of whom were involved in romantic and sexual relationships. There were no differences among the groups in the cumulative responses to scaled measures of love, compatibility, closeness of the relationship, and satisfaction from the relationship. Peplau and Cochran also asked the subjects to describe the best and worst things about their relationships. Typical responses were "The best thing is having someone to be with when you wake up" and "We like each other. We both seem to be getting what we want and need. We have wonderful sex together."

---

[d]The implicit caveat in the text reflects the reality that many marriages are not good marriages. In some cases the spouses are just not compatible. In other cases one partner exploits the other. There is, however, no reason to believe that same-sex marriages would be more afflicted with these problems than different-sex marriages already are.

The lesbian, gay, and straight couples reported statistically similar joys and troubles. They also reported similar levels of love and uncertainty about their relationships.

Same-sex couples reveal the same kind of interpersonal growth and love that different-sex couples do. Perhaps surprisingly, a large number of same-sex couples also provide homes for their children.[60] Many gay men, bisexuals, and lesbians have children from marriages to people of the opposite sex, and many have adopted children, a practice allowed in most states. Lesbians have children by means of artificial insemination, usually through anonymous sperm banks but increasingly through known gay donors. Gay men have children through surrogacy arrangements (permitted in most states) and through donor arrangements with female friends. The editors of the *Harvard Law Review* said in 1989, "Approximately three million gay men and lesbians in the United States are parents, and between eight and ten million children are raised in gay or lesbian households."[61] I think both figures are too high and doubt there can be precise figures at this point. What can be said with confidence is that a lot of gay people want to have children, do have children, and rear them in families.

In short, same-sex couples engage in productive and lasting human interconnections and contribute to the next generation of citizens. Not atypical is the story of Susan Silber and Dana Naparsteck. Silver-haired and stately, Silber is a successful lawyer and senior partner in one of the leading law firms in Takoma Park, Maryland. (She is now city counsel for Takoma Park.) Naparsteck is a therapist for Montgomery County; with raven hair and a ready smile, she is a nice complement to her serious partner. They have been a couple for eighteen years. Early in their relationship, Silber and Naparsteck decided to have a child, with Chris, a gay friend of theirs who worked for an international financial institution. Danielle Rachel Naparsteck Silber is now thirteen years old. Raised in Silber and Naparsteck's household, Danielle knows Chris as her father, whom she calls Papa. Chris and his former partner, Art (Danielle's other dad), have taken an active interest in Danielle's upbringing. Danielle is a brilliantly alert child and an unusually mature thirteen-year-old. She has two mothers, two fathers, and one little brother, Avi Benjamin. Danielle sees no disadvantage in not being raised in a more conventional family.

Indeed, she explains that she has more people to explain things to her and to help her, because she has "two mommies and two daddies." She understands family differently from traditionalists: "Family is people who all love each other, care for each other, help out, and understand each other," she said at age eight.[62] The new natural law advocates could learn something from her.

Silber and Naparsteck have established such a solid life together that marriage would add little if anything to their level of commitment. Still, they would like to get married, and their marriage would honor the institution. Their union reflects every family value and every virtue that even the most traditionalist thinker believes marriage is supposed to embody, except the belief that marriage must be between a man and a woman. The state should be proud to seal this union with its stamp of approval.

Prohibiting Same-Sex Marriage Is Antifamily

The stamp-of-approval objection to same-sex marriage is not only a bad argument but an "inverted" one. That is, the objectors say they favor family values, commitment, and the welfare of children. By opposing same-sex marriage the objectors are in reality subverting families, promoting promiscuity, and penalizing children. State prohibition of same-sex marriage is antifamily, anticommitment, and antichildren. It is uncivilized.

Virtually no respected authority believes there is anything the state can do to affect or change a person's sexual orientation.[e] A lesbian who is prohibited from marrying the woman she loves will not become a heterosexual. She might marry a man, as millions of lesbians did in the past. Such a marriage is likely to be dysfunctional (especially if the lesbian does not let her husband in on her secret orientation) and can be expected to become loveless over time. This is not a profamily scenario. For the lesbian herself, a more attractive scenario would be a

---

[e] This is common ground between libertarian Richard Posner and natural lawyer John Finnis, for example. Neither they nor I must have an opinion as to exactly what causes homosexuality to believe that its roots are early in life. All the respectable scientific theories accept this premise, whether the posited causative agent is a possible "gay gene" or some other genetic factor, pre- or postnatal hormonal influences, or early childhood experiences.

relationship with another woman. Such a relationship is likely to be fulfilling to her, and some studies suggest that the relationship is particularly satisfying if it is lasting and both partners are committed to it.[63]

What assures that a relationship will be a committed one? Two factors have been emphasized by researchers.[64] One is the strength of the relationship's advantages, including the presence of love and bonding between the partners, professional and economic synergy of the family unit, and cooperative endeavors such as the rearing of children. Another factor is the disadvantages of breaking up, including the costs of dismantling the household; the effect on third parties such as children and parents; and, for married couples, the expenses and complications of divorce. From the couple's point of view, the marriage option may be a wash. It may be just as likely to trap a couple in an unhappy marriage as to rescue a deteriorating one before it becomes irrevocably doomed. From a procommitment point of view, state-approved marriage is good for all couples because it creates additional advantages for the relationship and a big barrier to breakups. Under current law these advantages and this barrier only apply to different-sex couples; the law thereby misses an opportunity to contribute to the commitment of same-sex couples. In this admittedly twisted way state prohibition of same-sex marriage is anticommitment and anti-family.

Consider another consequence of the prohibition. For most people, gay or straight, it is easier to rear children in partnership with another person than to rear them as a single parent. (Even in the popular sitcom *Murphy Brown*, the independent Murphy needed a nurturing helper, housepainter Eldon, to help raise Avery, her child born outside of marriage.) Straight couples rearing children have an advantage gay couples do not; the legal recognition of their marriage creates additional incentives to stay together (divorce is expensive). By denying same-sex couples the right to marry in the name of procreation and childrearing, the state makes it a little bit harder for gay people to form lasting unions. This, in turn, makes it harder for gay people to raise children and probably discourages some gay people from having children at all.[65] This is an antiprocreation policy.

The state policy is also antichildren. Studies have repeatedly shown that children raised in gay and (especially) lesbian households are as

well socialized, as psychologically adjusted, and as capable of forming healthy peer relationships as children raised in different-sex or
single-parent households.[66] A few studies have found that children
raised in a two-parent lesbian household are better adjusted than children raised in a single-parent household, whether the single parent is
straight or lesbian.[67] These studies provide tentative support for the
intuitive proposition that two parents, whether of the same or different sex, are better for children than one. Yet state prohibitions of
same-sex marriage undermine the stability of the same-sex union
and therefore of the household. Such prohibitions also ensure that
children reared by different-sex married couples have an additional
advantage not afforded to children reared by same-sex couples: Each
married partner has a legal obligation to support the children (the
nonparent in a same-sex union has less of an obligation unless she or
he goes through a "second-parent adoption" procedure, allowed in
some states[68]). Finally, and not least importantly, the inability of same-
sex couples to marry leaves their children unusually vulnerable if the
biological parent dies. Consider the following story.

Janine Ratcliffe and Joan Pearlman formed a loving relationship in
the early 1970s and went through a commitment service to seal their
love.[69] Also sealing their love was the birth (after artificial insemination) of Pearlman's daughter, Kristen Janine Pearlman, in 1979. Soon
after Kristen's birth, however, Pearlman entered a period during
which she suffered one health complication after another; she died
when Kristen was just five years old. After Pearlman's death, Ratcliffe
continued to care for Kristen just as she had always done; Kristen
loved "Neen" as a parent. Pearlman had not left a will, but she had
left a letter to her daughter expressing her wish that she be raised by
Ratcliffe.[f] Pearlman's parents, Bernard and Rose, tentatively agreed.

---

[f] "I'm leaving you a wonderful person to love, my daughter, someone who was part of your
making, your birth, and up to now has shared with me all the responsibility of caring for you.
You love her face, voice, everything about her now (you are three months old). Please love Neen
and respect her. I leave your future and happiness in her hands. Love her as she loves you, love
her as she loves me.

"Forgive me, my little one, for leaving you, but know that no matter where I am I will
always be with you. You and Neen [are] in my heart and mind always. Make Neen proud of you.
Grow to be a proud but sensitive woman. Love life. Make good of yourself." Quoted in Laura
Benkov, *Reinventing the Family: The Emerging Story of Lesbian and Gay Parents*, 216 (New York:
Crown, 1994).

Later, they changed their minds. Because Ratcliffe had no legal relationship to the child or her mother, the Pearlmans were able to gain custody of Kristen.

Kristen's account of the separation is pitiable; the attorney "had to practically almost pry me away from my Neen to get me into the car."[70] Ratcliffe herself broke down and was hospitalized. The Pearlmans made visitation difficult for Ratcliffe, who faithfully sought contact. Kristen, for her part, was torn up by her separation. She wrote to the judge: "I love my Grandma and Grandpa, but my mommy wanted me and my Neeny to always be together. I have lived with my Neeny all my life and I want please to go back to my Neeny."[71] Deprived of her parent and living with septuagenarians in a nursing home, Kristen became overweight and lethargic; her grades plummeted. In response to a petition for custody, a judge finally spoke with the child. On the basis of that conversation and the testimony of experts, the judge returned Kristen to her family. "I ran down to the end of the block and I had this little dance I started to do and I started to scream because I felt so good. After that, my Neen came to pick me up. I'm real happy now," recalls Kristen.[72]

The Pearlmans considered their daughter's lesbian relationship a perversion. They sought legal custody of Kristen because they considered Ratcliffe an unfit parent.[73] They were wrong. The child recognized the truth all along, and ultimately so did a judge: Joan Pearlman and Janine Ratcliffe were good people joined in a good relationship that would have been a good marriage. It is the law, not its victims, that is perverted in denying this and other couples the rights that heterosexual couples have.

Note how the objections to same-sex marriage can be turned on their head. Objectors invoke interpersonal commitment, family values, and the procreative imperative. All of these values are sacrificed by the state's ban against same-sex marriages. All of these values are promoted once the state recognizes same-sex marriage. The only remnant of the stamp-of-approval argument is that the state should persecute gay people, an option that is unconstitutional (chapter 6) and nonsensical. As Andrew Sullivan put it, "even the most hardened conservatives recognize that gays are a permanent minority and aren't likely to go away. Since persecution is not an option in a civilized society, why not coax gays into traditional values rather than rail incoherently against them?" He concluded, "Given the fact that we already allow legal gay relationships, what possible social goal is advanced by framing the law to encourage those relationships to be unfaithful, undeveloped, and insecure?"[74]

PRAGMATIC OBJECTIONS

Most pragmatists should be open to my thesis that the state ought to accommodate the needs of same-sex couples and that traditional morality ought not to prevail. Judge Richard Posner, law's leading pragmatist and a conservative to boot, acknowledges that the burden of proof should be on those who would limit or prohibit same-sex marriages.[75] Nonetheless, Judge Posner stops short of endorsing same-sex marriage. Explaining why he thinks that sodomy law repeal is an easier call, Judge Posner first invokes the stamp-of-approval argument.[76] He does not think that popular disapproval should veto the idea completely, but he does think that disapproval requires incremental rather than dramatic change in the status quo. Relatedly, Judge Posner emphasizes the potential costs of recognizing same-sex marriage:[77]

> [The legal] incidents of marriage were designed with heterosexual marriage in mind, more specifically with heterosexual marriages with children. They may or may not fit the case of homosexual marriage. Do we want homosexual couples to have the same rights of adoption and custody as heterosexual couples? Should we worry that a homosexual might marry a succession of dying AIDS patients in order to entitle them to spouse's medical benefits?

Judge Posner concludes with a pragmatic pitch for proceeding slowly with the idea of same-sex marriage. He suggests a compromise solution for now, perhaps something like the Danish Registered Partnership Act (described in chapter 2).

Such pragmatic cost–benefit objections to same-sex marriage are not limited to intellectuals. When Governor Pete Wilson vetoed the California legislature's domestic partnership bill in 1994, he mentioned the costliness of extending marriage-like employment benefits to couples not previously eligible. Similar arguments were probably decisive in voters' endorsement of a referendum repealing the Austin, Texas, domestic partnership law the same year.[78] Concerns about cost and collateral consequences are substantial ones, particularly during a period of economic uncertainty. The factual record will reveal these to be greatly overblown, however. In any event, they must be balanced against the substantial benefits that same-sex marriage offers to society as a whole (not just to same-sex couples).

Marriage Law Easily Accommodates Same-Sex Couples

Consider Judge Posner's claim that the "incidents of marriage were designed with heterosexual marriage in mind." This claim, even if true, should have little normative consequence for a cluster of rights as important as marriage. Consider this form of argument in light of *Loving v. Virginia*, where the Supreme Court evaluated Virginia's prohibition of different-race marriages. Virginia could have argued that its "incidents of marriage were designed with same-race marriage in mind" and that the Court should be fearful about the consequences. Chief Justice Earl Warren's opinion in *Loving* eschewed such a narrowly consequentialist approach and, instead, focused only on the fairness of excluding different-race couples from an otherwise non-discriminating institution. In retrospect, Warren's focus on what is right and his rejection of consequentialism reveal the strength of the opinion, whose stature has only grown over time. Even the most ardent pragmatist has got to stand on principle some of the time.

More important, Judge Posner's generalization about the incidents of marriage is not accurate. Chapter 3 is an exhaustive listing of the legal benefits and obligations that flow from spousehood. Not a single one of them (go back and look) is any less applicable to homosexual couples than to heterosexual ones (or less applicable to childless couples than to those with children). The *legal* incidents of marriage involve rules protecting the privacy of the marital relationship, allowing the couple to act as one economic unit, allotting benefits and responsibilities to one's spouse when one dies or is incapacitated, and creating obligations of mutual support and fidelity. No informed person can deny that same-sex couples would profit from those legal incidents just as much as different-sex couples.

The legal benefits and obligations of marriage also do not directly relate to children.[g] If a couple has a child, that child has rights of support and good treatment whether the couple is married or not. If an unmarried man and woman have a child together but ultimately marry other people, both natural parents still have legally enforceable obligations to the child. All of these duties are as applicable to homosexual parents as they are to heterosexual parents. If a gay man marries a woman and they have a child, the gay man continues to have obligations of support after he leaves the household. If a lesbian has a child through artificial insemination by a known (gay male) donor, the donor father has legal obligations to the child just as the mother does. If a gay man has a child through a surrogate mother, both mother and father have legal rights and obligations relating to the child. Same-sex marriage would not disrupt any of these obligations to spouses or to children.

I would admit the following qualification to the foregoing argument. In their capacity for love, interpersonal growth, responsibility, childrearing, economic cooperation and joint financial planning, and maintaining a household, same-sex couples cannot persuasively be distinguished from different-sex couples. Both kinds of couples are also subject to the same calamities—death, illness, desertion, incapacitation—that marriage law regulates. However, none of this is to say that same-sex couples will be cookie-cutter replicas of different-sex couples. There will in fact be structural differences in these types of couples. Because procreation will necessarily involve a third party, children will introduce differences. For instance, third-party sperm donors and surrogate mothers (and perhaps their partners) are more likely to be part of the lesbian or gay family than is the case with heterosexual families. Lesbian and gay "families we choose" would, in the short term at least, be more extended than heterosexual families. (Recall Danielle Naparsteck Silber's "two mommies and two daddies.")

---

[g]Recognizing same-sex marriage might throw a monkey wrench into a California law providing that "the issue of a wife cohabiting with her husband, who is not impotent or sterile, is conclusively presumed to be a child of the marriage." California Evidence Code § 621(a) (1989), upheld against constitutional attack in Michael H. v. Gerald D., 491 U.S. 110 (U.S. Supreme Court, 1989). This complication would occur only if a court took the tendentious step of reading "wife cohabiting with her husband" to include same-sex couples.

There is also evidence to the effect that same-sex marriages would be more egalitarian. Lesbian couples in particular seem relatively more committed than gay or straight couples and seem more likely to structure their relationship on an equal basis. Silber and Naparsteck both work outside the home and share duties inside the home as well. Many lesbian couples specialize, of course, with one partner doing all the cooking, for example, but the specialization tends to depart from traditional marriage patterns. Rather than allocating all domestic duties to one partner, lesbian couples tend to share them; for example, one partner might be responsible for the cooking and the other for cleaning house, or one partner might be in charge of mowing the lawn whereas the other takes responsibility for raking the leaves.

My point is this: There will be systematic differences, especially at first and perhaps over time, between same-sex and different-sex married couples. Contrary to Judge Posner's view, the differences are legally irrelevant, because the law of marriage focuses on the interpersonal commitment and not the heterosexuality of the partners. To the extent the law of marriage focuses on children (by and large it does not), it is agnostic as to where the children come from. Generally, the law of marriage is highly accommodative. Not only can the law accommodate same-sex couples without strain, but the entry of same-sex couples into the institution of marriage will infuse it with much-needed fresh blood. To be blunt, it would be civilizing for the institution of marriage to welcome couples like Ninia Baehr and Genora Dancel, Susan Silber and Dana Naparsteck, and Joan Pearlman and Janine Ratcliffe.

Same-Sex Marriage Is Cost-Effective

The biggest cost of same-sex marriage would appear to be the greater employee benefits owed to a new wave of spouses. This is a cost whose fairness is completely justified. Fringe benefits such as health and life insurance are a substantial (usually more than a third) portion of the salary package of most American employees. Employers routinely subsidize coverage of spouses and children in these packages. Lesbian and gay employees are systematically discriminated against in employment because they cannot add spouses to their package. This argument based on fairness is complemented by one based on low cost.

Employers who have studied the issue have found that allowing same-sex domestic partners to share in fringe benefits adds very little or nothing to their overall cost.[79] Municipalities adopting domestic partnership coverage for their employees in the 1980s found in practice that the extra coverage added 1 to 2 percent (Seattle, San Francisco, West Hollywood) or virtually nothing (Berkeley, Laguna Beach, Santa Cruz) to their total insurance costs.[80] The main reason for the low costs is low enrollment, but employers are also finding that the per employee cost of domestic partnership coverage is substantially lower than it is for spousal coverage. Accordingly, employers are galloping to include domestic partners in their fringe benefit policies.[81] This market response signals that the biggest anticipated expense of gay marriage, higher fringe benefit costs for employers, is greatly exaggerated.

What of the other costs? Judge Posner worries, "Should we worry that a homosexual [man] might marry a succession of dying AIDS patients in order to entitle them to spouse's medical benefits?" Should we worry that a heterosexual or bisexual might marry a succession of dying AIDS patients? That a lesbian might marry a succession of dying breast cancer patients? There is no evidence that an appreciable number of people marry for medical insurance reasons. There is no evidence that gay or bisexual men would marry a succession of AIDS patients, and there is every reason to believe that lesbians (who are the group least afflicted with the HIV virus) will not. There is no evidence that AIDS claims would be disproportionately numerous for same-sex couples, and there is every reason to believe from private companies' domestic partnership experience that AIDS claims would not be expensive.[82] The succession-of-AIDS-patient-marriages argument is a lavender herring.[h]

---

[h] If one is just trying to make up scare examples, a better one is immigration. Heterosexuals do marry noncitizens in order for them to emigrate and become citizens in the United States, and the Immigration and Naturalization Service tries to monitor this practice. (It is the only serious state effort to police the integrity of marriage in the United States.) I suppose it could be argued that gay people, like straight people, might enter into sham marriages. So what? Unless one is willing to abolish or reform different-sex marriage, it is no argument to say that same-sex marriage will invite the same regulatory problems already associated with different-sex marriage.

Indeed, AIDS ultimately provides an argument for same-sex marriage that should appeal to reasonable pragmatists.[83] The early years of the AIDS epidemic were fueled by unsafe sex with multiple partners by gay and bisexual males. Safer sex has been an effective weapon against the epidemic, but safer sex within a monogamous setting is even more effective. Monogamy ought to be useful not only because it reduces the number of sexual partners but also because it fosters better monitoring and more honest sharing of information between sexual partners. State-recognized same-sex marriage would encourage committed monogamous relationships within a group at risk. (The state encourages committed heterosexual relationships by its anti-adultery rules and by its barriers to exit.) Secondarily, legalizing same-sex marriages might also encourage more open and informative discussions of sexuality and homosexuality, discussions that are important in slowing the spread of AIDS. State recognition of same-sex partnerships and prohibition of sexual orientation discrimination are key components in Sweden's successful anti-AIDS campaign.[84]

The One-Step-at-a-Time Argument

More telling is Judge Posner's strategic point: Before the law can tackle anything so controversial as same-sex marriage, it needs to wait for popular attitudes to move closer to the desired policy. If the law moves too fast, its sanction will do little good and may produce a backlash against lesbians, gay men, and bisexuals. If the law moves too slowly, on the other hand, it will perpetuate needless human anguish and waste. The trick is to find the optimal political compromise and to avoid bad timing.

This kind of strategy informed the Supreme Court's treatment of laws prohibiting different-race marriages. Virginia's Racial Integrity Act first reached the Court on appeal in 1955, when twenty-nine states had antimiscegenation laws and the South was seething over the antisegregationist gauntlet the Court had thrown down in *Brown v. Board of Education*. After hearing argument in *Naim v. Naim*, the Supreme Court remanded the case for a hearing, which the Virginia courts arrogantly refused to provide.[85] The Supreme Court declined to take up the law again until *Loving*. In the interim, the nation had come to accept the value of *Brown* and thirteen more states repealed their antimiscegenation laws. The shift in American culture over the decade between *Naim* and *Loving* facilitated a unanimous Court decision on an issue that still divides Americans morally.

The United States Supreme Court's temporizing between *Naim* and *Loving* finds a parallel in the Hawaii Supreme Court's temporizing in *Baehr v. Lewin*. The court found the state's prohibition against same-sex marriage to be sex discrimination in 1993 but remanded the case for trial to determine whether the state can demonstrate a compelling justification for its discrimination. The opinion has generated much debate in Hawaii, as the court knew it would, and a final disposition of the case (trial judgment through appeal) ought to take several years more. That opinion might be a wise pragmatic judgment on the part of the court: alert the body politic that same-sex marriage is an urgent issue; give the political backlash a chance to pass; and only then invalidate the prohibition, with the hope that hate-based politics cannot sustain its energy for the duration.

Judge Posner's pragmatism counsels not just delay but compromise. If the backlash against same-sex marriage in Hawaii is serious, proponents might fall back on a Danish-style proposal that gives same-sex couples marriage with all the trappings except the name and adoption rights. Such a compromise would be more broadly acceptable than a pure marriage right. Many of the religious leaders who bless same-sex relationships favor using a euphemism for *marriage* (e.g., *union*). Moreover, a Danish-style compromise would generate almost all the advantages noted for same-sex marriage in chapter 3, including tangible and intangible benefits flowing from the rights associated with marriage as well as the sense of commitment that arises from accepting the duties associated with marriage. It is not clear that such a compromise would have spared Kristen Pearlman separation from her beloved second mother, Janine Ratcliffe, but it would have saved Karen Thompson and Sharon Kowalski from their legal purgatory and would offer advantages to the family of Susan Silber and Dana Naparsteck.

The main thing that a Danish-style compromise would sacrifice is formal equality. How important is that sacrifice? I consider it critically important and would oppose a halfway house to marriage. As chapters 5 and 6 will demonstrate, the Constitution backs me up. It is a denial of the U.S. Constitution's equal protection clause and of state equal rights amendments for a state to discriminate against same-sex couples in issuing marriage licenses.

5

THE CONSTITUTIONAL CASE:
THE RIGHT TO MARRY

Same-sex couples have been bringing lawsuits seeking recognition of their marriages for twenty-five years. The state and federal constitutional issues presented by these lawsuits parallel the human and policy issues, and so I shall draw on the previous chapters and use plain English to make the legal case for same-sex marriage. This chapter analyzes and defends the claim that existing state policies discriminate unlawfully when, without substantial justification, they pick and choose the citizens granted the fundamental right to marry. The next chapter analyzes and defends the claim that existing state policies discriminate unlawfully when, without substantial justification, they exclude citizens from any right merely because of their sex or sexual orientation. Either claim can be expressed in terms of the equal protection clause of the U.S. Constitution's Fourteenth Amendment, which provides that no state may "deny to any person within its jurisdiction the equal protection of the laws."[a] The first claim can also be expressed in terms of the due process clause of the Fourteenth Amendment, which has been interpreted to assure that the state will not unduly disrupt people's privacy rights. Both claims can also be expressed as violations of equal rights or privacy provisions in state

---

[a]The main constitutional limits applicable to the states are found in the Fourteenth Amendment: "[N]or shall any State deprive any person of life, liberty, or property, without due process of law; nor deny to any person within its jurisdiction the equal protection of the laws."

constitutions. Any of these arguments would be a sufficient basis for constitutional invalidation of existing state policies.

The thesis of this chapter, in a nutshell, is that the state cannot arbitrarily allocate the right to marry and that there is no good justification for denying that right to same-sex couples. This thesis is amply supported by the Supreme Court's right-to-marry decisions, but it is hardly limited to American jurisprudence. Most of the arguments developed here would be applicable in other industrialized countries. The larger point is one of political morality. After a long period of being actively persecuted, lesbian, gay, bisexual, and transgendered citizens are out of the closet in increasing numbers. Many are joined in committed unions and would like to marry on the same terms that heterosexual couples routinely enjoy. We are citizens, and we insist on equal treatment. A polity that denies a responsible, even if beleaguered, minority group legal equality without good justification is a polity inviting wasteful as well as painful turmoil.

SAME-SEX COUPLES' RIGHT TO MARRY

A state's refusal to recognize same-sex marriage on the same terms as different-sex marriage is constitutionally problematic in two different ways. State policy might be seen as denying gay and lesbian couples a zone of protected privacy that citizens retain under the social contract. In law this is a *substantive due process* claim. Alternatively, state policy might be understood as discriminating against same-sex couples in the allocation of a bundle of important legal rights. In law this is an *equal protection* claim. Both kinds of claims are supported by Supreme Court precedents recognizing a fundamental right to marry. Although the Court's right-to-marry jurisprudence is not obviously supported by the text or original expectations of the Constitution,[1] it is consistent with and indeed required by America's constitutional traditions concerning citizens' freedom to make choices in matters of their intimate and familial relationships. For reasons that will be developed in the next part of this chapter, the equal protection version of this argument is the stronger one for gay and lesbian couples.

Constitutional Protection of Fundamental Privacy Rights

The United States Constitution does not explicitly protect against every injustice committed by the state. For example, it contains no provision assuring a general right to personal and relational privacy, as several state constitutions have,[b] yet the Constitution would not be complete without recognition that such a right is implicitly protected. Consider the following. For much of this century some states followed a practice of sterilizing people institutionalized for specified crimes or mental disabilities. A literal reading of the Fourteenth Amendment (see footnote a) would be hard put to fault this policy, unless it were arbitrarily applied. In 1927, Justice Oliver Wendell Holmes's opinion in *Buck v. Bell* upheld the sterilization of mentally disabled people essentially for this reason.[2] The principle underlying the decision is that courts should not second-guess legislative judgments unless they contravene a particular constitutional provision.

What kind of constitution was Justice Holmes interpreting, or creating? Would reasonable people have joined the social contract if they had thought that state power could be used to sterilize citizens without the most careful justification? Commentators have criticized Justice Holmes's decision intensely.[3] The Supreme Court had second thoughts about this issue in 1942, when it struck down a sterilization scheme applicable to certain classes of "habitual criminals" (such as thieves) and not others (such as embezzlers). Justice William O. Douglas's opinion for the Court in *Skinner v. Oklahoma* explains why judges ought to demand stronger justifications for such statutory schemes:[4]

> We are dealing here with legislation which involves one of the basic civil rights of man. Marriage and procreation are fundamental to the very existence and survival of the race. The power to sterilize, if exercised, may have subtle, far-reaching and devastating effects. . . . There is no

---

[b]Article I, § 6 of the Hawaii Constitution says: "The right of the people to privacy is recognized and shall not be infringed without the showing of a compelling state interest." To similar effect are Article I, § 22 of the Alaska Constitution; Article II, § 8 of the Arizona Constitution; Article I, § 1 of the California Constitution; Article I, § 23 of the Florida Constitution; Article I, § 12 of the Illinois Constitution; Article I, § 5 of the Louisiana Constitution; Article II, § 10 of the Montana Constitution; Article I, § 10 of the South Carolina Constitution; and Article I, § 7 of the Washington Constitution.

redemption for the individual whom the law touches. . . . He is forever deprived of a basic liberty.

Skinner stands for the proposition that when the state draws lines that affect the fundamental interests of a class of citizens, the state must show that the lines bear a close relationship to a substantial social goal. Even though the Oklahoma law reflected a eugenic theory of criminality widely accepted in that era, the Court held that the state failed to demonstrate why thieves and other blue-collar criminals should be subject to the penalty while embezzlers and other white-collar criminals were not.

Although invoking the equal protection clause to strike down the statute, *Skinner* reflects a broader principle, which is also found in Supreme Court decisions, protecting against undifferentiated state intrusions into people's private affairs. Justice Benjamin Cardozo had written in 1937 that the due process clause incorporates rights that are "implicit in the concept of ordered liberty."[5] The Court in 1923 had stated that the right "to marry, establish a home and bring up children is a central part of [that] liberty."[6] Two decades after *Skinner*, Justice John Harlan's dissenting opinion in *Poe v. Ullman* synthesized a century of case law when he stated that the due process clause protects rights "which are *fundamental*; which belong . . . to the citizens of all free governments," for "the purposes [of securing] which men enter into society."[7]

The most famous of all privacy cases is *Griswold v. Connecticut* from 1965. In his decision striking down Connecticut's anticontraception law, Justice Douglas ringingly declares:[8]

> We deal with a right of privacy older than the Bill of Rights—older than our political parties, older than our school system. Marriage is a coming together for better or for worse, hopefully enduring, and intimate to the degree of being sacred. It is an association that promotes a way of life, not causes; a harmony in living, not political faiths; a bilateral loyalty, not commercial or social projects. Yet it is an association for as noble a purpose as any involved in our prior decisions.

Griswold expands *Skinner*: The right of privacy not only disables the state from arbitrarily interfering with the individual's *personal* liberty (*Skinner*), but also from arbitrarily interfering with his or her *inter-*

personal or *relational* liberty (*Griswold*).ᶜ More subtly, *Griswold* and *Skinner* reflect different dimensions of sexuality. Whereas *Skinner* emphasizes the traditional goal of procreation when it protects against state sterilization, *Griswold* necessarily separates constitutional protection of private sexuality from procreation. (Arrested for proposing to use birth control, the plaintiffs were trying to *avoid* procreation.) *Griswold* instead stresses the social features of sexuality, the "harmony in living" and "bilateral loyalty" mentioned by Justice Douglas.

The Fundamental Right to Marry and Its Application to Same-Sex Couples

Consistent with Justice Harlan's *Poe* framework, *Griswold* did not address the state's "power . . . to say who may marry."⁹ That was a separate issue. Two years after *Griswold*, a unanimous Court invalidated state laws prohibiting different-race marriages in the ironically captioned *Loving v. Virginia*. Part I of Chief Justice Earl Warren's opinion found the law's race-based classification to violate the equal protection clause (this opinion is explored in chapter 6). Part II briefly presented an independent ground for striking down the law. "The freedom to marry has long been recognized as one of the vital personal rights essential to the orderly pursuit of happiness by free men," said the chief justice. "To deny this fundamental freedom on so unsupportable a basis as the racial classifications embodied in these statutes . . . is surely to deprive all the State's citizens of liberty without due process of law."¹⁰ Like *Griswold*, Part II of *Loving* recognizes a substantive due process right that cannot be denied by the state without strong justification. The Supreme Court has said that the right to marry is so important that the state may not easily take it away.

Loving's recognition of a due process right to marry was a potentially significant regulation of state decisions as to who can marry, but its scope was unclear. Was the right to marry constitutionally significant outside of the miscegenation (different-race marriage) context?

ᶜBy "personal" liberty, I mean what a person does with her or his own body, goods, or affairs. *Skinner* and *Roe v. Wade,* 410 U.S. 113 (U.S. Supreme Court, 1973), protecting a woman's right to abort, are examples. By "interpersonal" liberty, I mean how people relate to one another. *Griswold* and the cases discussed in this chapter are examples.

The Court so found in *Zablocki v. Redhail*.[11] For residents owing support obligations to children from a prior marriage, Wisconsin required proof of compliance with those obligations before the state would issue marriage licenses. The law's goal was to make deadbeat dads pay up, by preventing them from a new marriage. Justice Thurgood Marshall's opinion for the Court in *Zablocki* had no quarrel with the state's goal but struck down the state's method of achieving its goal. The Court held that no state restriction of the "freedom of personal choice in matters of marriage and family life" can be sustained under the equal protection clause unless the state can show that its restriction is narrowly drawn to serve a compelling social purpose.[12] Because there was no suspicious classification in *Zablocki* comparable to the race-based classification in *Loving*, the stricter judicial scrutiny had to be justified solely from its restriction of the right to marry. Justice Marshall observed that the right to marry should be "placed on the same level of importance as decisions relating to procreation, childbirth, child rearing, and family relationships," for "it would make little sense to recognize a right of privacy with respect to other matters of family life and not with respect to the decision to enter into the relationship that is the foundation of the family in our society."[13]

Zablocki establishes a doctrinal structure logically applicable to other cases: A state law or practice that places a "direct legal obstacle in the path of persons desiring to get married" denies those persons the equal protection of the laws unless the state policy is "supported by sufficiently important state interests and is closely tailored to effectuate only those interests."[14] This means that the burden of persuasion as to same-sex marriage lies with the opponents. The issue is not "Why gay marriage?" but is instead "Why *not* gay marriage?" This is precisely why Justice Lewis Powell refused to join Justice Marshall's majority opinion.[15] Although the majority rejected Powell's position, it sent mixed signals on the issue of procreation. Would the right to marry apply to couples who cannot or will not procreate? The next, and most recent, Supreme Court decision spoke to this question.

The issue in *Turner v. Safley* was whether the state could limit marriages of prison inmates to cases where the warden found a compelling reason to allow the marriages; in practice, the only compelling reason was a pregnancy or the birth of an illegitimate child. Justice Sandra Day O'Connor's opinion for a unanimous Court discreetly conceded the right of prisons to impose "substantial restrictions" on inmate marriages, probably referring to connubial visits, but insisted that *Zablocki* and *Loving* remained relevant:[16]

> Many important attributes of marriage remain, however, after taking into account the limitations imposed by prison life. First, inmate marriages, like others, are expressions of emotional support and public commitment. These elements are an important and significant aspect of the marital relationship. In addition, many religions recognize marriage as having spiritual significance; for some inmates and their spouses, therefore, the commitment of marriage may be an exercise of religious faith as well as an expression of personal dedication. Third, most inmates eventually will be released by parole or commutation, and therefore most inmate marriages are formed in the expectation that they will be fully consummated. Finally, marital status often is a precondition to the receipt of government benefits (e.g., Social Security benefits), property rights (e.g., tenancy by the entirety, inheritance rights), and other, less tangible benefits (e.g., legitimation of children born out of wedlock). These incidents of marriage, like the religious and personal aspects of the marriage commitment, are unaffected by the fact of confinement or the pursuit of legitimate corrections goals.

These elements taken together "are sufficient to form a constitutionally protected marital relationship," concluded Justice O'Connor. In short, procreation is not an acid test for the right to marry.

Turner adds nothing to the analytical structure created by *Loving* (due process) and *Zablocki* (equal protection). Because it arose in the prison context, where the Court is deferential to state rule making, the Court applied the lenient "reasonable relationship" approach developed in earlier prison cases. It is remarkable enough that the restriction on marriage fell even in this setting. More important, at no point in her opinion did Justice O'Connor mention procreation as a necessary justification for treating marriage as a fundamental right. Given her application of the right to inmates, some of them in prison for life, she was extending the right to marry to some people who would never consummate their relationships.[17] This is potentially important. *Loving* and *Zablocki* give some emphasis to the procreative goal of marriage associated with religious and natural law traditions. *Griswold*, in contrast, stresses the social, or unitive, goal of marriage, its "bilateral loyalty." Even more than *Griswold*, *Turner* emphasizes the unitive goal, where marriage is an institution of commitment. The shift in emphasis from *Skinner* (procreation) to *Turner* (commitment) reflects the evolution of American society from an agrarian one, where procreation was important for survival and economic progress, to an urban one, where procreation takes a back seat to personal and interpersonal fulfillment. This point is both descriptive and normative. American society has shifted from a procreative to a unitive understanding of marriage, and this is a good shift. Procreation is a lesser goal in the modern world. Baby production has narrowed women's personal choices, and a unitive understanding of marriage reflects greater equality between the marital partners. Finally, it is well recognized that children enrich a family whether or not they are the result of the parents' intercourse.

In light of the Supreme Court's precedents, a state's refusal to recognize same-sex marriages would seem to be both the denial of a fundamental liberty (*Loving*) and discrimination in the allocation of a fundamental right (*Zablocki*). In light of our society's emphasis on the unitive, "bilateral loyalty" goal of marriage, this constitutional requirement that states recognize same-sex marriages is a good requirement. Policymakers and judges should eagerly embrace it. As of 1996, however, no judge or attorney general in the United States has ever applied the foregoing jurisprudence to require the state even to justify its refusal to recognize same-sex marriages.[18] One possible reason for this phenomenon might be an accident of timing. The initial legal challenges to state laws excluding same-sex couples were brought in the early 1970s, after Stonewall but before the Supreme Court had elaborated on the right to marry in *Zablocki* and *Turner*. The first appellate decision on the issue, *Baker v. Nelson*,[19] dismissed the plaintiffs' right-to-marry argument based on Part II of *Loving* (the right to marry) by limiting *Loving* to its Part I (race discrimination). Losses in cases like *Baker* undermined similar arguments even after it was clear that *Loving* had established a right to marry beyond the miscegenation context. Another reason for the early losses may be incomplete factual records. *Baker* began its constitutional discussion with the premise that "[t]he institution of marriage as a union of man and woman, uniquely involving the procreation and rearing of children, is as old as the book of Genesis."[20] The Kentucky Court of Appeals dismissed a same-sex marriage claim in *Jones v. Hallahan* because "[m]arriage has always been considered as the union of a man and a woman and we have been presented with no authority to the contrary."[21] I need not repeat why these claims are factually improper.

In the *Baehr* litigation both the attorney general and the supreme court of Hawaii rejected plaintiffs' argument that they have a fundamental right to marry. Although the court found an equal protection claim for the state's sex-based classification (see chapter 6), the court ignored *Turner* and read *Zablocki* narrowly:[22]

> Implicit in the *Zablocki* Court's link between the right to marry, on the one hand, and the fundamental rights of procreation, childbirth, adoption, and child rearing, on the other, is the assumption that one is simply the logical predicate of the others.
>
> The foregoing case law demonstrates that the federal construct of the fundamental right to marry . . . contemplates unions between men and women. (Once again, this is hardly surprising inasmuch as such unions are the only state-sanctioned marriages currently acknowledged in this country.)

Restricting the state constitution to the federal approach, as it interpreted it, the Hawaii Supreme Court refused to recognize a state constitutional right to marry.

Like the history-definition argument accepted in *Baker* and *Hallahan*, the Hawaii court's insistence that marriage must involve procreation is normatively unjustified for the reasons developed in chapter 4. It is also inconsistent with *Griswold* and *Roe v. Wade*, which stand for the proposition that the state *cannot* impose a procreation goal on married couples. Finally, it is inconsistent with the analytical framework established by *Loving*, *Zablocki*, and *Turner*. This framework involves just two steps: Is there a "direct legal obstacle in the path of persons desiring to get married"?[23] If so, is that restriction "supported by sufficiently important state interests and . . . closely tailored to effectuate only those interests"?[24] The real problem with the Hawaii decision is its addition of an unauthorized third step: *Is the couple one that has traditionally been allowed to marry?* This unauthorized third step is unjustified for both due process and (especially) equal protection reasons.

No one disputes that same-sex couples have a prepolitical right to relational privacy in a polity of ordered liberty. The various definitional arguments discuss only same-sex marriage, arguing that it is unheard-of and therefore cannot be a prepolitical right. Yet a similar argument had been offered, and rejected, in *Loving*. Defending its antimiscegenation law, Virginia maintained that different-race marriages were contrary to the law of God and unknown to civilized jurisprudence. These claims are factually incorrect, but Chief Justice Warren brushed them aside as irrelevant to the due process right to marry. Part II of his opinion found a violation of the right to marry without any inquiry into whether different-race marriages had been recognized in other societies or other times. An implication of *Loving* is that the relational privacy involved in the right to marry is prepolitical, whether or not historical practice has specifically sanctioned it. Relational privacy is prepolitical because it is so necessary to the well-being of citizens that the state cannot easily disrupt it. The first half of this book provides many illustrations and refers to empirical studies that establish the importance of relational privacy for same-sex couples.

Definitional arguments are more starkly inconsistent with an equal protection analysis such as that in *Zablocki*.[d] An equal protection analysis starts from the proposition that marriage carries with it a bundle of important rights and duties. Marriage is fundamental not only because it is a prepolitical form of interpersonal liberty but also because it is a creature of law and generates many legal ripple effects. Recall *Turner*'s justification for protecting the right to marry of inmates, including those who could not consummate their marriages sexually. Because any line drawing by the state creates a category of

---

[d]Cass R. Sunstein, "Sexual Orientation and the Constitution: A Note on the Relationship Between Due Process and Equal Pretection," 55 *University of Chicago Law Review* 1161 (1988), maintains that due process arguments are relatively more backward-looking (Is this practice inconsistent with our traditions?") than equal protection arguments ("Is this practice invidiously discriminatory?"). Sunstein's thesis does not hold for *Loving*, which relied on both types of arguments, but it may be applicable to the same-sex marriage issue.

citizens who cannot partake of those associated rights and duties, that line drawing (that *discrimination*) must be justified as necessary to achieve an overriding social goal. For a *Zablocki*-type of argument to succeed, the plaintiffs need not show their historical pedigree; all they have to show is their exclusion from a state-created fundamental right. Justice Powell's concurring opinion in *Zablocki* made clear that Justice Marshall's opinion for the Court opened up the right to marry to historically excluded couples, a charge Justice Marshall did nothing to discourage.

Is There a Homosexuality Exception to the Right to Marry?

The persistence of arguments based on "the definition" of marriage or the "necessary" link between marriage and procreation surely owes something to the association same-sex marriage has with homosexuality. The large majority of committed same-sex couples are homosexual,[e] and many of the couples consummate their marriages with illegal acts. Justice Harlan's *Poe* dissent emphasized that the privacy right protecting the contraceptive practices of married couples does not necessarily protect "extramarital sexuality," such as "[a]dultery, homosexuality and the like."[25] Just as state decisions about who may marry were not at issue in *Poe* and *Griswold*, so state decisions about extramarital sexuality were not at issue in those cases. While the Court has consistently and firmly resolved the first issue, the Court has issued arguably inconsistent decisions on the second issue.

In *Eisenstadt v. Baird* the Supreme Court struck down a statute preventing unmarried couples from receiving contraceptives. Justice Brennan's opinion for the Court emphasized the right of "*the individual*, married or single to be free from unwarranted governmental intrusion into matters so fundamentally affecting a person as the decision to bear or beget a child."[26] In *Stanley v. Georgia*,[27] the Court held that the state could not regulate the private use of otherwise regulable obscene materials within the confines of one's own home.

---

[e]Not all same-sex couples are homosexual, because emotional affinity is not always linked with erotic affinity. See Lillian Faderman, *Surpassing the Love of Men: Romantic Friendship and Love Between Women from the Renaissance to the Present* (New York: Morrow, 1981). Moreover, I am unconvinced that all people can be easily pegged as homosexual or heterosexual.

Justice Marshall's opinion essentially suggested that private masturbatory fantasies, with pictorial aids, were beyond state interference. *Eisenstadt* and *Stanley* can be read to create constitutional protection for personal freedom in matters of sexual behavior.[28]

However, the Court limited this line of liberty in its famous *Bowers v. Hardwick* decision.[29] The case involved the prosecution (later dropped) of Michael Hardwick for practicing oral sex with a consenting adult male in his bedroom. A narrowly divided Court held that there is no due process "right of homosexuals to engage in acts of sodomy," by which the state meant oral and anal sex. Justice Byron White's opinion for the Court denied that the earlier cases insulated all private sexual conduct between consenting adults from state regulation. It distinguished its earlier privacy cases, *Skinner* through *Stanley*, from cases involving homosexuality: "No connection between family, marriage, or procreation on the one hand and homosexual activity on the other has been demonstrated" by the parties or the lower court. Without that link to the earlier cases, the Court essentially left the states free to regulate sodomy, with a likely exception for consensual sodomy within the confines of marriage.[30] The Court's disposition and reasoning have been criticized from every perspective known to law professors.[31] Even Charles Fried, solicitor general during the Reagan Administration and a law clerk to Justice Harlan, has urged that *Bowers* be overruled as inconsistent with the principles of the earlier precedents.[32]

Assume that *Bowers* is not overruled. Does it create a "homosexuality exception" to the right to marry? This depends in part on how broadly the Court reads *Bowers*, for there are many grounds for finding *Bowers*, a decision only about extramarital sexuality, irrelevant to the different decision about who can marry. *Turner* relied on this distinction, for example. The state can prohibit sex between inmates, can prohibit sex between inmates and outsiders, and can regulate and probably prohibit sex between inmates and their spouses. Nonetheless, the state cannot prohibit inmates from marrying without showing a factually supportable penological interest. The implication I draw from *Turner* is that the state has more freedom to regulate sex than it has to regulate who may marry. I read *Bowers* as standing only for the proposition that the states have fairly broad discretion in regulating nonmarital sexual activity and as saying nothing about the right to marry.

On the other hand, *Bowers* invites state regulation of same-sex intimacy and can be read more broadly. If the state can criminalize sodomy, one might argue, then surely the state can discourage sodomy by prohibiting institutions (marriage!) that would create opportunities for sodomy or that could be read as a stamp of approval of sodomy.[33] Consider the problems with such a broad reading of *Bowers*, however. Only twenty states have fully enforceable laws prohibiting consensual sodomy.[f] A state that does not prohibit or expressly condemn consensual sodomy (such as Hawaii in *Baehr v. Lewin*) ought not rely on *Bowers* to support its prohibition of same-sex marriage. Even in states that do make sodomy prohibition an important state policy, *Bowers* ought not dispose of the constitutional challenge, for several reasons. The prohibition of specified sexual acts is not as serious an invasion of personal and relational liberties as is the denial of the right to marry and its hundreds of associated rights.[g] This is the holding of *Turner*, decided a year after *Bowers*. To narrow *Turner* (a decision widely accepted as correct) by invoking *Bowers* (a decision universally condemned) would be irrational. It may seem odd to say that sodomy is illegal outside of marriage but legal between spouses at home, but that is the way some lower courts have interpreted their sodomy laws for straight couples.

A *Bowers*-based limitation of *Turner* would also face a problem of sexual reality. A great deal of heterosexual activity violates state

---

[f]As of June 1995 there are operative sodomy laws in Alabama, Arkansas, Arizona, Florida, Georgia, Idaho, Kansas, Louisiana, Maryland, Minnesota, Mississippi, Missouri, Montana (litigation pending), North Carolina, Oklahoma, Rhode Island, South Carolina, Tennessee (litigation pending), Utah, and Virginia. I am not counting, but others might be inclined to include, Texas and Michigan, where there are unchallenged lower court decisions invalidating the sodomy laws, and Massachusetts, whose sodomy laws have been partially invalidated.

[g]That sodomy laws are criminal laws and marriage rights only civil does not detract from the statement in the text. The defendant in *Bowers* was not sentenced to a prison term; the case against him was dropped. Few people are sentenced to prison for violating sodomy laws by their consensual conduct with another adult. Justice Powell's critical fifth vote in *Bowers v. Hardwick* explicitly said that a prison sentence would raise more serious constitutional issues that, on his understanding, the Court was not deciding. Sodomy laws have important and vile consequences for those harassed under their aegis. My point is only that denial of marriage rights has more serious and fundamental consequences.

sodomy prohibitions. Sodomy laws typically prohibit anal and oral sex, and the laws of sixteen states prohibit different-sex sodomy on the same terms as same-sex sodomy.[h] According to most studies of American sexuality, a large majority of heterosexual couples practice oral sex and a significant minority practice anal sex.[34] Indeed, popular American marriage manuals have advocated and taught methods of sodomitic foreplay since the early twentieth century.[35] Would the Court insist that states prevent any marriage that would be consummated by prohibited sodomy? Aside from being a silly and unenforceable idea, this would contravene the wall of marital privacy built by *Griswold*. Even if the state only prohibited marriages consummated by prohibited sodomy, many gay marriages would still qualify. Lesbian unions have long been consummated by a variety of activities that do not violate state sodomy laws, including kissing and caressing, mutual masturbation, digital stimulation, penetration by an object, bondage, spanking, and other intense and erotic physical contact.[36] Gay male couples engage in similar nonsodomitic practices, with the addition of frottage (male intercourse between the thighs). Because of the AIDS epidemic an increasing number of male as well as female couples refrain from sexual activity (primarily anal sex but also oral sex) that risks transmitting the virus that causes AIDS.[37] Consequently, a state prohibition of same-sex marriages in order to discourage sodomy would be both overinclusive and underinclusive. It would be overinclusive because it would prohibit marriages not involving sodomy and also because marriage would likely reduce the overall level of sodomy. It would be underinclusive because it would not reach different-sex marriages consummated by sodomy.

Only if *Bowers* is read as an openly homophobic opinion (declaring state war on homosexuals) can it override *Turner* and *Zablocki*. Even if the Court were to read *Bowers* so broadly, it is already clear that many states would not follow. Each of the fifty states has its own constitution. All the state constitutions have due process and equal

---

[h]Alabama, Arizona, Florida, Georgia, Idaho, Louisiana, Maryland, Massachusetts (partially invalidated), Minnesota, Mississippi, North Carolina, Oklahoma, Rhode Island, South Carolina, Utah, and Virginia.

ever the origins of a person's sexual orientation, they operate early in one's life. Most people do not make a conscious choice to be homosexual or heterosexual; they just turn out that way. If gay men and lesbians are prohibited from marrying the person they are likely to fall in love with, they will make do with an informal relationship or a construct-it-yourself union. Some, perhaps not many, of these same-sex couples will be significantly less willing to have children (through insemination, surrogacy, or adoption) because they do not have the commitment value that marriage bestows on a relationship. In this regard, state refusal to recognize same-sex marriage retards, rather than fosters, procreation.

Set against this, to be fair, is the modest effect state policy might have on bisexual men and women. Bisexuals have erotic feelings for people of both sexes. The state's refusal to recognize same-sex marriages presents bisexuals with an uneven set of choices. If the bisexual settles down with a different-sex partner, he or she has a choice of an informal relationship, a do-it-yourself union (through legal contracting), or marriage. If the bisexual settles down with a same-sex partner, he or she has only the first two choices, not the third. For those bisexuals who would like to be married *and* who would like to have children *and* who are more reluctant to have children in a same-sex union than in a different-sex marriage, the state bar to same-sex marriage has the effect of making the different-sex relationship and children more likely. The negligible size of this procreation effect renders absurd the argument that the state's refusal to recognize same-sex marriage will foster procreation on the part of bisexuals.

Any state policy of fostering procreation is not discernibly served, on balance, by state prohibition of same-sex marriage. Hawaii's stated procreation policy is also at war with its further argument that "a child is best parented by its *biological* parents living in a single household" (emphasis added). I am aware of no reliable evidence to support that statement, unless the emphasized language is deleted. There have been a few studies comparing children raised in a two-parent lesbian household with those raised in a household consisting of a single heterosexual mother. Dr. Susan Golombok and her colleagues compared twenty-seven families headed by lesbians (most of them with partners) with twenty-seven families headed by single (heterosexual) mothers.[43] The researchers found no differences between the children in the two groups along most dimensions, including sex role behavior, gender security, and the ability to form and maintain peer relationships. They did find a significantly higher percentage of children with psychiatric problems in the heterosexual mother group than in the lesbian mother group. The conclusion was that children raised by two adult women are better off than children raised by one adult woman.[44] This conclusion has been supported by at least two other studies.[45]

There is no evidence that children are better off being raised by their biological parents. Genetic ties are not to be denied, but there are plenty of bad biological parents and good adoptive or stepparents. Furthermore, children are competently raised by lesbian, gay, and bisexual parents. Recall thirteen-year-old Danielle Naparsteck Silber's story in chapter 4. Danielle has been raised by her biological mother, Susan Silber, and her nonbiological mother, Dana Naparsteck. Danielle regards both women as her parents and thinks she is lucky to have "two mommies." I told her about Hawaii's argument that "a child is best parented by its biological parents living in a single household." She replied that families are created out of love and mutual concern, not biology. As to officials who make these kinds of arguments, she had this to say: "They're biased. They're afraid of what they don't know." Amen.

Despite the inequities flowing from their inability to marry, the Silber–Naparsteck household is an unusually secure one, because of the partners' long-lasting relationship and their good health. Other same-sex parents face uncertainties that would be eliminated or lessened if their union could become a legally binding marriage. Recall the story of Kristen Janine Pearlman in chapter 4. Because her biological mother died and her grandparents disapproved of her other mother, Kristen was dragged crying from her surviving mother, Janine Ratcliffe, and spent five miserable years separated from the only family she knew. Kristen was a victim of the state's discriminatory policy. Because state bars to same-sex marriage undermine the stability of some same-sex households, they are not only bad for procreation but bad for the children of those households.

State Interest in Promoting Tourism

Let us turn now to a wackier state justification for barring same-sex marriage. Need it be argued that Hawaii's fear that allowing same-sex marriages "will alter the State of Hawaii's desirability as a visitor destination" is not the sort of "compelling" state interest needed to justify denying people fundamental rights? By this logic, Hawaii could kick all homely, overweight, and disabled people out of the state, making it a haven for "beautiful people." Tourists would probably flock to a paradise populated only by tanned, toned, and trendy men and women, but this boon to the state cannot justify the deprivation of fundamental rights to some of its citizens. I am aware of no American court that has ever held tourism to be a compelling state interest.

Just for fun, consider whether the state's bar to same-sex marriage would serve any pro-tourism policy. Would lots of heterosexuals stay away from Hawaii if the state allowed same-sex marriage? Do heterosexuals hate gays so much that they would boycott a state that gave us legal rights? While this degree of hysteria might be true for *some* heterosexuals, it is surely not true for most. In any event, whatever heterosexual tourism would be lost because of Hawaii's recognition of same-sex marriage would be more than offset by increased homosexual tourism. Consider the following calculus.

Professor Jennifer Brown argues that the first state—either Hawaii or some other state, probably a small, progressive one—that recognizes same-sex marriage will generate a great deal of additional tourism income, immediately and for a long time to come.[46] On the basis of conservative assumptions about (1) the number of homosexuals in the United States, (2) the percentage who would desire to be married, and (3) how much they would spend in Hawaii, Brown argues that because of a large pent-up demand, many would flock to the state to marry, much as those bent on a quickie marriage flock to Las Vegas or Reno, thus increasing its coffers. She estimates that lesbian and gay partners coming to Hawaii would yield an immediate tourism windfall of between $1 billion and $10 billion for the state. Additionally, a steady flow of same-sex couples would troop to the state every year to take advantage of the state's marriage law. Even without a pent-up demand, Brown speculates that the normal cycle of marriages would generate $1.7 billion for Hawaii in the first year, tapering off to $344 million per year after the twentieth year. That is still a lot of money. Brown considers the costs of potential loss of heterosexual tourism and finds them much more speculative and almost certainly much lower.

Brown's argument is well informed, carefully developed, and fun to take on. I would be even more conservative in setting the short- and medium-term advantages of being the "first mover" on this issue. Because of still-pervasive homophobia, numerous gay couples will not marry, fearing employer and other retaliation for "flaunting" their homosexuality by marrying. The initial increase in revenue from tourism would likely be a trickle. It also remains to be determined whether other states would recognize same-sex Hawaiian marriages.[47] It is likely that decades will be spent working through the issue whether other states would—or, under the Constitution's full faith and credit clause, must—give effect to Hawaiian same-sex marriages. Notwithstanding any quibbles, Brown's overall point is unimpeachable: Any state that is the first to recognize same-sex marriages will reap a tourism windfall, both immediately and over time. It pays to be tolerant ahead of the crowd.[i]

State Interest in Avoiding the Appearance of Approval of Nonheterosexual Orientations

Finally we come to the critical justification offered by Hawaii, both legally and psychologically. Hawaii's fear that "allowing same-sex couples to marry conveys in socially, psychologically, and otherwise

---

[i]Brown makes an excellent point when she observes that gay people show an intense loyalty to products and states that befriend them first. She notes that Absolut vodka was the first liquor to advertise in gay publications and that this gesture has inspired a firm loyalty of gay drinkers to that beverage. Brown is "absolutely" right to say, "Even after other states start celebrating same-sex marriages, gay people and their friends would remember that the first-mover state was the groundbreaker. Loyalty to that state could continue to generate substantial tourism revenue even after same-sex couples start to celebrate their marriages in other states." Jennifer Gerarda Brown, "Competitive Federalism and the Legislative Incentives to Recognize Same-Sex Marriage," 68 *Southern California Law Review* 745, 800 (1995).

important ways approval of nonheterosexual orientations and behaviors" probably is the reason Hawaii and other states do not allow same-sex marriage. The procreation and tourism arguments are little more than pretexts for this argument. What the state wants to foster is heterosexual procreation and families. What the state wants to encourage is heterosexual tourism. The state's policy is compulsory heterosexuality.

Compulsory heterosexuality is a problematic constitutional justification, however. One problem, developed in chapter 4, is that the state does not view its authorization of marriage as conveying any kind of approval. State agencies hand out marriage licenses like lollipops at a doctor's office. No other category of people is subject to a marriage ban, as gay people are. Convicted murderers and drug dealers, admitted spouse abusers, deadbeat dads, and the like are justifiably condemned for hurting other people, yet the state allows them to marry. The Constitution, in fact, requires the states to allow such marriages. Gay people are condemned even though we are responsible and have done nothing to hurt others. This is both unfair and unconstitutional, if *Turner* and *Zablocki* mean what they say.

Popular disapproval cannot be the important state interest required by *Zablocki*. Virginia's defense of its antimiscegenation law included the argument that the state did not want to convey approval of unions its citizens condemned. In *Loving*, Chief Justice Warren was right to find that argument insufficient to justify *either* race-based discrimination against interracial couples (next chapter) *or* deprivation of interracial couples' right to marry (this chapter). The Burger Court repeatedly struck down laws pandering to popular prejudice, because "objectives such as 'a bare desire to harm a politically unpopular group,' are not legitimate state interests."[48] This is a sound constitutional proposition. Discriminations and invasions of liberty whose justification boils down to penalizing a group of despised citizens are unhealthy for the polity. Group bashing without any larger social justification risks a competition of bashing; the bashed group lashes back at its perceived oppressors, who in turn retaliate with more bashing. A healthy polity is not one that allows the mechanisms of government to be used for group warfare.

THE SLIPPERY SLOPE:
POLYGAMOUS, INCESTUOUS,
AND CHILD MARRIAGES?

There is a final consideration that might explain why the courts, including the sympathetic Hawaii Supreme Court, have uniformly refused to find a right to marry for same-sex couples. If the state must, as a matter of constitutional necessity, recognize same-sex marriage, must the state also recognize polygamous, incestuous, and child marriage? This is called a "slippery slope" argument. Once you start going down the slope, you tend to slip to the bottom. The first, attractive, step leads to a tumble that is manifestly unattractive. Slippery slope arguments are powerful in constitutional cases. If Policy A and Policy B are based on the same principle and if that principle together with Policy A are held unconstitutional, then Policy B is also probably unconstitutional. The principle underlying the state's prohibition of same-sex marriage (Policy A) is the traditional Anglo-American construction and therefore limitation of marriage. If Policy A is invalidated, then other traditional restrictions on marriage (Policy B) might also be invalidated. Three such restrictions are that marriage be limited to two people, that the two people not be related, and that both be over the age of consent. These restrictions seem natural and just to most people. Would they not be vulnerable if same-sex marriage is accepted?

To begin with, it is important to remember that slopes can slip in more than one direction. Slippery slope arguments buttress rather than undermine the case for same-sex marriage. If one starts with the principle that traditional Anglo-American limitations on marriage define what marriage can be, then one might prohibit not only same-sex marriage (Policy A) but also different-race marriage, marriage by people with mental disabilities, and marriage by people with sexually transmitted diseases (Policy B). All of these prohibitions have enjoyed great popularity in American history. Do they define marriage? If they do, then *Loving*, the miscegenation case, was wrongly decided and the Americans with Disabilities Act has been incorrectly interpreted to preempt state prohibitions inconsistent with its non-discrimination rule.[49] To travel further down this alternative slope, if it is constitutional for the state to prohibit same-sex marriages because they are not procreative, then it ought similarly to be constitutional to prohibit marriage by couples who are sterile or use contraceptives or are too old. Finally, if it is constitutional for the state to prohibit same-sex marriages because they offend many citizens, what is there to protect other unpopular groups from being denied basic liberties? If the citizens of one state are anti-Semitic, can that state constitutionally prohibit Jews from marrying? Can Roman Catholics be denied the right to marry in a state that desires to persecute them? These examples will seem so ridiculous and stupid as to be inconceivable to many readers, but from the perspective of lesbians, gay men, and transgendered people this is precisely the effect of current state policy on us.

Note, too, that the right to marry is not absolute. *Zablocki* holds that a statute placing a "direct legal obstacle in the path of persons desiring to get married" is unconstitutional *unless* it is "supported by sufficiently important state interests and is closely tailored to effectuate only those interests."[50] There is no neutral state interest supporting the state's prohibition of same-sex marriage, but there are better arguments for the state's regulation of child, incestuous, and polygamous marriage. The discussion of these different kinds of marriage that follows will be suggestive rather than conclusive, for my goal is not to lay out a constitutional regime for marriage regulation. But I shall exploit a point I have been making in this chapter (and that I made in the previous one). If the overriding or necessary goal of marriage were procreation, it would be hard to fault polygamy and child marriage, and surprisingly hard to fault incestuous marriage. Our culture does not rely on the procreation goal, and the Supreme Court has rejected that goal in *Griswold* and other cases. As expressed in *Turner*, the dominant goals of marriage are the unitive goals of equal companionship, mutual support backed up by law, and expression of love and commitment. With these unitive, rather than procreative, goals in mind, the state has potential interests to regulate these other forms of marriage. Ironically, the scare scenarios imagined by some opponents of same-sex marriage (polygamy would flourish and children would marry!) only underscore the invalidity of procreation as the linchpin for modern thinking about marriage.

Prohibiting Child Marriage

Assume that two adolescents want to get married. Under special circumstances, they can do so. In all fifty states and the District of Columbia, eighteen-year-olds can marry. If the children's parents consent, all fifty states plus the District of Columbia allow seventeen-year-olds to marry as well. Forty-nine states (all but Oregon) allow sixteen-year-olds to marry under such circumstances. Forty states[j] allow fourteen-year-olds to marry; usually a court order as well as the consent of the child's parents are required for these marriages. Nine states allow children under eighteen to marry if the female is pregnant or has borne a child by the male; in these cases parental consent is usually not required.[k]

At first blush it is not clear that state laws regulating child marriage deprive adolescents of their right to marry. Does the state place a "direct legal obstacle in the path" of two sixteen-year-olds who want to get married? Yes and no. The sixteen-year-olds must obtain the consent of both sets of parents. This is a formal "obstacle" and frequently one that cannot be surmounted. But even if the sixteen-year-old children cannot successfully negotiate parental consent, they are not absolutely deprived of the right to marry (as lesbian and gay couples are), because all the children have to do is wait two years. When they reach age eighteen, they are free to marry one another. The age-of-consent rule, at worst, only delays their marriage and is not an absolute legal obstacle.

Age-of-consent laws, with the parental consent escape hatch, do not materially obstruct the constitutional right to marry.[l] Even if they

---

[j]Alabama, Alaska, Arkansas, Arizona, California, Colorado, Connecticut, Delaware, Florida, Georgia, Idaho, Kansas, Kentucky, Louisiana, Maine, Maryland, Massachusetts, Michigan, Missouri, Mississippi, Nebraska, Nevada, New Hampshire, New Jersey, New Mexico, New York, North Carolina, Ohio, Oklahoma, Pennsylvania, Rhode Island, South Carolina, Tennessee, Texas, Utah, Vermont, Virginia, Washington, West Virginia, and Wyoming. In all but five of these states, children under fourteen can theoretically marry.

[k]Arkansas, Delaware, Georgia, Kentucky, New Mexico, North Carolina, Oklahoma, South Carolina, Virginia.

[l]On the other hand, *Zablocki* suggests that the right to marry is implicated by prerequisites as well as by absolute prohibitions. The case involved a state requirement that marriage licenses would

did, the laws are rather easily "supported by sufficiently important state interests and [are] closely tailored to effectuate only those interests." The case for state regulation does not rest on the procreation goal, which would be served by allowing abundantly fertile sixteen-year-olds to marry. Instead, the case for state regulation rests on the unitive goals of marriage. Empirical as well as casual evidence demonstrates that adolescents are immature decision makers. They are prone to bad decisions because they lack the experience necessary to evaluate data and consequences, tend to sacrifice future benefits for present pleasure much more than adults do, and respond extravagantly to immediate stimuli and peer pressure.[51] Our society does not allow fifteen-year-olds to vote or drive cars, diverts their criminal prosecutions into a more lenient juvenile justice system, and requires them to attend school. Most important, the state empowers their parents or legal custodians to supervise adolescents' decision making as to matters of finance, commercial transactions, and sexuality. Given adolescent immaturity and their own normally beneficial motivations toward their offspring, parents are well situated to monitor and veto adolescent decisions.

Marriage is the most important economic as well as emotional decision most people make in their lives, and the burdens of marriage make bad decisions especially costly. The decision-making delay required by age-of-consent laws, with parents available to permit expedition, seems well justified in our society. No decision recognizing a constitutional right for same-sex couples to marry would have any effect on state regulation of child marriage.

---

not be issued to divorced persons with support obligations unless they could demonstrate that they were not in arrears in their obligations. Like parental consent rules, this prerequisite to marriage was only contingent. Unlike parental consent rules, this contingency was formally within the control of the parties desiring to marry. Nonetheless, the Supreme Court held that this was a "direct legal obstacle" triggering constitutional concern. *Zablocki* can be distinguished from age-of-consent laws on the ground that many deadbeat dads will be completely unable ever to satisfy their support obligations. Once the former spouse has fallen behind, it is often hard to catch up, because the arrears are in addition to the regular payments owed every month. Whereas time is the nemesis of the deadbeat dad, it is the friend of the sixteen-year-old, who only has to wait a couple of years to enjoy full marriage rights.

Prohibiting Polygamous Marriages

Suppose a married man desires to take a second wife. All fifty states and the District of Columbia forbid the issuance of a marriage license for a bigamous marriage. In cases decided before *Loving*, the Supreme Court upheld prohibitions against polygamous marriages among Mormons. The reasons given by the Court were not the best. In one case the Court said polygamy has "always been odious among the northern and western nations of Europe, and, until the establishment of the Mormon Church, was almost exclusively a feature of the life of Asiatic and of African people"[52] (including, by the way, the Old Testament Israelites). In a later case the Court inveighed against polygamy as "a notorious example of promiscuity,"[53] an observation that would have stunned Solomon and other biblical polygamists. I would not consider these old cases dispositive on the right-to-marry issue. If anything, they are as ill informed as the state cases denying same-sex couples the right to marry.

Again, the initial question is whether state prohibitions against bigamy represent a "direct legal obstacle in the path of persons desiring to get married." Under an antibigamy law the married man cannot marry a second wife simultaneous with his first marriage, but he can do so *seriatim*. That is, the married man can divorce his first wife and marry the second. What prohibitions against polygamy do is force a choice on the married person: you can retain your current spouse, or you can divorce and marry another. In states where divorce is essentially available on demand, *de facto* polygamy is possible by *seriatim* marriage, divorce, and remarriage to another person. Still it seems fair to assume that antibigamy laws substantially restrict the right to marry.

Antibigamy rules are hard to defend if marriage is justified as an engine of procreation. Without such rules a man could marry several women, and procreation would be made more efficient. (The issue is muddier where women can marry several men.) Again, any state interest would have to relate to the unitive goals of marriage. The argument would run something like this: If people were allowed to take more than one spouse, the central goals of marriage, namely, its companionate and social insurance features, would be compromised.[54] If a man had more than one spouse (probably the typical case), the intensity of his emotional bond to any one wife would likely be diluted. There would often be rivalry between the two wives for his affection, time, and even spousal benefits. Who, for example, would have decision-making responsibility in the event of the husband's incapacitation? The husband or the law would have to choose one wife (giving each a veto power would seem unworkable), thereby creating an uncompanionate tension. This rivalry might extend to childbearing and would often sour the household for the children, especially those of a disfavored wife.

Most important, allowing a man to take two wives might create or exacerbate hierarchical structures within the marriage. As the center of competition, the husband would be able to play one wife against the other. Because the husband would have to deal with at least twice as many wives, it is probable that he would establish a more authoritarian structure for the marriage. This not only defeats the companionate goal of marriage but contributes to gender inequality. In a society such as ours, where men not only hold more economic and political power than women but also are less numerous, the typical pattern would be that a man would take more than one wife but a woman would take only one husband. While polygamy of this sort is the dream of some men, it is a nightmare for many women. Because it could severely reduce women's position within the household, polygamy could be a major setback for women's equality in the United States. The state's interest in gender equality is a compelling one.[55] Therefore, if it can be shown that polygamy undermines women's equality, state antibigamy laws could be upheld on this ground alone.[56]

Prohibiting Incestuous Marriages

Assume two persons related to one another desire to get married. All fifty states and the District of Columbia prohibit "incestuous" marriages, including parent–child, grandparent–grandchild, aunt–nephew, uncle–niece, and brother–sister marriages. Thirty-eight states prohibit marriages by first cousins.[m] Eleven states[n] and the District of Columbia prohibit marriages by step–relatives, that is, persons related within the prohibited degree but only by marriage and not by blood. Two states (Alaska and Louisiana) prohibit persons within four degrees of consanguinity from marrying. One state (Utah) prohibits persons within five degrees from marrying.

As applied to related adults, these state consanguinity regulations are a "direct legal obstacle in the path of persons desiring to get married." Like the state's prohibition against same-sex marriage, its prohibition against incestuous marriage by adults is an absolute bar that time will not dissolve. Under *Zablocki*, this regulation abridges the right to marry and should be struck down unless it is "supported by sufficiently important state interests and is closely tailored to effectuate only those interests."[57]

Religious and social taboos ought not to suffice as a basis for regulating incestuous marriage, but other state interests should be considered.[58] One possible justification is genetic: Allowing closely related people to marry and procreate increases the chance that harmful recessive genes will pair up and produce defects in offspring. I am dubious that genetic engineering by the state constitutes an "important" state interest, for the same reason that I think *Buck v. Bell*, where the Supreme Court allowed sterilization of people judged to be mentally disabled, was wrongly decided. A eugenics-based rationale is also overbroad, for it does not justify prohibiting incestuous marriage between people who cannot have children with one another because of the age, infertility, or sterilization of one or both partners. The rationale is also overbroad in light of scientific evidence that the recessive gene problem is slight for most incestuous couples, including aunt–nephew, uncle–niece, and first cousin pairs, and not as impressive as formerly believed even for sibling and parent–child unions.[59] Again, the procreation goal of marriage provides little justification for current state policy.

---

[m]California, Colorado, Connecticut, the District of Columbia, Florida, Georgia, Hawaii, Massachusetts, New Mexico, New Jersey, New York, North Carolina, and Virginia allow first cousins to marry. Arizona, Illinois, and Indiana allow first cousins to marry if they are older than sixty-five, fifty, and sixty-five, respectively.

[n]Connecticut, Georgia, Maryland, Massachusetts, Michigan, Mississippi, Oklahoma, Rhode Island, South Carolina, South Dakota, Tennessee.

The most promising justification for regulating incestuous marriage draws from the unitive goals of marriage and the rationales developed above for regulating polygamous and child marriage.[60] That justification would rely on something like the following theory of family dynamics. The family is the main context for children's socialization and developing sexuality. The typical pattern finds the adolescent reaching beyond the family and setting up her or his own extrafamilial relationships. The process by which each generation reaches beyond the family unit and forms new ones is very useful for society and, perhaps, necessary for the individual as well. Not only does sexual interaction within the family interfere with this development of the individual, but sexual interaction between a child and a trusted adult can have traumatic effects on the child. The foregoing justification finds support in the academic literature and has intuitive appeal, but I should emphasize that this is tentative rather than established.

The large majority of incest cases involve relationships between an adult and a child (mainly men and their daughters or step-daughters).[61] Regulation of incestuous marriage would appear easiest to justify under these circumstances. The difficult cases are adult relatives who desire to marry but not procreate and adult step-relatives who desire to marry. A few states have limited exceptions for the former,° and I am open to the argument that such exceptions are constitutionally required. I am also sympathetic to the one state court decision that applied *Zablocki* to invalidate state prohibitions against marriage between adult adoptive siblings.[62] The fundamental right to marry does call into question the more broadly written state regulations of marriage by relatives.

The foregoing discussion has gone beyond Hawaii's stated justifications to consider other possible justifications. None exist. There is no neutral reason for the state to exclude same-sex couples from marriage. Ergo, they cannot do so, and courts should so hold.

°Wisconsin allows first cousins to marry if the woman is fifty-five years old or older or if either party is sterile. Wisconsin Statutes § 765.03(1) (1993). Arizona, Illinois, and Indiana have similar rules allowing first cousins to marry after they reach a certain age.

Will they? There is reason to doubt it. Indeed, it is the same reason advanced by Hawaii: antihomosexual sentiment. Despite fact, notwithstanding reason, and in spite of human need, judges who harbor such feelings or fear their backlash may not support same-sex marriage. Yet it only requires a few judges in one state to reverse the presumptions established by homophobia, and that state promises to be Hawaii. Chief Justice Ronald Moon and Associate Justices Steven Levinson and Paula Nakayama of the Hawaii Supreme Court have tentatively taken a position that cuts the Gordian knot. In the case brought by Ninia Baehr and Genora Dancel they have relied on a different equal protection argument to require the state to justify its discrimination. The next chapter explores their bold constitutional move.

6

THE CONSTITUTIONAL CASE: DISCRIMINATION

L oving v. Virginia,[1] the leading case for the right to marry, is mainly a discriminatory classification case.[a] Although Loving's creation of an independent right to marry is directly applicable to state prohibitions of same-sex marriage, its race discrimination holding seems on its face inapplicable to the same-sex marriage issue. But is it? Both in the legal world and outside it, we make arguments by analogy. Those on one side argue, "How can we ban gay marriage if we don't ban marriage among transvestites or transsexuals?" Those on the other ask, "If gay marriage, then why not bigamy? Why not incestuous marriage?" This chapter explores the politically charged analogy of interracial marriage, like that in Loving, to gay marriage, like that in Baehr.

The history of Virginia's law prohibiting different-race marriage, including its downfall, bears on the state's prohibition of same-sex marriages. They are parallel histories. Those defending the prohibitions in both cases relied on arguments that deny marriage's social and contingent features. Specifically, the supporters of antimiscegenation statutes made the same kind of definitional and natural law arguments that supporters of statutes barring same-sex marriage now

---

[a]Chief Justice Warren's discussion of the right to marry is an alternative basis for the Court's disposition in Loving. The primary reasoning of the Court was that the Virginia antimiscegenation statute was an "invidious" racial classification that violated the equal protection clause of the Fourteenth Amendment because it was not justified by a compelling state interest.

make. *Loving* rejected all those arguments and exposed them as pretexts for a discriminatory race-based classification for which the state could advance no compelling interest. Following the Hawaii Supreme Court in *Baehr*, this chapter maintains that *Loving* can be applied to require the state to justify its discriminatory sex-based classification in statutes prohibiting same-sex marriage. *Loving* can also be extended to require the state to adduce a neutral justification for discriminatory sexual-orientation-based classifications such as the same-sex marriage bar.[b]

THE MISCEGENATION ANALOGY

Recall the recurring argument made by opponents of same-sex marriage, namely, that marriage *by definition* cannot include same-sex couples (chapters 4 and 5). To support this definitional argument, opponents cite historical practice, natural law's emphasis on procreation, and religious text and tradition. The strategy of opponents has been to essentialize the social institution of marriage around the concept of husband and wife. The same strategy was followed by opponents of different-race marriage, who essentialized marriage around the concept of racial purity. To support their definitional argument, opponents cited historical practice, natural law's abhorrence of procreative mixing, and religious text and tradition. And for almost all of American history, opponents prevailed. *Loving* was a rejection of this way of thinking, however. Its reasoning provides support for other challenges to natural law thinking about the legal institution of marriage.

American Antimiscegenation Laws

Few traditions are as pervasive in American legal history as laws prohibiting different-race marriages.[2] Virginia's antimiscegenation law was first adopted in 1691, its stated purpose being to prevent "abominable mixture and spurious issue."[3] This law was characteristic

---

[b]Chapter 5 demonstrates that the state cannot produce a compelling justification for prohibitions on same-sex marriage, and I shall not repeat that discussion here.

of those prevailing in the colonies before the Revolution. After independence, antimiscegenation laws were enacted at one time or another by thirty-eight states. The laws were viewed as recognition of a natural order, but a more directive purpose was also articulated. A Virginia juror said in 1833, "The law was made to preserve the distinction which should exist between our two kinds of population, and to protect the whites in the possession of their superiority."[4]

The Civil War and the Reconstruction amendments to the Constitution did virtually nothing to undermine such laws. Although opponents of the Fourteenth Amendment charged that it would lead to interracial marriages, supporters of the amendment assured Congress that antimiscegenation laws would not be disturbed by the amendment's guarantee of "equal protection of the law" for African Americans.[5] Accordingly, few states repealed their laws after the Fourteenth Amendment was ratified, and antimiscegenation laws were a centerpiece of the Jim Crow regime of *de jure* segregation in the South after Reconstruction. Whites in both the North and South firmly opposed different-race marriage for reasons that were to them fundamental. Senator James Doolittle of Wisconsin put it most broadly, "By the laws of Massachusetts intermarriages between these races are forbidden as criminal. Why forbidden? Simply because natural instinct revolts at it as wrong."[6] Others rooted their opposition in the desire to "maintain the purity of white blood, [to] assure for it that natural superiority with which God had ennobled it."[7] Most opponents sooner or later invoked an argument that African Americans were genetically inferior and that different-race marriages would produce inferior children. The eugenics movement of the late nineteenth century provided scientific respectability for a view long defended by reference to the Bible and theories of white supremacy.[8]

Legal challenges to state antimiscegenation laws in the nineteenth century were uniformly rejected under both federal and state constitutions. State court decisions upholding antimiscegenation statutes emphasized the same religious and scientific arguments made in the social and political arenas. For example, the Georgia Supreme Court upheld its statute in part because "amalgamation of the races is . . . unnatural," yielding offspring who are "generally sickly and effeminate, and . . . inferior in physical development and strength, to the full-blood of either race."⁹ The court also rested its judgment on the view that

> equality [of the races] does not in fact exist and never can. The God of nature made it otherwise, and no human law can produce it, and no human tribunal can enforce it. There are gradations and classes throughout the universe. From the tallest arch angel in Heaven, down to the meanest reptile on earth, moral and social inequalities exist, and must continue to exist through all eternity.¹⁰

The Missouri Supreme Court went further to opine "as a well authenticated fact" that "if the issue of a black man and a white woman, and a white man and a black woman, intermarry, they cannot possibly have any progeny, and such a fact sufficiently justifies those laws which forbid the intermarriage of blacks and whites."¹¹ Such reasoning might seem bizarre to us today, but it was fully consistent with the mind-set of those opposing different-race marriage in the late nineteenth century.

The United States Supreme Court resolved the issue in favor of such laws, but on narrower grounds. The Court in *Pace v. Alabama*¹² held that antimiscegenation laws do not offend the equal protection clause because their prohibition applies equally to all races. That is, a black person is just as much constrained by such laws as a white person. Because both races are equally disadvantaged, the Court reasoned, there is no equal protection problem. *Pace*, decided in 1883, was a harbinger of the "separate but equal" philosophy offered by the Court later in *Plessy v. Ferguson*,¹³ the decision upholding racial apartheid in general. *Pace* was the parent of *Plessy* in another way, for the popular appeal of segregation in housing, public accommodations, and schooling was based on white fear of interracial mixing and different-race marriage.

The early twentieth century saw the creation of more elaborate legal regimes to regulate different-race marriages. Virginia, for example, updated its antimiscegenation law in the Racial Integrity Act of 1924.¹⁴ The new statute sought the same goal as the former one (avoiding "pollution" of the white race by interracial sexual relations) but sought to implement the policy more thoroughly. The 1924 law made it "unlawful for any white person in this State to marry any save a white person" and set forth a definition of "white person" for purposes of Virginia law.[15] The law charged local registrars to keep on file certificates of "racial composition"[16] and marriage license officials to require verification of applicants' declarations as to their race.[17] Virginia law not only prohibited a "white person" from marrying someone other than a "white person" but made it a felony to do so; it also made it a felony to file an inaccurate statement of one's race.[18] Post-1924 Virginia law punished interracial couples with one to five years in the state penitentiary.[19]

The Decline and Fall of Antimiscegenation Laws

Pace and the eugenics craze pretty much ended challenges to antimiscegenation laws until after World War II. Thirty states had such laws at the war's end.[c] These laws were increasingly viewed as problematic, partly because of their similarity to the racist regime of the recently defeated Nazis. Added to this, the civil rights movement and its challenge to *de jure* racial segregation drew worldwide attention to American antimiscegenation laws. In his widely read book on American apartheid, Dr. Gunnar Myrdal observed in 1944 that "[t]he ban on interracial marriage has the highest place in the white man's rank order of social segregation and discrimination."[20] Ironically, African Americans did not target these laws as the primary object of legal reform, and two early postwar challenges were brought by couples who were Latino-Caucasian and Asian-Caucasian. Nevertheless, the judicial response to these postwar challenges was mixed. The California Supreme Court struck down its law in *Perez v. Lippold*,[21] while the Virginia Supreme Court upheld its statute in *Naim v. Naim*.[22] Invoking precedent from other states as well as its own policy of racial integrity, the Virginia Supreme Court held that "the natural law which forbids [the Naims'] intermarriage and the social amalgamation which leads to a corruption of the races is as clearly divine as that which imparted to them different natures."

---

[c]Alabama, Arizona, Arkansas, California, Colorado, Delaware, Florida, Georgia, Idaho, Indiana, Kentucky, Louisiana, Maryland, Mississippi, Missouri, Montana, Nebraska, Nevada, North Carolina, North Dakota, Oklahoma, Oregon, South Carolina, South Dakota, Tennessee, Texas, Utah, Virgina, West Virginia, and Wyoming.

In the wake of its controversial decision in *Brown v. Board of Education*, the Warren Court left the divergent state resolutions alone in the 1950s. The Court did act decisively in the 1960s, after half the states had repealed their antimiscegenation laws. In *McLaughlin v. Florida* the Court applied the antidiscrimination principles of *Brown* to invalidate a statute criminalizing interracial cohabitation. Implicitly overruling *Pace*, the Court held that *any* classification based on race is an "invidious discrimination forbidden by the equal protection clause," unless it can be justified by some "overriding state purpose."[23] *McLaughlin* set the stage for the Warren Court's showdown with antimiscegenation laws.

Mildred Jeter and Richard Loving were convicted of violating Virginia's Racial Integrity Act in 1959. Their one-year prison sentence was suspended on condition that they leave Virginia, which they did. Later, the Lovings sought to have their conviction overturned in state court. Notwithstanding *McLaughlin*, they lost in the Virginia courts— for reasons straight out of the nineteenth century. Consistent with the Virginia Supreme Court's reasoning in *Naim*, the trial court held:[24]

> Almighty God created the races white, black, yellow, malay and red, and he placed them on separate continents. And but for the interference with his arrangements there would be no cause for such marriages. The fact that he separated the races shows that he did not intend for the races to mix.

The Virginia Supreme Court adhered to its decision in *Naim*, where the court had held that the state must have the power "to regulate the marriage relation so that it shall not have a mongrel breed of citizens. We find there is no requirement that the State shall not legislate to prevent the obliteration of racial pride, but must prevent the corruption of blood even though it weaken or destroy the quality of its citizenship."[25]

The Lovings appealed to the United States Supreme Court. The Supreme Court unanimously reversed the Virginia ruling. Confirming that *McLaughlin* had overruled *Pace*, Chief Justice Warren's opinion held that race-based "classifications" of any kind require a "heavy burden" of state justification. The opinion also rejected the argument that the original intent of the Fourteenth Amendment's framers was not to interfere with antimiscegenation laws. Although many such statements could be found in the historical record, such an intent was inconsistent with the "broader, organic purpose" of the amendment. In two sentences bursting with history, the chief justice concluded Part I of the opinion by summarily dismissing three centuries of Virginian public policy:[26]

> The fact that Virginia prohibits only interracial marriages involving white persons demonstrates that the racial classifications must stand on their own justification, as measures designed to maintain White Supremacy. We have consistently denied the constitutionality of measures which restrict the rights of citizens on account of race.

Sixteen state antimiscegenation schemes were thereby constitutionally dissolved. Even though most Virginians and many Americans still do not like different-race marriages, thousands are performed each year in the United States, with no fuss.

The Implications of Loving for Same-Sex Marriage

The second part of the *Loving* decision, which recognizes that different-race couples have a fundamental right to marry, bears directly on the right of same-sex couples to marry. The first part of *Loving*, where the Court discusses issues of race discrimination, does not directly implicate same-sex marriage, but its logic is relevant to gay and lesbian challenges to state bars against same-sex marriage.

To begin with, *Loving* rejects defenses similar to those routinely advanced to deny same-sex marriage. For a hundred years definitional arguments had been accepted as sufficient legal justification for antimiscegenation laws. Virginia and other states maintained that different-race marriages are "unnatural"; contrary to American religious and legal traditions; and inconsistent with the overriding purpose of marriage, namely, procreation. The first two arguments are simply the same as those made by opponents of same-sex marriage. The procreation argument is slightly different. Opponents of same-sex marriage claim that same-sex couples cannot procreate whereas opponents of different-race marriage (with some exceptions, such as the Missouri Supreme Court's opinion, quoted earlier) admitted that different-race couples can procreate but lamented the consequences. Both sets of opponents essentialize marriage around procreation and then exclude couples who cannot procreate in the desired way.

By rejecting these arguments *Loving* cautions us to think twice before we claim that marriage is "inherently" such and such. Neither history nor the Bible nor the imperative of procreation establishes what marriage *must* be, as a matter of law. Marriage is an important social and legal construction, and it is what we *make* it to be. In America marriage has been opened up to virtually any couple who want to take advantage of its legal benefits and obligations. There are few restrictions on who may marry, thanks in part to the Supreme Court decisions protecting the right to marry. Most of the restrictions, such as the bar to different-race marriage, are legally constructed practices reflecting divisive social prejudice rather than sound policy. *Loving* is at odds with the philosophy that historical pedigree alone justifies a dividing practice restricting who may enjoy state benefits. Many arrangements accepted as natural by the founding generation of our society are constitutionally unacceptable in today's world. Slavery and bans on interracial sexuality head the list, which also includes the exclusion of women from political citizenship and their economic and social inequality, the death penalty for sodomy, extraordinary penalties for adultery and fornication, bars against contraception and abortion, limits on who can serve on juries, and property or wealth requirements for voting and other rights of citizenship.

Loving not only rejects the definitional arguments but dismisses them as irrelevant. Although Chief Justice Warren could have cited social science literature (as he did in *Brown*) to refute Virginia's "mongrel race" assumption, he did not bother to do so. In the two sentences quoted earlier the Court noted that the statute only prevented Caucasians from marrying outside their race (Asian- and African-American citizens, for example, could marry one another). What this reasoning revealed was that the statute's goal boiled down to "White Supremacy," a goal that was not only uncompelling but confirmatory of the invidiousness of the racial discrimination effected by the law. What *Loving* rejects, therefore, is not just an essentialist view of marriage but a caste system and its philosophy of white supremacy.

I would read *Loving* in light of the history it reflects. Apartheid was a web of institutions reflecting a caste system in which whites were privileged and blacks subordinated. One institution key to apartheid was marriage, which was defined so as to avoid "pollution" of the white caste, and to prevent confusion as to the caste arrangement generally. As anthropologist Kingsley Davis put it in 1941, "either intermarriage must be strictly forbidden or racial caste abandoned."[27] Dissenting from the Court's sanction of separate-but-equal racial segregation in *Plessy*, Justice John Harlan had warned against the perpetuation of a "caste system" in the United States. "In respect of civil rights, all citizens are equal before the law," he said. *Brown* had adopted Justice Harlan's result. *Loving* adopted Justice Harlan's philosophy and extended it to strike down the dividing practice that was dearest to apartheid. This chapter argues that the state's prohibition of same-sex marriages reflects two related caste systems: an apartheid of the kitchen harmful to women and an apartheid of the closet harmful to gay people.

Either system can be understood as an invidious discrimination violating the constitutional guarantee of equal protection. In both *McLaughlin* and *Loving* the Court seized on the racial *classification* to discredit the states' argument that racial *classes* were being treated equally (whites were just as prohibited as blacks from different-sex marriages). A classification-based attack on bars to same-sex marriage is straightforward because the bars classify according to sex. I am a man. Therefore, I am barred from marrying another man while permitted to marry a woman. This is unequal. Sex-based classifications are subjected to heightened scrutiny under the United States Constitution and state constitutions. You do not get much more sex-based than heterosexual marriage. From another angle, the prohibition against same-sex marriage is even more discriminatory than the prohibition against different-race marriage. Even under *Pace* the states could not enact a law saying African Americans could not marry one another. Yet this is how current state law affects the class of so-called homosexuals: we cannot marry one another. I shall argue that sexual orientation classes should be given some level of constitutional protection against popular prejudice and for the same reasons race and gender classes are protected.

The sex-classification argument and the sexual-orientation-classification argument in this chapter are independent arguments under the equal protection clause. Either is sufficient to invalidate state prohibitions against same-sex marriage under either the national or state constitutions. I make both arguments, and they complement one another.

PROHIBITING SAME-SEX MARRIAGE AS SEX DISCRIMINATION

Relying on Washington State's equal rights amendment, lawyers for John Singer and Paul Barwick were the first to argue in court that the state's refusal to give marriage licenses to same-sex couples is sex discrimination. The state court of appeals rejected their argument in 1974.[28] For the next decade and a half the argument lay dormant, until Professors Sylvia Law and Andrew Koppelman revived it with more sophisticated (feminist) theory and analysis.[29] Ultimately speaking for a majority of the Hawaii Supreme Court, Justice Steven Levinson's opinion in *Baehr v. Lewin* adopted the Law–Koppelman argument as its interpretation of Hawaii's equal rights amendment.[30] The Hawaii court made the right decision, and its logic should be extended to other state constitutions and, ultimately, to the United States Constitution. This part of the chapter lays out the argument, develops a counterargument suggested by *Loving*, and responds to the counterargument.

Same-Sex Marriage Prohibitions Are Sex Discrimination

The state prohibition against same-sex marriage in *Baehr* is on its face sex discrimination in exactly the same way that the prohibition against different-race marriage was held to be race discrimination by *Loving*. In *Loving* a marriage between a *black* man and a black woman was legal, but one between a *white* man and a black woman was not. The only variable (the item that changed, in italics) was the race of one partner. *Loving* held that to be a classification-based race discrimination. In *Baehr* a marriage between a *man* and a woman was legal, but one between a *woman* and a woman was not. The only variable (the italicized term) was the sex of one partner. *Baehr* held that to be a classification-based sex discrimination.

Loving held that race-based discrimination is invidious and invalid unless justified by a compelling state interest. The Court did so by interpreting the equal protection clause of the Fourteenth Amendment. Although that amendment does not mention race as a classification meriting special attention, as an element of the Reconstruction amendments adopted after the Civil War it nonetheless clearly targets race-based classifications. The Hawaii court was applying Hawaii's equal rights amendment, which is more specific than the federal equal protection clause and reads as follows: "No person shall . . . be denied the enjoyment of the person's civil rights or be discriminated against in the exercise thereof because of race, religion, sex, or ancestry."[31] Sixteen other state constitutions explicitly prohibit discrimination on the basis of sex.[d] It should be clear where I am heading.

How can one avoid the conclusion that a state bar against same-sex marriage is sex discrimination? Judges resisting this conclusion have argued that same-sex couples are denied marriage licenses because of the "recognized definition of marriage," and not because of their sex.[32] Not only is such a definitional argument factually wrong, but it is exactly the same kind of definitional argument Virginia made, and lost, in *Loving*. The Washington Court of Appeals decision denying relief to Singer and Barwick also offered this justification: "The [state] ERA does not create any new rights or responsibilities, such as the conceivable right of persons of the same sex to marry one another;

---

[d]Provisions similar to Hawaii's, where *sex* is specifically inserted into a broader equal protection clause, are Alaska Constitution, Article I, § 3 (*sex* added 1972); Connecticut Constitution, Article I, § 20 (added 1974); Illinois Constitution, Article I, § 17 (1970 revised constitution); Massachusetts Declaration of Rights, part I, Article I (added 1976); Montana Constitution, Article II, § 4 (1972 revised constitution); New Hampshire Constitution, part I, Article 2 (added 1974); Texas Constitution, Article I, § 3a (added 1972); Virginia Constitution, Article I, § 11 (added 1970); Wyoming Constitution, Article I, § 3 (1889 Constitution).

Some states have clauses specially protecting against sex discrimination, such as Colorado Constitution, Article II, § 29 (equal rights amendment added 1972): "Equality of rights under the law shall not be denied or abridged by the State . . . or any of its political subdivisions on account of sex." To the same effect are Illinois Constitution, Article I, § 8 (equal rights provision in 1970 revised constitution); Maryland Declaration of Rights, Article 46 (added 1972); New Mexico Constitution, Article II, § 18 (added 1972); Pennsylvania Constitution, Article I, § 28 (added 1971); Utah Constitution, Article IV, § 1 (1896 Constitution); Washington Constitution, Article 31, § 1 (added 1972).

rather, it merely insures that existing rights and responsibilities as may be created in the future, which previously might have been wholly or partially denied to one sex or to the other, will be equally available to members of either sex."[33] The same argument has been made by the Hawaii legislature in response to *Baehr.* "There is simply no class of individuals under [the marriage law] that have been discriminated against in relation to another group of similarly situated individuals. Because all men and all women are treated alike by [the marriage law], there is no sex- (i.e., gender-) based classification."[34] Yet this is precisely the form of argument that had been accepted in *Pace,* which upheld antimiscegenation laws because all "rights and responsibilities" of marriage were "equally available to members of either" race. Whites were barred from different-race marriages in the same manner as blacks. Just as *McLaughlin* and *Loving* overruled *Pace,* so these current precedents cannot be read for any other proposition than the one originally pressed by Singer and Barwick and now invoked by Ninia Baehr and Genora Dancel, namely, that the sex-based classification itself triggers the exacting judicial scrutiny.

Baehr is the correct approach to state equal rights amendments protecting against sex discrimination and ought to be followed in the sixteen other states having such amendments (see note d), as well as in the District of Columbia, which has an equal rights superstatute protecting against sex discrimination.[35] *Baehr's* reasoning is also applicable to the federal equal protection clause and to analogous state clauses that do not mention "sex." In *Craig v. Boren* the United States Supreme Court interpreted the federal equal protection clause to require that "classifications by gender must serve important governmental objectives and must be substantially related to achievement of those objectives."[36] The Court has repeatedly applied *Craig* to invalidate sex-based classifications, especially where "the statutory objective itself reflects archaic and stereotypic notions."[37] The only issue that remains open is whether sex-based classifications are as completely suspect as race-based classifications are.[38] However that issue is resolved, it is clear that any sex-based classification requires substantial justification under the federal equal protection clause, and state courts are at least as liberal when interpreting their general equal protection provisions.

In short, sex discrimination is now constitutionally questionable in every state and at the national level. As a result, we must carefully examine *all* laws that employ sex-based classifications. Such laws cannot survive constitutional scrutiny unless their defenders can adduce compelling reasons of social policy. Put another way, the burden of proof is now on *opponents* of same-sex marriage because the bar is a sex-based classification.

Must There Be a Link Between Classification and Class?

Baehr was correct to reject the old definition-of-marriage response to the *Loving* analogy, but there is a better objection: Is it not odd that constitutional protection against sex discrimination is invoked to protect gay people? Why should *gay men* benefit from a constitutional protection that is supposed to benefit *women*? The following is a legal way of putting the objection.

Loving holds that the state's use of a racial classification requires a compelling justification, but that holding is expressed in the context of the core purpose of the Fourteenth Amendment, namely, the rejection of a philosophy of white supremacy. In the context of that philosophy the racial classification was revealed to be sinister in a way *Pace* and later *Plessy* refused to recognize: The classification was part of a legal "caste system" subordinating African Americans and other racial groups. *Loving*, therefore, might be narrowly limited as a decision where a particularly invidious classification is used to suppress a group whose identity is defined by that classification. *Baehr* may not be a sex discrimination case in the same way *Loving* is a race discrimination case. The classification in *Baehr* is sex, but the class being disadvantaged is defined by sexual orientation (lesbians, gay men, bisexuals, and some transgendered people), not by sex (women). The philosophy that justifies their disadvantage is "compulsory heterosexuality," that is, the requirement that citizens be (or pretend to be) heterosexual. This may not be the quintessential sex discrimination case, where a sex-based classification disadvantages women on the basis of a philosophy of sexism.

This doctrinal argument parallels the commonsense objection. *Baehr* is not like the classic sex discrimination case because the classification (sex) does not match up with the disadvantaged class (sexual orientation minorities). That match fails to occur because the disadvantage is the result of compulsory heterosexuality rather than sexism. *Baehr* is also unlike *Loving* for the same reason. Table 1 maps the differences among the cases.[e]

The argument in Table 1 is doctrinally oversimple in one dimension, the middle column (Disadvantaged Class). In *Loving*, for example, the immediately disadvantaged class is composed of people who fall in love with someone of another race. Such people are a minority among both whites and blacks. While African Americans may ultimately have been disadvantaged by the classification, many did not feel that way in 1967 and many do not feel that way now. Racial minorities were disadvantaged by the classification only by reasoning from the ideology (racism or white supremacy). Hence, the middle column in *Loving* reflects an indirect reasoning process rather than direct harm. The Equal Rights Amendment (ERA) line must be qualified in the same way by reference to *Craig v. Boren*, the case that established heightened scrutiny for sex-based classifications. In *Craig* the disadvantaged group was eighteen-to-twenty-one-year-old boys who were denied the right to buy low-alcohol beer, which eighteen-to-twenty-one-year-old girls enjoyed. Justice William Brennan's opinion for the Court emphasized that sex-based classifications ostensibly benefiting men are just as objectionable as those ostensibly benefiting women when they reflect "'archaic and overbroad generalizations'" about women or "outdated misconceptions concerning the role of females in the home rather than in the 'marketplace and world of ideas.'"[39] When sexist assumptions animate a sex-based classification and gender stereotypes are reinforced, women as a group suffer (at least indirectly). Again, the middle column only reflects indirect harm, deriving from the underlying philosophy (sexism) and not from the classification in a particular case (women can buy drinks earlier than men).

This subtler analysis of the miscegenation analogy leaves one question unanswered: Does constitutional doctrine disapproving sex-

---

[e]I developed Table 1 as a way of commenting on the Law–Koppelman thesis at a panel sponsored by the American Association of Law Schools in January 1995. Professors Law and Koppelman both responded to the doctrinal argument captured by Table 1. I consider their responses persuasive, and they are reflected in the discussion.

TABLE 1

	Classification	Disadvantaged Class	Philosophy
Loving	Race	Racial minorities	Racism
ERA	Sex	Women	Sexism
Baehr	Sex	Sexual orientation minorities	Compulsory heterosexuality

based classifications rooted in sexism apply to sex-based classifications rooted in compulsory heterosexuality? More simply, does the prohibition of same-sex marriage serve sexist goals? Professors Law and Koppelman have suggested reasons why it does.

Homophobia as a Weapon of Sexism

There is no inevitable connection between the prohibition of same-sex marriage and sexism, as the history in chapter 2 illustrates. Embracing companionate marriage, medieval Christianity represented an advance in women's status, yet it was more (and increasingly) hostile to same-sex male unions than ancient Greece and imperial Rome were. Conversely, ancient Greece was severely sexist by modern standards yet tolerated same-sex unions, especially male unions. Some anthropologists view the African institution of woman marriage as reinforcing patriarchal stereotypes, because the "female husband" takes on the male role. Nonetheless, in the context of modern Western culture there is a strong connection between antihomosexual rules and sexism. Indeed, the construct of "the homosexual" is one modern response to gender equality.[40]

Western history has long stigmatized the "passive" partner in a same-sex male relationship on the ground that he was compromising his "superior" male identity by taking an "inferior" female role. In the modern era, starting no later than the eighteenth century for England, men who lusted after other men were stigmatized as "effeminate sodomites," whatever role they took in intercourse. This represented a historical transition from stigma because of acts to stigma because of identity. The transition was completed in the late nineteenth century by the appearance of the construct of "the homosexual," the person defined by the new concept of "sexuality." This is the chronology generally accepted by historians of homosexuality. More speculative are the reasons why these cultural changes occurred.

Historian Randolph Trumbach maintains that the effeminate sodomite stigma came when and because "a patriarchal morality that allowed adult men to own and dominate their wives, children, servants and slaves was gradually challenged and partially replaced by an egalitarian morality" of women's equality.[41] Men reacted to this new equality by creating differently defined gender roles. Marriage became a secure refuge of the striving urban bourgeoisie. In a companionate relationship men and women were formally "equal" but functionally unequal. This was possible because their equality was conceptualized by considering each supreme in a separate but equal sphere, that is, men in the workplace and women in the home. This new middle-class equilibrium was necessarily temporary inasmuch as it became possible for women to be economically independent of men. Nineteenth-century feminists demanded not only personal equality for women but also political and social equality. Opponents of women's equality have traditionally argued that it would destroy the family and undermine the institution of marriage. Although still accepted in some quarters, these arguments slowly gave way to women's increasing political clout. As women made gains in politics and the marketplace, middle-class anxiety about gender and the family was displaced onto another object: the homosexual.

Homophobia became one way modern urban culture responded to women's political and social equality.[42] Nervous that their manhood was under seige from the "new woman" (Carroll Smith-Rosenberg's term) and from an increasingly hierarchical economic structure, middle-class men latched onto the class of male "inverts" or homosexuals as their object of special scorn. By setting up the male homosexual as the antithesis of the normal heterosexual, men were reassured of their own sexuality and virility. Power and satisfaction derived from classification and deviance. Homosexual men were threats to the idea of masculinity, for the possibility that a man could "cross over" into roles and dress traditionally reserved for women impeached the supposed superiority of the masculine role. Although the focus on sexual deviation did not include lesbians at first (but did so by World War II), lesbians, too, came to be seen as threats to male virility: they were the apotheosis of men's fears about feminism, namely, women who had no need for men. The "effeminate man" and "mannish woman" became virtual synonyms in the twentieth century for the male homosexual and the lesbian.

This account is not a demonstrated thesis so much as a coherent hypothesis. Consider other sources of support for the hypothesis. Most feminists (at least among those I have read or talked to) believe that resistance to women's equality, by women as well as men, is associated with antihomosexual patterns of belief. For example, a popular reproach to feminists has long been that they are lesbians and that women's equality will lead to gay marriage and other affronts to family values.[43] Persuasive theories of feminist psychology maintain that the Western concept of masculinity is itself a psychological reaction to men's childhood anxieties about their relationship to their mother and a displacement of those anxieties. Feminized men and masculinized women become objects of intense hatred by men hoping to reaffirm a manhood about which they are deeply uncertain.[44]

Independent survey evidence supports the account given by historians of sexuality and these feminist theorists. Scholars have been studying male homophobia for a quarter century. Many studies emphasize a correlation between antihomosexual feelings and "a belief in the traditional family ideology, i.e., dominant father, submissive mother, and obedient children," as well as "traditional beliefs about women, e.g., that it is worse for a woman to tell dirty jokes than it is for a man."[45] A few studies claim a causal link: "A major determinant of negative attitudes toward homosexuality is the need to keep males masculine and females feminine, that is, to avoid sex-role confusion."[46] One study found a significant correlation between antihomosexual attitudes and one's own conformity to traditional gender roles.[47] Of course, these studies should be read cautiously. Most of them involved small or unrepresentative samples, and causal claims are always suspect.

The Kinsey Institute published an unusually thorough survey using sophisticated statistical analyses in 1989.[48] These researchers found a host of variables positively correlated with antihomosexual attitudes. They were able to map a complicated array of factors associated with those attitudes, and their model employed regression analysis that permitted them to sort out causal from simply associated factors. One variable significantly linked to antihomosexual feelings was respondents' own fears and anxieties about the opposite sex. The researchers believe that people who feel threatened by the opposite sex are hostile to homosexuality as a defense mechanism, displacing an identity-shattering fear onto a socially safe object (gender-bending queers). "Accordingly, we may condemn the homosexual in order to reduce sex role confusion."[49]

Consider the implications of these studies and surveys, of feminist psychology, and of historical theory for the *Baehr* argument. Denying a marriage license to two women simply because one of the partners is not a man is discrimination by reason of a sex-based classification. The ideology that drives this discrimination is deep-seated and arouses fierce emotion in many people. Otherwise, the state would simply make the requirements gender neutral (two persons can get married, rather than a man and a woman), just as the state has since the 1970s routinely rewritten old laws to make them gender neutral (e.g., alimony is now owed to a financially dependent party in a divorce rather than to the wife).

One might simply say that those who oppose same-sex marriage hate homosexuals, but few people will admit that anymore in public discourse.[f] Instead, they will shop around for arguments that support their visceral positions. They may say that it is "unnatural" for two women to get married or that it is "impossible" for men to marry one another. "Who will be the wife?" is a typical crack, usually made in private. (This is a revealing comment, because it signals the under-

---

[f] For a recent example, the current majority leader of the House of Representatives referred to the openly gay representative Barney Frank as "Barney Fag" in a press meeting. The majority leader went to great lengths to cover his tracks, first attacking the media for reporting an allegedly off-the-record remark, then attacking the media for reading antihomosexual implications into a "slip of the tongue," and then apologizing to Representative Frank and indicating his own distaste for homophobic utterances. The slip-of-the-tongue explanation is particularly striking.

lying fear: If two men can get married, one of them must play housekeeper or the gendered nature of marriage will be lost.)

The idea that everyone must be heterosexual is closely associated with the idea that every wife must have a husband, which is in turn correlated (though not absolutely) with a belief that the wife rules the home while the husband supports the family. At the level of common sense as well as theory, there is a connection between compulsory different-sex marriage and sexist assumptions. Requiring the state to recognize same-sex marriage (*Baehr*) will not deliver us a world of gender equality any more than requiring the state to equalize beer-drinking ages for men and women did (*Craig*). Both moves do eliminate unjustified sex-based classifications, and they confront traditional views of women's role in society. The federal equal protection clause and state equal rights amendments are more than enough to require the state to show a compelling justification for its discrimination in barring same-sex marriage.

Table 2 maps the result of the foregoing analysis. Parentheses are used for the middle column in order to suggest that the identity of the disadvantaged class is based on inference from the underlying philosophy. In this table, *Baehr* is the same as *Craig* and analytically indistinguishable from *Loving*. *Baehr* and *Craig* involve sex-based classifications derived from a philosophy viewing men and women in traditional (i.e., gendered) terms. In both cases the state is obligated to show a strong interest to justify the continuing discrimination. Likewise, *Baehr* and *Loving* both involve classifications (sex and race, respectively) that restrict the right to marry. As the Supreme Court has interpreted the federal equal protection clause, both classifications

TABLE 2

	Classification	Disadvantaged Class	Philosophy
Loving	Race	(Racial minorities)	Racism
Craig	Sex	(Women)	Sexism
Baehr	Sex	(Women)	Sexism

are "suspect," for they are red flags triggering heightened scrutiny. Just as the state was unable to carry its burden to justify the invidious discrimination in *Loving* and *Craig*, it will be unable to do so in *Baehr* (for reasons laid out in chapter 5).

Prohibiting Same-Sex Marriage as Sexual Orientation Discrimination

There is a transvestite quality to the argument adopted by the *Baehr* majority. It dresses a gay rights issue up in gender rights garb.[g] Such legal transvestism is not uncommon, and this one is persuasive. But consider a complementary and more direct argument: Prohibiting same-sex marriage is invidious discrimination on the basis of sexual orientation. Several state courts have held that the states have an obligation under their state constitutions to justify such discrimination by reference to a compelling or at least neutral state interest.[50] Judge William Norris has articulated a similar interpretation of the U.S. Constitution.[51] For the reasons that follow, Judge Norris's position ought to be adopted as the standard for the equal protection provisions of both the state and federal constitutions. As we have seen, the exclusion of lesbian and gay couples from marriage would flunk any form of heightened scrutiny.

Issues Suggested by the Racial Classification Cases

The Supreme Court's decisions in *Loving* and *Washington v. Davis*[52] suggest threshold issues for a sexual orientation claim under the equal protection clause. In *Davis* the Supreme Court refused to apply heightened equal protection scrutiny to evaluate the state's use of a personnel test that had the effect of excluding a disproportionate number of African Americans from the civil service. "Standing alone, [disproportionate impact] does not trigger the rule that racial classifications," such as those in *Loving*, "are to be subjected to the strictest

---

[g]This is even more true of the *Baehr* concurring opinion by Justice James Burns, who believes Baehr and Dancel's equal rights amendment claim can only be justified if they show their sexual orientation to be "biologically fated," or immutable, and therefore part of their "sex." *Baehr*, 852 P.2d at 69–70 (Burns, J., concurring in the judgment).

scrutiny and are justifiable only by the weightiest of considerations."[53] *Davis* raises a question whether there is a sexual orientation "classification" akin to the racial classification struck down in *Loving* and the sex classification struck down in *Craig* and invoked in *Baehr*.

On the other hand, *Davis* denied that "a law's disproportionate impact is irrelevant. . . . A statute, otherwise neutral on its face, must not be applied so as invidiously to discriminate on the basis of race."[54] For this proposition *Davis* cited *Yick Wo v. Hopkins*,[55] where the Court had invalidated as race-based discrimination a seemingly race-neutral rule that laundry houses must not be constructed of wood. *Yick Wo*'s classification operated as a race-based one because it excluded all Chinese American applicants for licenses to run laundries and allowed all but one non–Chinese applicant for such a license. The operation of the state's ban on same-sex marriages is almost as lopsided as the rule in *Yick Wo*, for the large majority of same-sex couples who would desire to get married are homosexual couples. That lopsided effect of the law is no accident, because the state's requirement that marriage involve partners of different sex is animated in large part by the state's insistence on compulsory heterosexuality. Some states express the obvious, providing (as Virginia does) that "homosexual marriage" is prohibited in the jurisdiction. In short, the pervasive class-based effect of the same-sex marriage ban permits challenge of that ban as a discriminatory classification.

A harder issue under *Davis* and *Loving* arises from their shared view that "[t]he *central purpose* of the equal protection clause of the Fourteenth Amendment is the prevention of official conduct discriminating on the basis of *race*."[56] Ratified in 1868, the Fourteenth Amendment sought to consolidate a new legal regime made possible by the North's victory in the Civil War. The equal protection clause is soaked with race and blood. Why should a constitutional provision concerned with race discrimination be expanded to police issues of sexual orientation? Would the framers of the Fourteenth Amendment have intended such coverage?

To begin with, the equal protection clause is not by its terms limited to racial discrimination. Its assurance that no "person" shall be denied the "equal protection of the laws" is so open textured that the job of the Court has been to narrow its limitless ambit. Serious judicial scrutiny of legislative classifications will only occur when the legislature is *either* abridging fundamental rights (chapter 5) *or* relying on suspect classifications (this chapter). The phrase *suspect classification* (or sometimes *class*) has become famous in civil rights debates. Often forgotten is that the idea of a *suspect* classification is inspired by the Court's desire to limit the exceedingly broad language of the Fourteenth Amendment.

Does the framers' original intent limit the Court's creativity? The Supreme Court's answer to this question has repeatedly been no. The Court's equal protection jurisprudence finds little support in the framers' original intent. Given pervasive white support for antimiscegenation laws in the 1860s, the Supreme Court in *Loving* did not adopt the pretense that it was simply applying original intent.[57] It was, instead, applying the general antidiscrimination principle when it struck down Virginia's race-based marriage rules. Similarly, the Court's decisions applying heightened scrutiny to sex-based classifications have not been justified by reference to the framers' intent.[58] The framers of the reconstruction amendments made a deliberate decision not to include protections against sex discrimination, and several leading feminists of the 1860s opposed one or more of the amendments for that reason. Scores of sex-based classifications went unchallenged after the adoption of the Fourteenth Amendment, and the Supreme Court upheld these classifications in every case it heard until 1971. As Judge, now Justice, Ruth Bader Ginsburg conceded in 1979, "Boldly dynamic interpretation, departing radically from the original understanding, is required to tie to the Fourteenth Amendment's equal protection clause a command that government treat men and women as individuals equal in rights, responsibilities and opportunities."[59]

Loving and decisions strictly scrutinizing sex-based classifications arguably cut against the intent of the framers, who filled the historical record with their views about different-race marriage (against it) and sex-based exclusions (for them). Ironically, an interpretation of the equal protection clause that subjects antigay discrimination to heightened scrutiny would only reach beyond (not necessarily against) the framers' original intent. Because sexual orientation was not even a coherent category of thought in the 1860s (recall the status of Walt Whitman, discussed in chapter 2), the framers would have had no serviceable intent as to the rationality of laws classifying on the basis of sexual orientation. The framers would have been familiar with sodomy laws, but the laws they knew applied equally to different-sex and same-sex sodomy[h] and had no connection to the not-yet-born idea of sexual orientation. The concept of homosexuality was formulated by a German doctor in 1869, a year after the Fourteenth Amendment was ratified. Although state marriage laws were on their face limited to different-sex marriage in 1868, the concept of gay marriage, which dominates the current debate, was inconceivable. In any event, *Loving* found irrelevant the overwhelming state practice of prohibiting different-race marriages in 1868 and thereafter.

In short, the U.S. Supreme Court and state high courts have not followed an original intent approach to elaborating the equal protection clauses of the federal and state constitutions. Instead, they have pragmatically adopted a category-by-category approach to determining which classifications are "suspect" under the broadly phrased clause.[i] The U.S. Supreme Court has held that classifications based on race, ethnicity, sex, illegitimacy, and (because of the First Amendment) religion are "suspect" and therefore require heightened scrutiny.[60] Over dissents, the Court has held that classifications based on age, income level, physical or mental disability, addiction, and marital status do not require heightened scrutiny.[61] In which grouping does sexual orientation belong? By analogy to the classifications previously categorized (especially sex, the most recent addition) and the reasoning behind their categorization, a neutral analysis would place sexual orientation in the first group.

---

[h]If the framers had read the sodomy cases that had been reported as of 1868, they would have found that the large majority of cases involved different-sex sodomy (typically between a man and an underage girl) and bestiality, namely, sex between men and barnyard animals. This will be documented in William N. Eskridge, Jr., *Gaylaw*, chapter 1 (Cambridge, MA: Harvard University Press, in press).

[i]Several states (including Hawaii) have equal rights provisions that contain lists of suspect classifications. The argument in the text works less well for these states, unless the category of sexual orientation can be shoehorned into that of sex, as Justice Burns tried to do in *Baehr* (note g above).

Sexual Orientation as an Irrational Classification

Justice Brennan's plurality opinion in *Frontiero v. Richardson* is the Court's primary explanation for why sex-based classifications are suspect. "[W]hat differentiates sex from such non-suspect statuses as intelligence or physical disability, and aligns it with the recognized suspect criteria, is that the sex characteristic frequently bears no relation to ability to perform or contribute to society."[62] *McLaughlin* had made a similar point about race-based classifications, finding them "in most circumstances irrelevant" to any legitimate state purpose.[63] The same is intuitively true of ethnicity, illegitimate birth, and religion inasmuch as those personal characteristics have no rational relationship to the person's ability to do a job, participate in society and politics, and carry on a productive life. Relatedly, drawing lines based on race, ethnicity, religion, sex, and nonmarital birth is typically motivated by stereotypical rather than fact-based thinking. "These factors are so seldom relevant to the achievement of any legitimate state interest that laws grounded in such considerations are deemed to reflect prejudice and antipathy," the Court has said.[64]

Conversely, the Court has denied heightened scrutiny to classifications that a neutral decision maker will often want to consider. A critical reason the Court gave for declining to subject age-based classifications to heightened scrutiny is that aged people have not been "subjected to unique disabilities on the basis of stereotyped characteristics not truly indicative of their abilities."[65] Age affects people's judgment, physical abilities, and mental capacity, all of which are considerations policymakers ought to be able to take into account. Likewise, the Court declined to give special attention to classifications based on mental disability because "those who are mentally retarded have a reduced ability to cope with and function in the everyday world."[66] The Court's approach to classifications based on income, addiction, and marital status has relied on a similar judgment that these classifications typically serve legitimate social functions and are not pretexts for prejudice.

Sexual orientation classifications almost never serve legitimate state goals. Although once pervasive in American law, most such classifications have been abandoned because neutral observers concluded that they serve no rational purpose and are, instead, animated by ignorance or prejudice. The case of the immigration exclusion is representative.[67] The McCarran-Walter Act of 1952 prohibited entry into the United States of any person "afflicted with psychopathic personality." This phrase was widely considered a code phrase for "homosexuals" because of medical and psychiatric beliefs that such people are sick.[68] Those beliefs were based on no rigorous neutral or empirical research. As researchers published more rigorous studies, these beliefs came under fire. The evidence has become overwhelming that sexual orientation per se has no connection with intelligence, personality disorder or psychopathy, capacity to interact with others, or the ability to mate and raise a family.[69] After unprecedented debate, the American Psychiatric Association (APA) delisted homosexuality as a mental illness in 1973 on the basis of increasing evidence that "homosexuality per se implies no impairment in judgment, stability, or general social or vocational capabilities."[70] Other professional groups followed the APA's lead, and in 1979 the Public Health Service (PHS) announced that it would no longer cooperate in the exclusion of gay and lesbian immigrants on the basis of the "psychopathic personality" exclusion of the immigration law, which the PHS administered. Lacking the PHS's cooperation, the Immigration and Naturalization Service adopted a "don't ask, don't tell" approach to enforcing the provision, and it went virtually unenforced. In 1990, Congress repealed it. Senate floor manager Alan Simpson, Republican of Wyoming, explained that the exclusion of homosexuals was irrational and grounded on obsolete thinking.[71]

Like the immigration exclusion, one classification after another has been discarded as evidence of its irrationality became too overwhelming to ignore. No impartial judge, no executive officer, no respected professional, no competent senator, no unbiased observer of any scruple is willing to say that sexual orientation bears any relation to lesbian and gay people's ability to participate in and contribute to society. The leading antigay regulation currently in force, the marriage exclusion, is ultimately justified not by any neutral reason but by people's hostility to gay marriage. In short, sexual orientation as a classification is irrational along both dimensions emphasized by the Supreme Court's cases; that is, it is linked to no characteristic neutral policymakers would normally consider and it is often a pretext for prejudice.

Some judges and commentators have urged that suspect classifications should be limited to those which are immutable.[72] This is an unfortunate attempt to say that in all areas where one has a choice society can make political decisions to reward or punish. Would anyone seriously extend that logic to religion? It makes little sense of the cases or of constitutional theory to require that the identifying characteristic be one that literally cannot be hidden or changed at all. Although sex is widely considered an immutable characteristic, people can successfully conceal their sex and many have changed their sex. Race and, even more so, ethnicity can be concealed. The status of nonmarital children can be changed legally. It is easy to conceal or change one's religion. These suspect classifications are much more mutable than nonsuspect classifications such as age, intelligence, and most forms of disability. To the extent that there is an immutability element in suspect classification law, "a trait [is] effectively immutable if changing it would involve great difficulty, such as requiring a major physical change or a traumatic change of identity."[73]

Sexual orientation may be biologically immutable for at least some people, according to new genetic discoveries and to studies of identical twins separated at birth. This remains an unresolved scientific issue.[74] What is resolved among scientists is that sexual orientation is a characteristic formed early in one's life and that the person has little control over this feature of her or his identity.[75] People can more readily change their religion than change their sexual orientation and can just about as easily change their sex. In all cases (religion, sex, orientation), people's actions can go against their category: Protestants can take Catholic communion and go to confession, women can dress like men, and gay people can date persons of the opposite sex. Passing is possible, but should the benefits of the law depend on denying features of one's personhood? Judge Norris put the immutability question this way: "Would heterosexuals living in a city that passed an ordinance banning those who engaged in or desired to engage in sex with persons of the *opposite* sex find it easy not only to abstain from heterosexual activity but also to shift the object of their sexual desires to persons of the same sex?"[76]

Gay People as a Subordinated Minority

In deciding which classifications should be suspect, the Supreme Court has considered the extent to which the classifications have been used to persecute particular groups in American history.[j] Thus, Justice Brennan's plurality opinion in *Frontiero* emphasized how sex-based classifications had been used to suppress women's interests. Although women had not as a group been subjected to slavery, during most of American history women could neither vote nor hold public office and the law limited their ability to manage property, obtain employment outside the home, or even serve as legal guardians to their children. While "the position of women has improved markedly" in the last three decades, "it can hardly be doubted that, in part because of the high visibility of the sex characteristic, women still face pervasive, although at times more subtle, discrimination in our educational institutions, in the job market and, perhaps most conspicuously, in the political arena."[77] Similarly, racial, ethnic, and religious minorities have all been subjected to legal as well as societal disabilities at various points in American history. All can testify to a history of group discrimination.

Conversely, the Court has sometimes, but not always, emphasized the absence of a history of discrimination when declining to hold a classification suspect. This was the main reason the Court declined to apply heightened scrutiny to age-based classifications, for example. The elderly "have not experienced a 'history of purposeful unequal treatment' or been subjected to unique disabilities on the basis of stereotyped characteristics not truly indicative of their abilities."[78] Although people with disabilities have been objects of prejudice, the

---

[j]The genesis of the idea is footnote 4 of Carolene Products v. United States, 304 U.S. 144 (U.S. Supreme Court, 1938), where the Court indicated, in dictum, that more searching judicial scrutiny of legislation is justified when it harms "discrete and insular minorities." The Court assumed that such minorities tend to be ill represented in the political process—see John Hart Ely, *Democracy and Distrust* (Cambridge, MA: Harvard University Press, 1980)—and tend to be objects of popular prejudice. For reasons developed by Bruce Ackerman, "Beyond *Carolene Products*," 98 *Harvard Law Review* 713 (1985), I do not rely on the "discrete and insular minorities" formulation in the text. Women, for example, are neither insular (everywhere you find men you find women) nor a minority (they are more than half the population). Lesbians and gay men are a minority but are typically anonymous or closeted rather than discrete (you cannot tell by looking) and are often dispersed rather than insular (though there are gay ghettoes in most major cities).

Court believed that "lawmakers have been addressing their difficulties in a manner that belies a continuing antipathy or prejudice and a corresponding need for more intrusive oversight by the judiciary."[79] As a result, the Court declined to subject disability-based classifications to heightened scrutiny.

People who commit sodomy have been punished, with varying severity, in Western culture for six hundred years or more. Since the creation of the category of sexual invert or homosexual in the latter half of the nineteenth century, there has been distinctly group-focused persecution by individuals and by the state.[80] Being known as a homosexual or associating with known homosexuals triggered all sorts of legal disadvantages as recently as the 1950s: you could not have a job in the federal or most state civil services, have a national security clearance, serve in the armed forces, immigrate to the United States or (if you slipped in by mistake) become a U.S. citizen, use the U.S. mails for your informational magazines, obtain some professional and business licenses, dance with someone of the same sex in a public accommodation, loiter in a public place, hold hands with someone of the same sex anywhere, or (heaven forfend) actually have intercourse with someone of the same sex.[81] Even statutes that were gay neutral on their face, such as vagrancy laws, were used by the police to target gay people and destroy their subculture. For much of this century gay people faced dismissal from their families, private violence and discrimination, and all-out war from the state.

Particularly after the Stonewall riots—when drag queens, dykes, and hangers-on actually resisted police violence against them—gay people have been able to press for the repeal, nullification, or amelioration of sexual orientation classifications. Nonetheless, lesbians, bisexuals, and gay men still live under a cloud of pervasive social homophobia and legal disability. Most gay people have been an object of hate crime or violence. An overwhelming majority of gay people conceal their sexual orientation at work, and a substantial minority have nevertheless suffered workplace discrimination.[82] Societal homophobia affects the ability of gay people to organize politically. Because most gay people are in the closet, their voices are not heard in the political arena. Because gay people remain unpopular, they are available scapegoats for politicians interested in scoring easy points with voters. Even scrupulous politicians are reluctant to oppose gay bashing, because they reasonably fear a backlash because of their association with a disliked group.

For these reasons, protection of legitimate gay rights has been hard to come by in the political process. Gay rights regulations have been possible mainly in relatively tolerant jurisdictions where they are least needed. Even where such regulations have been adopted, proponents have often had to defend those victories against antihomosexual initiatives and referenda, just as civil rights advocates had to do in the late sixties and early seventies. Antigay amendments proposed in the U.S. Senate are regularly adopted by huge margins, even though they are often dumped behind the closed doors of a conference committee. In short, for every two steps forward the gay rights movement often suffers a step or two backward because of sometimes hysterical backlash against homosexuality.

Classifications according to sexual orientation have no legitimate role in neutral governance. In the past, such classifications have only served invidious goals. The equal protection clause has in the past been a politically necessary means of cleansing American law of classifications based on race, sex, and ethnicity and is just as needed against sexual orientation classifications today. The state's prohibition of same-sex marriage is the primary example of sexual orientation discrimination by the state. Like the immigration exclusion, it should follow the dodo bird's path to extinction.

The analogy between same-sex marriage and miscegenation can now be completed. Table 3 maps the completed analogy.

TABLE 3

	Classification	*Disadvantaged Class*	*Philosophy*
Loving	Race	(Racial minorities)	Racism
Baehr I	Sex	(Women)	Sexism
Baehr II	(Sexual orientation)	Sexual orientation minorities	Compulsory heterosexuality

Denying same-sex couples a marriage license is on its face a sex discrimination and in its effect a sexual orientation discrimination that is motivated by desire(s) both to suppress lesbian and gay couples and to preserve traditional gender roles. Either or both discriminations should trigger heightened scrutiny, and the state's justifications for opposing same-sex marriage are either insufficient or rest on a philosophy of rigid gender roles (the sex discrimination claim) or compulsory heterosexuality (the sexual orientation claim).

In trying to justify its discrimination against this two-pronged attack, the state may face argumentative dilemmas. For example, if it argues that the sexual orientation discrimination is justified by the state interest in procreation (see chapter 4), the state is helping to prove the sex discrimination case, which posits that it is an unacceptable gender stereotype that women get married so that they can be baby producers. If the state argues that the sex discrimination is a benign classification not aimed against women (about the only argument that occurs to me to justify the sex discrimination), it is helping to prove the sexual orientation discrimination case, which posits that the classification is targeted at lesbian and gay couples. The double-barreled argument of sex and sexual orientation discrimination ought to be enough, standing alone, to shoot down the state's prohibition against same-sex marriages. When you add the constitutional arguments based on citizens' fundamental right to marry, the constitutional case becomes irrefutable.

EPILOGUE: FEAR OF FLAUNTING

America's anxiety about same-sex marriage is logically inexplicable. Most same-sex couples, like Ninia Baehr and Genora Dancel, are nice people who share America's values (chapter 1). Indeed, it is the values of love, commitment, and family that impel couples like Baehr and Dancel to marry. There is nothing intrinsically weird about their impulse; human history is filled with examples of culturally tolerated same-sex unions and legally recognized same-sex marriages (chapter 2). Such marriages serve important psychological functions for gay and lesbian couples (chapter 3). Constitutional traditions at both the national and state level require the state to recognize same-sex marriages; legal arguments to the contrary are factually wrong or unprincipled (chapters 5 and 6). Even God, often the last refuge of bad legal argument, offers little support for rejecting same-sex marriage (chapter 4).

At first blush, the nonsense frequently found in the objections examined in this book may suggest that arguments against same-sex marriage rest only on ignorance and antihomosexual hysteria. That is probably the case for many people. The only strategy for persuading such persons is to urge them to work through their homophobia with a therapist. For most people, however, a more subtle motivation explains continued resistance in the face of fact and reasoned argument. It is a fear of flaunting.

America is still a sex-ambivalent society, alternately fascinated and repelled by sexuality. Our culture manages to be both pervasively prurient and puritanical, tolerant and judgmental. This balance is reflected in our nation's libertarianism. Americans have strong feelings and beliefs about sexual morality, but at the same time they adhere to a "live and let live" attitude about sexual practices. The tension between substantive morality and procedural freedom is mediated by the public–private distinction in both law and society. Sex in the bedroom is fine, sex in a public park is not. Sexual pillow talk is fine, published prurience is not. A spouse's striptease is fine if done in the home but not if done in a nightclub. Filming the striptease is fine but not if it is intended for commercial distribution. Law professors regularly deconstruct the public–private boundary, but it remains a critical phenomenon of our culture.

I grew up in a small town in West Virginia. My aunt, Ms. Mildred Burke DeJarnette, once explained to me how small towns accommodate homosexual couples. Same-sex couples can live together all their lives in a small town, and everybody will understand that they are committed partners in the same way that husband and wife are partners. The partners can hold responsible jobs, and their families and neighbors will know to invite them both to social events. Gossips who speak maliciously against the couple will be disciplined by polite society, and the police will come down hard against harassers. My aunt's impression, and mine too, is that same-sex couples can often, though not always, live normal middle-class lives in small towns. The tradeoff is that the couple is expected not to flaunt their sexuality. They should not kiss romantically in public, probably should not wear pink triangles and speak as open lesbians or gay men, and definitely should not marry one another in a big, splashy church ceremony.

Some Americans consider the foregoing attitude homophobic; others consider it excessively tolerant. Many consider the small town's accommodation of homosexual couples an arrangement that works. My aunt's analysis also reflects the state of American law for gay people: So long as we do not flaunt our sexuality, we have equal rights. *Bowers v. Hardwick* notwithstanding, sodomy laws are almost never enforced against lesbians, bisexuals, or gay men within private spaces. Public hate crimes against us are often prosecuted by the police. Homosexual social clubs have sprouted all over America like mushrooms after a spring rain. Employers usually do not openly discriminate against discreet (yes, a spongy term) gay employees. Even the nation's only openly antihomosexual employer, the United States armed forces, says its policy is "don't ask, don't tell." The homosexual can serve but must remain in the closet. The situation is similar for homosexual couples: They can create some of the tangible benefits and commitment value of marriage through private contracting (the states "don't ask" what is going on), but their unions are not legally recognized marriages ("don't tell").

Americans' fear of flaunting is deep-seated. It reflects ambivalence about sexuality in general and about homosexuality in particular. It is beyond my competence to psychoanalyze Americans' complex emotional reaction to open homosexual expression, but medical professionals generally consider antihomosexual feelings mentally unhealthy. I maintain that it is politically unhealthy for our polity, any polity, to push its lesbian, gay, bisexual, and transgendered citizens into a closet.

THE INJUSTICE OF THE DOUBLE STANDARD

Melrose Place is a trashy, sexy nighttime soap opera for and about Generation Xers. In the 1994–1995 season the apartment complex was populated with six or seven randy heterosexuals (Alison, Amanda, Billy, Jake, Jane, Jo, and sometimes Sidney) and one discreet homosexual (Matt). The show is considered progressive in part because it has a "nice" (i.e., could pass for straight) gay character, but the show in all its progressiveness illustrates the double standard imposed by the fear of flaunting. At the drop of a cocktail, the heterosexuals toss off their clothing, fall into passionate embraces, and mate like bunnies. They are in contrast to chaste Matt, whose shirt remains resolutely buttoned as he pines for one closet case after another. Matt's closest call with on-screen romance came when a man apparently kissed him in the Melrose Place courtyard. I say "apparently" because the camera cut away at the crucial moment, and we the audience viewed the touching of lips only through the shocked eyes of Billy, the most vacant of the heterosexual tenants. *Melrose Place*, or its censors, were caught up in the fear of flaunting; anything beyond a hug by a gay character is too morally controversial for a show whose straight characters have been known to violate all of the Ten Commandments in a single episode.

Thus, it is considered sweet for a boy to kiss a girl but perverted for a boy to kiss a boy. It is natural for a girl and boy to cuddle and snuggle but unnatural for two girls to do the same. A wife's enthusiasm for life with her husband is sociable while a woman's aspiration for life with another woman is a sure conversation stopper. An engagement ring, the proposal, the wedding, and the honeymoon are American traditions for straight couples but an American abomination if enjoyed by same-sex couples. Marriage is a constitutional right for heterosexuals but a ticket to the unemployment office for gay people who try it.[1]

The foregoing paragraphs describe a double standard in which precisely the same sexual conduct that is socially permissible and legally protected for different-sex couples is socially questionable and sometimes legally prohibited for same-sex couples. The effect of this compulsory heterosexuality is that the more closeted the lesbian, bisexual, or gay person is, the more legal rights he or she has. The gay person who passes as straight can get married, can serve in the military, and can sue his or her employer under federal law if fired for appearing too butch (for a woman) or too effeminate (for a man).[2] Gay people who are as open about their sexuality as straight people are cannot get married, cannot serve in the military, and can sue for employment discrimination only in those states that have employment laws protecting against sexual orientation discrimination.[a] The purpose and effect of this double standard is public suppression of the lesbian or gay person's sexuality.

Most people concur with this purpose and are happy with this effect. They should not be. In the short run, homosexuality might be less visible. In the longer run, suppression is destructive for both the suppressed and the suppressors. Sexual orientation is a characteristic over which we have little and perhaps no conscious control. In our society it is a fundamental characteristic, pervasively affecting one's social and emotional life. Sexual orientation is part of one's identity—and a more fundamental identity feature for most people than

---

[a]As of January 1996 those states are California (1992), Connecticut (1991), the District of Columbia (1977), Hawaii (1991), Massachusetts (1989), Minnesota (1993), New Jersey (1992), Rhode Island (1995), Vermont (1992), and Wisconsin (1982).

their religion, ethnicity, or profession. Most respectable psychiatrists and psychologists today think that social or state suppression of that identity harms the individual without offering any larger social advantage, such as diminishing the amount of homosexual preference or activity.[3] The harm is tangibly illustrated in the extraordinary suicide rates for gay teenagers and the high alcoholism rates for gay adults. Should this be surprising?

Consider the following scenario. At an early age you are sexually attracted to left-handed people. This feels natural and good. However, through cultural osmosis you perceive that your family and surrounding society consider it deeply perverted for people with different dexterities to interact sexually. With horror you realize that you are left-handed and that your natural attraction is therefore perverted. You hide your feelings, and the biggest part of yourself, from your friends and family and pretend attraction to right-handed people. What feelings would you have? Anxiety? Shame? Hypocrisy? If you can imagine yourself in this situation, you can appreciate some of the pain felt by gay adolescents. Is this pain necessary to serve any larger social purpose?

What happens when you, the left-hander attracted to other left-handers, become an adult? The stigma of this attraction will press you into a public and perhaps even a private denial of your feelings. You might even marry a right-hander in order to persuade others and perhaps yourself of your normalcy. The marriage is not likely to be satisfying to you or your partner. Is this pain, yours and your unaware partner's, justified by any larger social purpose? Is there any good reason why the state should not accommodate the needs of this minority of its citizens to marry the people they choose? Does *Loving v. Virginia* not stand for precisely this proposition?

John Rawls maintains that the conditions of the social contract should be constructed as if the drafters were devising them behind a "veil of ignorance."[4] That is, the drafters do not know what their own situation will be in the polity. They do not know whether they will be rich or poor, male or female, heterosexual or homosexual. If you were behind the veil of ignorance, would you be willing to deny equal rights to gay couples? This is not an entirely speculative enterprise. If you are heterosexual and desire to have children, are you willing to sacrifice the mental health of a potential gay child in order to adopt a double standard based on sexual orientation? Are you willing to press that child toward a greater chance of committing suicide?

THE INSTABILITY OF THE DOUBLE STANDARD

Gay people did not create the idea of sexual orientation. The ideas of heterosexuality and homosexuality were for the most part created by self-styled heterosexuals (Carl Westphal, Havelock Ellis, and Sigmund Freud and his followers). The ideas were a big hit in America in the early twentieth century. One effect they had was to divide the citizenry into two groups: the "normal" heterosexual group and a "perverted" homosexual group. In the middle part of the twentieth century the law ruthlessly persecuted the latter group and contributed to its social isolation. The goal of the law was, bluntly, to eradicate homosexuals.

At the height of the law's assault (the 1950s) the persecuted group began an organized resistance to legal and social persecution. The homophile movement represented a new consciousness among those who had been singled out for opprobrium, a consciousness that included the following premises: We are good people, we are being asked to compromise our identities for no neutral reason, and we are going to stand up as a group to oppose this unfair treatment. The law was generally unresponsive to this petition. Gay liberation movements following the 1969 Stonewall riots were more militant in their insistence on equal treatment. Thousands of people "came out" as gay. We have organized into hundreds of political action groups, and we are determined. How should the law respond to a group that is no longer willing to tolerate the double standard?

One response is to dismiss the group as a cultural joke. This was long the law's response to women's demands for equal rights. The problem with this strategy is that it depends on denial; once the subordinated group is too important or numerous to be denied, a strategy of ridicule collapses. Once women became well organized and insistent against double standards of sex and gender, the law began to relent and formal inequalities came tumbling down. Another strategy is to try to crush the group. That was the philosophy of the McCarthy era toward homosexuals, and of the South toward African Americans demanding an end to apartheid. The American people do not have the stomach for group destruction without tangible evidence that the group threatens the nation or its people. And if the group being targeted for destruction is robust, a genocidal approach creates enormous anger. There is every reason to believe that group anger cannot be contained by a political system. If the anger blows up against the dominant group, it might yield a synergy of anger and hatred that is very destructive of the polity.

From the viewpoint of the polity as a whole, is a double standard of rights and duties rational? Consider the following statement of political philosophy:

> [I]n view of the Constitution, in the eye of the law, there is in this country no superior, dominant, ruling class of citizens. There is no caste here. Our Constitution . . . neither knows nor tolerates classes among citizens. In respect of civil rights, all citizens are equal before the law. . . .
>
> . . . [More than two hundred] millions of [heterosexuals] are in no danger from the presence here of [five to twenty] millions of [gay people]. The destinies of the two [groups], in this country, are indissolubly linked together, and the interests of both require that the common government of all shall not permit the seeds of . . . hate to be planted under the sanction of law. What can more certainly arouse . . . hate, and more certainly create and perpetuate a feeling of distrust . . ., than state enactments, which in fact proceed on the ground that [gay] citizens are so inferior and degraded that they cannot be allowed to [participate in institutions] occupied by [heterosexual] citizens.

This statement of political philosophy is adapted [with bracketed inserts] from Justice John Harlan's dissenting opinion in *Plessy v. Ferguson*,[5] the case that upheld racial apartheid. As Professor Philip Frickey originally pointed out to me, the objections to racial apartheid that resonate today parallel objections to what I call "the apartheid of the closet," the double standard applied to gay citizens.

America's denial of marriage to same-sex couples is multiply destructive. On the one hand, it formally announces, and its defenders confirm, that gay couples are so "inferior and degraded" that they cannot participate in an institution that welcomes heterosexual felons and fiends. This is needlessly divisive and insulting. The destinies of gays and straights are "indissolubly linked together, and the interests of both require that the common government of all shall not permit the seeds of . . . hate to be planted under the sanction of law." On the other hand, the prohibition of same-sex marriage denies our society the opportunity to establish connections between gay and straight people.

EQUAL CITIZENSHIP IN THE RESPONSIBLE STATE

A final matter deserves attention. A lot of Americans find lesbian and gay couples disgusting, and no amount of argument will change their attitudes. How should the state deal with people who dislike one another? In my view, the state should neither encourage nor tolerate intergroup discrimination. The only productive way is to tell each group that the state will treat both with strict equality and will not tolerate intrusions by one group into the other's liberties.

Consider an analogy Justice Antonin Scalia has made.[6] He analogizes the state to a family with lots of children. The children will bicker and jockey for position within the family, and some of the children will not like one another. The father of nine children, Justice Scalia wisely advises parents: Keep order in the family, and for God's sake apply the rules with a sense of strict equality. If one child is treated either more or less favorably as a formal matter, there will be hell to pay. The duty of the parents, like the duty of the state, is to announce formal rules and then apply them with strict neutrality. An underlying assumption of this regime of rules is that every child is valued and no child is treated as more valuable than the others. This parallels Justice Harlan's dissenting message in *Plessy*: Do not create a caste system, and do not treat one group differently from the others.

How does the family, or the state, deal with bickering? A few of the children might strongly dislike a gay sibling (this example is not from Justice Scalia). Good parents, in my view, will not side with the homophobic children. Such a response risks destruction of the persecuted child, which violates the most basic precepts of parenthood. It also threatens the health of the family unit because it creates resentment among the gay-friendly children and encourages an unhealthy intolerance among the children generally. Good parents will try to keep peace among the children and to teach them to communicate and cooperate productively. They might try to have each child understand the viewpoint of the others and to instill in them a "live and let live" attitude. Most important, parents should back up their words with action, setting rules that apply with scrupulous equality to all the children, including rules keeping the children from hurting one another.

Three grown children want to get married. The parents are delighted with one marriage: A son wants to marry a woman the parents consider highly desirable. The parents are not delighted with the other two marriages: A daughter wants to marry a man the parents do not like, and another daughter wants to marry a woman. Should the parents denounce the latter two children and embrace only the first? While a natural impulse, it is also immature. Parents can exercise moral suasion and provide information to their grown children, but at some point they have to let go—or even learn from their children. Bless all three marriages and hope that you have taught your children well enough that they can make good judgments. You are sure to be surprised. The marriage that privately delights parents often turns out much worse than ones parents feel are unwise.

As Justice Scalia argues, the good state must be like the good parent. It must protect every citizen in a fair and equal way, and it must invade no citizen's liberty just because he or she is unpopular. Required by Justice Scalia's analogy is the conclusion that the good state will allow its gay citizens to marry on the same terms as its straight citizens. Justice as well as law requires nothing less.

APPENDIX

Letters from the Faithful on the
Legal Recognition of Same-Sex Marriage

This appendix excerpts selected letters collected by the plaintiffs in *Dean v. District of Columbia*, Docket No. CA 90-13892 (District of Columbia Superior Court). All of the letters were written during the summer of 1991 to the Honorable Shellie Bowers, the trial judge in that case, and all were filed as part of the public record in the case, both at the trial level and on appeal. I have edited the letters to identify the authors and their affiliation at the beginning of each letter and to delete extraneous matter.

Reverend Elder Troy D. Perry

Universal Fellowship of Metropolitan Community Churches
Los Angeles, California

I am President of the Universal Fellowship of Metropolitan Community Churches. Our denomination is listed in *The Yearbook of American & Canadian Churches*, published by the National Council of Churches of Christ in the U.S.A.

Our Church's clergy are authorized to conduct Holy Unions for same-sex couples worldwide. Theologically, our definition of marriage is defined as a covenant relationship between two individuals. Our definition of marriage does include same-sex couples, and we bless those relationships.

Four months ago I received a copy of *National Geographic Magazine* which had an article on the State of Virginia. Included in the article was a photograph of the Episcopal Bishop of that state blessing the hounds for the fox hunt which was taking place that day. If the Christian Church can bless the hounds for a hunt, then surely the Christian Church can bless the relationship of two individuals who are in love.

Our Church has been performing Holy Unions for same-sex couples since 1968. I, personally, have performed over 1000. Our denomination probably performs about 2000 of these ceremonies each year. Enclosed please find a copy of one type of liturgy (as with most clergy, I have several) that I have used, myself, to perform a Holy Union.

SERVICE OF HOLY UNION

[Opening Song]

Dearly beloved, we are gathered together here in the sight of God and in the face of this company to join together these two (women/men) in Holy Union; which is an honorable estate, instituted of God, and therefore is not by any to be entered into unadvisedly or lightly; but reverently, discreetly, advisedly, soberly, and in the fear of God. Into this holy estate these two persons present come now to be joined. If any person can show us cause why they may not be joined together, let them speak or else hereafter forever hold their peace.

I require and charge you both, as you will answer at the day of judgement when the secrets of all hearts shall be disclosed, that if either of you know any impediment, why you may not be joined together in Holy Union, you do now confess it. For be well assured, that if any persons are joined together otherwise than as God's word does allow, their union is not binding.

Let us pray . . .

[Name], do you promise, with God's help, to live together with [Name] in Union. Will you love (her/him) comfort (her/him) honor and keep (her/him) in sickness and in health so long as there is love?

(Response: I will.)

[Name], do you promise, with God's help, to live together with [Name] in Union. Will you love (her/him) comfort (her/him) honor and keep (her/him) in sickness and in health so long as there is love?"

(Response: I will.)

[Song]

We are reminded in Scripture of the story of two women who confessed their love one to the other. In the Hebrew Scriptures we read the story of Ruth and her words to Naomi when she said, "Intreat me not to leave thee or to return from following after thee; for whither thou goest, I will go; and where thou lodgest, I will lodge; thy people shall be my people and thy God my God. Where thou diest, will I die, and there will I be buried; the Lord do so to me, and more also, if ought but death part thee and me." Ruth and Naomi stuck together through great adversity. They traveled a long distance to stay together, looked after each other when they were hungry and protected each other from danger. They expressed their love through physical affection in kissing and holding each other (Ruth 1:9, 11). They respected family and community customs and still retained the integrity of their love.

In 1978, Kate Millett said in Los Angeles: " . . . I would like us to act with the memory and the power of our passion, all the power of our many loves, all the times you made it and it was good. This is your experience—be proud of it. It is what has made you alive, what had made your life even happen, so that you didn't almost live, so that you didn't not live. This even, through all the tortuous tunnels of love. How really difficult it has been to survive against, to maintain this love against, all that pressure—all that pressure in the other person, in ourselves, in the great world around us, strangling us. This has been our energy, our force, our strength, our power. They had made it hell, and we made it beautiful. Never forget the nights of your love and the days of working for its freedom, its expansion to fill the world with the roses of those moments out of time. An army of lovers make a revolution. If a revolution is music ultimately, and not war, an army of lovers not only can't fail, but they could convert revolution into music, into the power of Eros. In fact what was it we wanted to bring into this place, if it wasn't love. . . ."

[Homily]

[The couple recites their own vows to each other. The minister requests rings and says a prayer over them; then gives the ring to the first party and has them repeat after him]:

> I give you this ring as a token of our covenant, vowing to live in close friendship and love and to strive for fuller knowledge of your being and to care for you above all others. I pledge myself to love you even as I love myself. May God be between me and thee forever.

For as much as [names of partners] have consented together in Holy Union and witnessed the same before God and this company, and thereto have given and pledged their vows, each to the other, and have declared the same by exchanging rings and joining hands, I declare that they are joined together in Holy Union. In the name of God the Creator. Amen.

God the Creator bless, preserve, and keep you; the Lord mercifully with favor look upon you, and fill you with all spiritual benediction and grace; that you may so live together in this life, that in the world to come you may have life everlasting. Amen.

The Reverend Scott W. Alexander

Director, Office of Gay and Lesbian Concerns
Unitarian Universalist Association
Boston, Massachusetts

I write you . . . as an official of the Unitarian Universalist Association, which has long sought to support and nurture gay and lesbian couples and families. . . . [Our] religious denomination, which is one of the oldest in America, has for the past twenty years been working proactively in our congregations and societies to ensure that gay and lesbian individuals and couples receive the same rights and affirmation that are universally assumed for heterosexual persons.

[In] the document entitled "Resolutions on Lesbian, Gay Men, and Bisexuals" in 1984 our General Assembly (which is the governing body of our denomination representing all our congregations) voted to affirm the growing practice in our religious movement to conduct services of holy union for gay and lesbian couples. Since then, such services have become widely and commonly performed in our congregations and ministry. Unitarian Universalist congregations and ministers have sanctified thousands of gay and lesbian partnerships with union services and have welcomed these families into our churches, where they receive the same support and affirmation a heterosexual couple might expect.

While such unions are not yet recognized by civil authorities, our church recognizes and sanctifies them with the same authority and affirmation we do for a heterosexual marriage. The only difference in our tradition is that when the union being performed is between a heterosexual man and woman, the minister conducting the service is obliged to sign a marriage license and return it to local authorities. Unitarian Universalists are working in our society to ensure that someday gay and lesbian couples will receive the same recognition and support of their committed, caring, and loving relationships. We of the Unitarian Universalist Association have followed the case over which you are now presiding with great interest, and sincerely hope that the union of Craig Dean and Patrick Gill can be formally affirmed by the District of Columbia. . . .

The Reverend John H. Mack

Pastor, First Congregational United Church of Christ
Washington, D.C.

. . . Perhaps the first thing to be said is that the Bible is not much concerned with marriage. It is, however, consumed with the issue of love. In marriage services there are two scriptures which are most commonly used. The Hymn of Love from First Corinthians, chapter 13, is actually an instruction written by Paul to the whole church in Corinth, instructing them on the subject of love in the church and the community, not romantic love. The second most commonly used scripture in weddings is from the book of Ruth, chapter 1 ["Entreat me not to leave you . . ."]. This statement of dedication in love is given by a woman to her mother-in-law, a same-sex love relationship which the entire book celebrates.

There are other references to marriage in the Bible, of course. Not as many as most people expect. And most of them are so bound in cultural mores which no longer apply that the modern couple finds them certainly uninspiring, as well us unusable. Virtually all churches have dropped Paul's admonition for wives to obey their husbands, for instance.

The critical biblical chapter on this topic is Genesis 1, which I take the liberty of quoting:

> In the beginning God created the heavens and the earth. The earth was without form and void, and darkness was upon the face of the deep; and the Spirit of God was moving over the face of the waters . . . (v. 27). So God created man in his own image, in the image of God he created him; male and female he created them . . . (v. 31). And God saw everything that he had made, and behold it was very good.

Either God created people who find romantic love among those of their same gender or this condition is a fall from grace, a sin. Since the incidence of same-sex love occurs in all times and cultures in approximately the same proportions, many have come to consider it a part of God's creation. The attraction is inherent to the createdness of each person.

The realm of sin, in biblical terms, has to do with those areas over which we have some control. Most notable in the Bible is the fidelity one exhibits in relationship to God and to one's fellow humans. Therefore, religious and societal ethics have to do with fidelity in love. Is this not what marriage is about?

There are those who will pick a small text here or there, interpret it completely out of context, so trying to make "God" speak in inflexible categories about subjects which were clearly of little import to our great ancestors in the faith. There are more texts in Leviticus on religious ritual laws, to which hardly anyone pays any attention except for reasons of anthropology, than there are on same-sex love relationships.

In my opinion, it is extremely easy to interpret the profound teachings of our religious scripture to apply to same-sex relationships. It is extremely difficult to find clear condemnation of them within the religious literature. And the systemic persecution of those who find romantic love with a person of the same sex violates virtually every major law and teaching of both Judaism and Christianity.

For too long we in the religious communities and we in positions of authority have demanded that this form of love exist outside the bounds of laws and ethics. Untold numbers have been destroyed as a result. That we are now seeing same-sex couples asking that the blessing of the church and the covenantal laws of society be applied to them is a wonderful stride forward toward the kind of loving, humane society which Jesus called "the kingdom of God." I hope I live to see it occur. Presently only the very best and the very strongest couples are able to survive, intact, in this atmosphere that mitigates so forcefully against fidelity.

The last verse of Paul's Hymn to Love says that faith, hope and love abide—these three—but the greatest is love. I, as a minister of this book, argue that we are all created in God's image, that God is pleased with creation, and that our mission is to be good stewards of God's love both for the world and for each of us. . . .

Father James P. Mallon, Ph.D., C.A.C.

Dignity Philadelphia
Philadelphia, Pennsylvania

The following is an attempt to present some relevant data and reflection regarding the theological basis for same-gender unions. I myself, an ordained Roman Catholic priest, have presided at several same-gender unions and consider them to be appropriate and graced when entered into by mature, loving, and honest persons. . . .

Since the close of Vatican II, and animated by its directives for renewal, much Catholic theological reflection has been given to the subject of human sexuality. Previously one might have concluded that the last word had been uttered and all discussion would be confined to how best to implement the "traditional teaching". . . . Clearly and simply, human sexuality and human genitality were suspect. An acceptable justification for sexual gratification was procreation, but possible offspring would require stable nurturing and formation as might be found in the permanent and binding commitment between the parents. . . . Genital intimacy could be justified between a committed couple so long as any such intimacy did not deliberately preclude the possibility of pregnancy.

This preoccupation with justifying any expression [of] genitality was so pervasive that marriage became codified accordingly. It was the only acceptable status in which human genitality could be expressed without serious sin. But even in marriage serious sin could only be avoided if no deliberate exclusion of pregnancy was attempted.

The preoccupation was carried still further, and a valid marriage required that the possibility of offspring was not precluded by intent or by physical condition. The circle was complete. Procreation had at first been considered the acceptable justification for genital expression in a committed relationship and now an openness to procreation became the only legitimate "excuse" for entering such a relationship. The theological reason which would justify genital activity became the only finality which could validate a marriage. From this perspective of procreation, it "naturally" follows that only a man and a woman can be married.

. . . It is because of this limited perspective that any consideration of same-gender relationships has been deemed unacceptable because contradictory to "traditional" church teaching. . . .

[Vatican] II's *Gaudium et Spes* (Pt. II, ch. 1) in the context of reflections on "The Dignity of Marriage and the Family" presents the outlines for developing a Catholic theology of human sexuality as it reaches beyond the confines of the previous "traditional" position:

> [But] marriage is not merely for the procreation of children; its nature as an indissoluble compact between two people and the good of the children demand that the mutual love of the partners be properly shown, that it should grow and mature. Even in cases where despite the intense desire of the spouses there are no children, marriage still retains its character of being a whole manner and communion of life and preserves its value and indissolubility.

The essence of marriage in recent church documents has been defined at different times as an intimate partnership, a community of love, a conjugal covenant, a mutual gift of two persons. For this very reason an acceptable definition of marriage is "the ultimate form of friendship achievable by sexually attracted persons" (*Dimensions of Human Sexuality*, p. 130). Such a definition does not require heterosexual orientation. As a matter of fact, reproduction is neither necessary nor feasible for every union and thus it is not essential to every marriage.

As in the case of a heterosexual marriage, so also with regards to a same-gender union, relationship and activity are much wider than mere genitality. Heretofore it would seem that theological reflection was obsessed with genitality. Currently the person(s) have a right to consideration for what they are rather than merely for what they might do.

A lesbian or gay couple enter into relationship and by that union they seek to "sustain each other, heal each other and help each other to grow. Insofar as they do this they make real for each other the work of the sustaining Father, of the redeeming and healing Son, of the transforming Spirit. A truly Christian vision [of this] can be found in the person of Christ, accepting, caring, reconciling, healing; calling and challenging, suffering and enduring, trusting and persevering—and all for love" (Bishops of England and Wales Secretariat, *Pastoral Care of Marriage and Family Life*).

Recent documents issued from Rome and the U.S. Catholic Bishops have consistently acknowledged the homosexual person's right to an intimate, lasting, supportive, and maturing friendship. Therefore Dignity Philadelphia has a policy and a procedure for same-gender unions. The Philadelphia chapter offers counseling for the couple as they prepare for commitment, the chapter furnishes guidelines for the couple as they prepare for commitment, the chapter furnishes guidelines the couple may follow in formulating their own liturgical ceremony, and the chapter prides itself in being a community in which the couple may express publicly their love for each other. I myself have officiated at several of these commitment ceremonies.

Rabbi Yoel H. Kahn

Congregation Sha'ar Zahav
San Francisco, California

THE *KEDUSHAH* OF HOMOSEXUAL RELATIONSHIPS[a]

. . . [I]f the goal of Jewish life is to live in *kedushah* (sanctity), can we sanctify and bless homosexual relationships without compromising

---

[a]This was a paper presented at the Central Conference of American Rabbis, Cincinnati, Ohio, on May 26, 1989. The paper was published in the *Central Conference of American Rabbis Yearbook* (1990).

the integrity of our tradition? If we do wish to bless these relationships, can we reconcile this new stand with the historical Jewish
teaching in favor of heterosexual, procreative marriage as the normative and ideal form of Jewish family life? . . . We will examine this
question in relation to God, Torah and Israel.

GOD

I begin with the most fundamental yet unanswerable question: What
does God want of us? As a liberal Jew, I am usually reluctant to assert
that I know precisely what "God wants." For me to begin by stating
that "God calls us to affirm the sanctity of homosexual relationships"
(a statement I believe to be true) would be to assert a privileged claim
as little open to dispute as the counter-assertion by Rabbi David
Bleich that these relationships today remain *"to'evah"* (an abomination).[b] How would one respond to such an argument?

Thus, although our assertion of what God wants properly begins
our debate, in fact it cannot. Our conclusions about God's expectations of us in a particular matter develop against the background of
our unfolding, wider understanding of what God summons us to
do—rooted in what we know about God and God's nature. In the
foreground is all that we have learned from the scientific disciplines,
from universal ethics, from Jewish tradition, and from our own
prayerful conscience. It is when they touch, where the background
of what we have already learned of God's expectations of us and
God's nature meets foreground of knowledge, prayer, and conscien-
tious reflection about a subject, that we may discern God's will.

My teacher Eugene Borowitz writes that he does not hear a clear
message from God about homosexuality, as he has in other areas.[c] I
differ from Rabbi Borowitz. I believe that we can hear and affirm
what God expects of us in this matter. My understanding of what
God wants emerges from the background of God's justice and compassion, and is shaped in the foreground by religious interpretation

[b]J. David Bleich, *Judaism and Healing: Halakhic Perspectives,* 69 (New York: Ktav, 1981).

[c]Eugene B. Borowitz, "On Homosexuality and the Rabbinate, a Covenantal Response," in *Homosexuality, the Rabbinate, and Liberal Judaism: Papers Prepared for the Ad-Hoc Committee on Homosexuality and the Rabbinate,* 2 (New York: Central Conference of American Rabbis, 1989).

of the insights of modern science. It is this foreground which has changed in recent years and leads me to dissent from the teachings of our received tradition.

The overwhelming consensus of modern science—in every discipline—is that homosexual relations are as "natural" to us as heterosexuality is. Now, to call something "natural" is a descriptive act; what occurs in nature is not inherently good or bad. Assigning of meaning is a religious act. I, along with many others, have come to recognize sexual orientation as a primary, deep part of the human personality, inseparably bound up with the self. Science does not know what creates homosexual attraction in some people, heterosexual attraction in others; yet today we recognize that some people can only be fulfilled in relationships with people of the same sex. What do we say to them? What does God expect of them and of us?

I do not believe that God creates in vain. Deep, heartfelt yearning for companionship and intimacy is not an abomination before God. God does not want us to send the gays and lesbians among us into exile—either cut off from the Jewish community or into internal exile, living a lie for a lifetime. I believe that the time has come, I believe that God summons us to affirm the proper and rightful place of the homosexual Jew—and her or his family—in the synagogue and in the Jewish people. . . .

TORAH

When we confront the text honestly, we face a twofold challenge: first, we must dissent from an explicit Biblical injunction which has been in force until modern times. Now, dissenting from Leviticus has not been an obstacle for us before; Reform Judaism has long abandoned the Biblical and rabbinic proscriptions in the area of ritual purity in marriage. Robert Kirschner . . . argues convincingly that the Biblical and rabbinic injunctions forbidding male homosexual acts are no longer applicable to the situation of homosexuals today.[d]

---

[d]Robert Kirschner, "*Halakhah* and Homosexuality: A Reappraisal," 37 *Judaism*: 4 (Fall 1988); reprinted in *Homosexuality, the Rabbinate, and Liberal Judaism: Papers Prepared for the Ad-Hoc Committee on Homosexuality and the Rabbinate*, 2 (New York: Central Conference of American Rabbis, 1989).

It is important for us to realize that the Biblical authors proscribed particular sexual acts, the motivation for which they could only understand as sinful.

We begin from an entirely different perspective than our ancestors did. If we grant that homosexual acts are not inherently sinful, then can a homosexual relationship be sanctified? When two Jews, graduates of our schools, alumni of our camps and youth movements, members of our synagogues, promise to establish a Jewish home, pledge to live together in faithfulness and integrity, and ask for God's blessing and our own on their union, is this *to'evah* or is it *kedushah*?

Do we look at this committed and loving couple from an I–It perspective, which sees a particular act and condemns it, or with I–Thou understanding, which affirms the propriety of sexual intimacy in the context of holistic and enduring relationship? Let me be clear: I do not propose merely that we politely overlook the historical Jewish teaching condemning homosexual behavior but that we explicitly affirm its opposite: the movement from *to'evah* to *kedushah*. This transformation in our Jewish standard, from a specific act to the evaluation of the context in which acts occur, seems to me entirely consistent with Reform Jewish thought and practice.

Many are prepared to affirm that for some Jews homosexuality is the proper expression of the human need for intimacy and fulfillment. Still, I know that some are reluctant to endorse *kiddushin* (sanctified covenantal union, usually translated "marriage") for same-sex couples because these relationships apparently disregard the historical and continuing Jewish preference for what Eugene Borowitz and others have called "the procreative family." How can we grant Jewish sanctity, they ask, to a form of family which by its essence precludes procreation, a primary purpose of *kiddushin*?

My reply has three parts. First, we cannot hold homosexual families to a higher standard than we do heterosexual ones. We do not require proof of fertility or even an intention to become parents before we are willing to marry a heterosexual couple. Is the homosexual couple who uses adoption, artificial insemination, or other means to fulfill the Jewish responsibility to parent so different from the heterosexual family who does the same?

Second, does *kiddushin* require procreation? While Judaism has always had a preference for procreative marriage, our tradition has also validated the possibility that some unions will not produce children. *Halachah* states that a woman who does not bear children after ten years can be divorced by her husband. But the evidence that his law was reluctantly or negligibly enforced is precisely the type of historical example Reform responsa often cite to support the explicit expansion of a value we find implicit in our historical tradition. The Jewish tradition has never insisted that the sole purpose of sexual expression is procreation, as evidenced by the numerous rabbinic discussions on the *mitzvah* of sexual intimacy and pleasure.[e]

Third, the situation of the gay and lesbian Jews among us points out the need for new categories in our thinking. Reform Judaism is committed to affirming the responsibility of the individual. Can we not teach that a heterosexual relationship is the proper form of *kedushah* for many and a homosexual relationship may be a proper form for others? Can we not create a plurality of expressions of convenantal responsibility and fulfillment and teach that different Jews will properly fulfill their Jewish communal and religious responsibilities in different ways?[f]

Finally, I would like to introduce into this discussion of Torah a different text than those which have shaped our debate so far. Mine is a classic Jewish text, the record of a uniquely Jewish form of revelation—the text of our history. The history of our people, writ large, has been a continuing source of revelation. For our own generation the recollection of events that we witnessed has assumed the force of Torah, and makes demands upon us as a people and as individual Jews. But our history is not only writ large—history is also written in the small, daily events of our lives. . . .

When I arrived to assume my pulpit in San Francisco four years ago, deep down I still believed that gay and lesbian relationships and families, were, somehow, not as real, not as stable, not as committed

[e]See David Feldman, *Marital Relations, Birth Control and Abortion in Jewish Law,* chapters 2, 4, 5, esp. pp. 65–71, 103–105 (New York: Schocken, 1968).

[f]Eugene Borowitz, *Liberal Judaism,* 448–449 (New York: Union of American Hebrew Congregations, 1984). This section ("Accepting the Single Jew") begins, "It will not do, however, to give the impression that one must be married to be a good Jew."

as heterosexual marriages. I could tell many stories of what I have learned since. There are the two women who have lived together for many years without familial or communal support, who have endured long distances and job transfers, because employers thought them both single and admitting their homosexuality would have endangered their livelihoods, women who have cared for each other without benefit of insurance coverage or health benefits or any legal protection. They came to me one Friday night and simply asked: "Rabbi, this is our twenty-fifth anniversary, will you say a blessing?"

Mine is a synagogue living with AIDS. I have been humbled by the unquestioning devotion of the man who, for more than two years, went to work each morning, calling intermittently throughout the day to check in on his partner, and spent each night comforting, talking, preparing meals, and waking in the middle of the night to carry his loved one to the bathroom. Who would have imagined, when they first chatted twelve years before, that their life together would take this path? The loving caregiver stayed at his partner's side throughout the period of his illness and until his death.

These many lives have taught me about the possibility of enduring loyalty, the meaning of commitment, and the discovery of reservoirs of strength in the face of unimaginable pain and suffering. If the covenant people are summoned to be God-like, then these Jews live their lives *b'tzelem Elohim* and these relationships are surely of true covenantal worth. *Kiddushin* is, in Eugene Borowitz's words, "Judaism's preferred condition in which to work out one's destiny. . . . Because it is a unique fusion of love and demand, of understanding and judgment, of personal giving and receiving, nothing else can teach us so well the meaning of covenant." If "[i]t is the situation where we are most thoroughly challenged to be a Jew and where . . . we may personally exemplify what it means to be allied with God in holiness," then the Torah scroll of lived history records the *kedushah* of these relationships.

ISRAEL

I would like to conclude with a word about *kiddushin* and the Jewish people. I have been repeatedly asked, If we elevate homosexual families to an equal status with heterosexual families, will we not undermine the already precarious place of the traditional family? I do not believe that encouraging commitment, stability, and openness undermines the institution of family—it enhances it. At present, many gay and lesbian Jews are estranged from the synagogue, the Jewish community, and their families of origin because of continued fear, stigma, and oppression. Welcoming gay and lesbian families into the synagogue will strengthen all our families by bringing the exiles home and by reuniting children, parents, and siblings who have been forced to keep their partners and innermost lives hidden. *K'lal yisrael* (the community and unity of the Jewish people) is strengthened when we affirm that there can be more than one way to participate in the Covenant.

Reverend Carla B. Gorell

Westminster Presbyterian Church
Washington, D.C.

. . . As Executive Director of Food & Friends, which provides home-delivered meals to people with AIDS, I have the privilege of working with the gay and lesbian community. This ministry has given me the opportunity to know hundreds of gay people and their families. I have experienced their hospitality, shared their joys, and heard their concerns. I know the positive contributions gay and lesbian people are making to the wider community. And I see them living their daily lives with courage, caring, and moral integrity.

I receive occasional requests to perform a religious ceremony for gay men or lesbians who have made a commitment to live together as life-partners. The first of these requests led me to study the meaning of gay and lesbian unions as they relate to the Bible, Reformed theology, and our denomination's constitution. In this search I have found no prohibition against a religious ceremony to bless the solemn decision by gay couples to take vows to enter into a faithful covenant relationship. These long-term relationships function like a marriage between a man and a woman, except that the partners were born with an orientation to love and to bond with a member of their own sex.

Condemnation of homosexuality has been based on a literal interpretation of a few texts from the Bible, which have a particular historical context. It took long experience and self-examination for the church to confess that it has used Scripture to perpetuate the injustices of racism, sexism, and anti-Semitism. Today, a growing number of clergy from mainline denominations throughout the country agree that new knowledge about the etiology of human sexuality and modern Biblical scholarship makes it impossible to perpetuate discrimination based on old interpretations of Biblical texts.

Unfortunately, homophobia in the church and society is a barrier to changing public opinion. The question is, When will our civil and religious systems take the lead to overcome unseasoned prejudice, as was necessary in earlier movements for African American and women's rights? . . .

Reverend William H. Carey

Pastor, Lighthouse Apostolic Church
Schenectady, New York

. . . We believe that marriage is based upon an agreement between two people that they will live together as one and be faithful to each other. We feel that such an agreement, in and of itself, constitutes a marriage and that public ceremonies, receptions, etc., are simply a recognition of a relationship that already exists. The concept of marriage licenses, although not biblical, does not violate biblical principle, nor does it, in our opinion, alter the basic definition of marriage.

From a biblical perspective, we find that an agreement of this type existed between the prophet Daniel and Ashpenaz, the prince of the Babylonian eunuchs. We find no biblical evidence that either of them ever violated that agreement by marrying or being intimate with anyone else.

Recent historical research by the Catholic scholar Boswell has indicated that until around the thirteenth century the Roman Catholic Church routinely performed wedding ceremonies for homosexual couples. This practice ceased only when the social tide turned against homosexuals.

As can be seen above, the concept of marriage between persons of the same sex is not a new one. From my own personal experience as a minister, I can say without hesitation that such marriages are quite common today, the government's refusal to recognize them notwithstanding. I currently pastor a small Apostolic Pentecostal church in the city of Schenectady. Schenectady has a population of somewhere between 60,000 and 70,000. This city could hardly be compared to San Francisco or New York City. And yet, in this medium-sized city in upstate New York I perform between ten and fifteen wedding ceremonies for same-sex couples each year. My colleagues in other cities of comparable size around the nation inform me that the number of such unions that they perform is similar. I realize that New York State won't recognize the marriages I perform, but I believe with all my heart that God does.

It may be asked why a fundamentalist minister would perform such ceremonies, given the usual fundamentalist stance of opposition to homosexuality. There is more than one answer to this question. First, I find by reading the scriptures in their original languages that they do not express the antihomosexual sentiment that the English translations do. I therefore do not believe that God is, or ever was, anti-Gay. Secondly, in the past the homosexual community has been much accused of promiscuity. To a large extent this has been true. But when a group of people are forbidden to marry and are forced to hide their sexual orientation to protect jobs, housing, etc., we have little right to expect them to follow any type of moral standard of monogamy or celibacy. By performing weddings for same-sex couples, I offer them the opportunity to live according to a moral standard that many of them obviously do believe in. Finally, I perform these ceremonies because I have been convinced of the validity of love between persons of the same gender and find it to be a holy and powerful thing, no less holy and powerful than the love between a man and woman.

As is the case in any type of wedding, be it heterosexual or homosexual, the couple is offered some choice in the type of ceremony they wish to have. I do find, however, that the majority of couples I marry, whether two men, two women, or a heterosexual couple, opt for a standard ceremony. I use a modified version of an Episcopalian ceremony. The modifications include alteration of pronouns to match gender and the inclusion of more scripture, particularly the thirteenth chapter of Paul's first epistle to the Corinthian Church. One final note on the durability of homosexual marriages: Since I was ordained in 1981, the majority of couples I have married, both heterosexual and homosexual, are still together. I find no difference between types of couples when it comes to holding their marriages together. If they truly love each other and are willing and able to communicate with each other, they'll usually make it. . . .

Jay W. Wright

Clerk, Penn Valley Meeting of Friends
Kansas City, Missouri

As a spiritual family, we of Penn Valley Meeting affirm the validity of same-sex relationships and find within our hearts no cause for treating them in any different manner than heterosexual relationships. A same-sex marriage has taken place under the care of our Meeting and is considered both valid and sacred by consensus of our members.

We enclose our printed statement of belief upon these matters, and feel couples such as Craig Dean and Patrick Gill seek no special privileges, simply the rights supposedly guaranteed to us all as U.S. citizens. Equality of law under justice. We believe same-sex relationships and love must cease being denigrated and relegated to the bars, the baths, and the bushes. Now is the time to bring same-sex love into the home and welcome same-sex couples into the human family without prejudice and discrimination. . . .

PENN VALLEY MEETING OF FRIENDS
MINUTE ON MARRIAGE

Penn Valley Meeting of the Religious Society of Friends affirms the traditional Quaker concept of marriage as a special, committed relationship between two people who share their lives, a partnership between spiritual equals. We believe that such a partnership has religious dimensions and is appropriately solemnized in ceremony at an appointed meeting for worship before God and Friends. It is our belief that both the meeting and partners are nourished when a celebration of marriage takes place within the meeting and that this mutual nourishment continues.

We believe marriage is based upon a loving relationship and involves sharing on all levels—spiritual, physical, emotional, intellectual. Loving relationships are essential blocks in the foundation of the Society of Friends and undergird a just and peaceful society for all.

Penn Valley Meeting affirms the equal opportunity of all couples, including members of the same sex, to be married within the framework of the meeting process. We recognize and accept that some couples may prefer terminology other than "marriage" to describe their union. It is not the wish of the meeting to name the relationship, only to signify it.

Penn Valley Meeting recognizes the Certificate of Marriage signed by the couple and those present at the Ceremony as the only public expression necessary to certify the marriage. A couple united in marriage under the care of this meeting who wish to legally certify their union will be assisted by the oversight committee. At the present time, it would, according to the laws of Missouri, be necessary for one of these persons to be a member of the meeting.

In marriage, as in all aspects of life, it is our wish to recognize as fully as we can the Light Within us all through keeping open to the many reflections of that Light.

Approved by consensus
August 2, 1987

Denise Chrysler

Convenor, Worship & Pastoral Care Committee
Red Cedar Monthly Meeting of Friends
East Lansing, Michigan

. . . On March 6, 1988, the Red Cedar Monthly Meeting approved the following Minute at its Monthly Meeting for Worship for Business:

This Meeting offers to all persons our support and care for their relationships. We now affirm our willingness as a Meeting to hold celebrations of love and commitment under our care for both opposite sex and same-sex couples, in accordance with our traditional procedures, when one or both of those partners participate in our meeting community as members or attenders and share our religious experience. We want our meeting community to be a place for lesbians and gay men to express among us tenderness and affection toward partners and friends. We commit ourselves to such efforts and learnings as are required for this to happen.

At the time this Minute was approved, the Meeting was not yet clear on the use of the term *marriage* and the application of that term to both different-sex and same-sex relationships. Following Friends' procedures for decision making, consensus was reached regarding the use of the term *marriage,* and on June 2, 1989, at a special called Meeting for Worship for Business, the Meeting approved the following:

It is the sense of Meeting to provide procedures, support, and celebrations under the care of Meeting in accordance with usual Friends' practices, for all committed relationships of same-sex and different-sex couples, leaving it to the couple to request that the relationship be described as a Marriage Under the Care of the Meeting or by some other name.

Thus, as stated in the Minutes, quoted above, the Red Cedar Monthly Meeting treats same-sex and different-sex couples who ask for marriage under its care the same, following Friends traditional procedures for marriage for both. The Red Cedar Meeting recognizes marriages under its care fully and equally, whether the partners are of the same or of different sexes. Thus far, the Red Cedar Meeting has had one same-sex marriage under its care, which occurred in December 1989.

The only difference in treatment between same-sex and different-sex couples which may arise is whether a marriage license is completed and filed with the state of Michigan. Michigan law is unclear about same-sex marriage, defining marriage as simply "a civil contract" between consenting parties. This Meeting is not aware of litigation by a same-sex couple attempting to obtain recognition of their marriage by the state of Michigan. In the event that a same-sex couple seeking marriage under our Meeting's care should wish to pursue recognition of their marriage by the state of Michigan, the matter would be considered in accordance with Quaker process to help the couple become clear on their proposed course of action concerning the state and how our Meeting may assist or support them in such an endeavor.

Reverend Richard E. Stetler

Minister, Capitol Hill United Methodist Church
Washington, D.C.

. . . Please maintain absolute clarity that I am not speaking on behalf of the United Methodist Church. These are my personal thoughts which have distilled themselves through my experience of dealing with same sex relationships. . . .

The church is the slowest of all societal groups to react to change. The upside of that is that many of our values are timeless and are the ones historically which have held societies together during traumatic upheavals. Without the maintenance of commonly held values, individuals tend to develop their own under the heading of "enlightened self-interest," which have tended to produce chaos.

The downside is that on the cutting edge of change society has raised issues demanding decisions as is evidenced with *Roe v. Wade*. . . . We have arrived at a day where nearly any position can thoroughly be justified, tossing our traditional "right" and "wrong" values to the wind. The issues we face tomorrow will only increase in their complexity. Genetic engineering, euthanasia, and a host of new frontiers have caused society to ask questions of itself never before imagined. At the moment, mainline churches in the United States are in an identity crisis as they realize that many of the answers they have lack clarity and relevance to the issues on the cutting edges of tomorrow.

In considering homosexual unions, I could launch into an essay on what constitutes a wholesome relationship. The irony here is that many homosexual couples know and understand far more about commitment and the essential ingredients of a wholesome relationship than do their heterosexual counterparts.

In today's world such commitment not only has the pressures that all couples experience, but homosexual couples also have the added pressures placed on them by a rigid, judgmental society. We live in a society which has yet to become honest with itself concerning its understanding of sexual expression. Our beliefs are strong and quite verbal as evidenced by any number of highly visible personalities who have rapidly "fallen from grace" because of embarrassing relevations. Yet when we consider our daily habits and behavior, society speaks volumes about itself in countless other directions.

Society doesn't understand homosexuality, and there is little sign on the horizon that it desires to be educated about the matter. Most education requires an opened mind, and that mental state is not within the grasp of society at the moment. . . .

. . . Permit one example which is all too commonplace. A year ago, a colleague of mine watched two people's lives become torn apart by our legal system. One was dying of AIDS while the other— the caregiver—remained helpless to make any decisions on his lover's behalf because he was not considered "family." The caregiver struggled with agency after agency all to no avail. Finally, when the partner with AIDS died, his mate stood by while all the funeral arrangements were made by the biological family, arrangements which were against the deceased's desires. The family proceeded to take all of the deceased's belongings. All the caregiver wanted were mementos of their lives together, but the family, living out its denial, left him with nothing but memories. . . .

Jesus said that we will recognize whole people by the fruits they display in their daily lives (Matt. 7:16, 20), not by their gender preference in their relationships and not by some legal document which decrees their status as married. The burden of proof always rests with the individual, but society doesn't need to stand in the way and make life more difficult for what two people are very determined to do anyway. . . .

Reverend Jan Griesinger

Director, United Campus Ministry at Ohio University
Athens, Ohio

. . . I have been ordained in the United Church of Christ since 1970. I performed my first same-sex ceremony in 1974 in Dayton, Ohio.

Since that time I have performed two or three per year, most of them in this rural area of Appalachian Ohio. I have performed them in the college chapel, in local churches, and in private homes for gay and lesbian people of all ages, incomes, races. These couples have used the word *marriage* to refer to their ceremonies and understand it to be a permanent commitment which they would do legally if they were able.

The United Church of Christ has a denomination of 1.6 million people and over six thousand churches across the U.S. . . . Hundreds of our clergy are now performing such ceremonies, and many have been for over twenty years. Our denomination leaves such decisions to the conscience of each member of the clergy.

Our national denominational conference, called the General Synod, meeting in Washington, D.C., July 1–5, 1977, passed a motion which includes this statement: "Encourages the congregations of the United Church of Christ, assisted by Conferences and Instrumentalities, to study and experiment with liturgical rites to celebrate important events and passages in human experience and relationships of commitment between persons." The United Church of Christ has continued to state publicly its witness against laws which discriminate against lesbians and gay men. . . .

The Reverend Jack Seymour

Pastor, Chapel in the Woods
Upper Marlboro, Maryland

. . . Heterosexuals [when they are united in committed] relationships (when a man and woman wish to be legally united for a lifelong relationship) call the ceremony a marriage ceremony. Traditionally this is the only legal relationship recognized as valid. In the situation where two same-sex persons desire to mark their lifelong relationship, only what has been called a "Holy Union" and a "Gay Marriage" has had to suffice. This nonlegal relationship permits them to "be" together but not in the eyes of the state. As a result, a number of problems arise:

1. Many health benefits open only to a husband–wife relationship are closed to them.

2. In some cases where husband and wife can share certain legal and credit benefits, [those benefits] are not open for them.

3. A most critical matter arises regarding medical decisions and funeral decisions in which a person who has loved another for years finds that the parents of the one who is ill, or who has died, step in and make all final arrangements (when to conclude medical treatment, funeral arrangements, and where the person is to be buried).

Most of these matters can be understood by heterosexuals and even the most homophobic person should be able to feel sympathy, especially in item 3 above.

Legalization of "union" ceremonies means a great deal to homosexuals, not only for the needs and benefits above but so that family/friends/business associates and others will recognize them, too. . . .

Beyond all these considerations it is necessary to look at certain aspects of homosexuality:

1. It is generally accepted that homosexuality is not a "decided" act. A person is born with certain genes and proclivities regarding sexual matters. Indeed, many homosexuals, if given a choice, would become heterosexual. To put yourself in a state that homosexuals find themselves to be living with—social persecution, economic and religious persecution—would require the person to be insane. The reason for the insanity is from the legal and social standards imposed by a heterosexual society.

2. . . . [H]omosexuals have proved their creative abilities to the world in art, science, and all other aspects of living.

3. Why should homosexuals be deprived of their rights in this country, a country that goes to war over the rights of people in other lands yet discriminates against homosexuals in their own country? Countless numbers of homosexual men and women have served in their country's armed services (although anonymously). Homosexuals have been discriminated against in countless ways for no reason other than their sexuality.

It will not be possible to right all of the wrongs done to homosexuals by permitting them to marry, but it will be a step in the right direction.

Homosexuals do now observe their relationships before God, friends, and families in what is generally called a "Holy Union." Requirements vary but most persons conducting Holy Unions have general standards requiring persons to attend counseling sessions, to have known each other for a time (usually a year) and to have lived together (thus knowing each other better), to have demonstrated love and concern, and to be financially stable. I once counseled two women who desired to have such a ceremony when one of them, a woman who had been in a heterosexual marriage, said to me, "If I had to go through all this in my male–female marriage, I would never have gotten married!"

I have been performing Holy Unions for nearly ten years and have been impressed by a number of things:

1. Most couples entering into a Holy Union are doing so out of sincere love and affection for each other and they wish to give witness to this love in a *religious* (not civil) ceremony.

2. In this time of AIDS we find that persons who have had Holy Union ceremonies demonstrate love and affection through the illness and death of a loved one far more than in many heterosexual marriages. (It is truly a tragedy when the heterosexual parents of the one who has died do not permit the survivor to make burial plans and often invade their home and take away goods that both of them have worked for and shared together.)

The legalization of Homosexual Holy Unions or Marriages will not relieve many of the injustices to homosexuals but it would give more rights to homosexuals desiring to avail themselves of such services. One thing is certain: it would give homosexual couples more rights in relation to determinations needed in times of illness and death. Such recognition will alleviate unnecessary pain during these circumstances.

NOTES

Chapter 1. Civilizing Gays, Civilizing Straights

1. Letter from Warren Price, III, Hawaii Attorney General, to John C. Lewin, Director of Health (December 27, 1990), p. 2, quoting Zablocki v. Redhail, 434 U.S. 374, 386 (U.S. Supreme Court, 1978).
2. Jones v. Hallahan, 501 S.W.2d 588, 589 (Kentucky Court of Appeals, 1973), quoted in Price letter, p. 2.
3. Letter from Alvin T. Onaka, Assistant Chief and State Registrar, Office of Health Status Monitoring, to Genora Carios Dancel and Ninia Leilani Baehr (April 12, 1991).
4. A plurality opinion by Justice Steven Levinson (speaking only for himself and Chief Justice Ronald Moon) held that the state's denial of marriage licenses to same-sex couples is sex discrimination under the equal rights amendment to Hawaii's constitution. Baehr v. Lewin, 852 P.2d 44 (Hawaii Supreme Court, 1993). When the court clarified its mandate in response to the state's motion for reconsideration, newly appointed Justice Paula Nakayama joined the Levinson–Moon group, ibid., 74 (three of five Justices signed the order clarifying the proceedings on remand, consistent with the Levinson opinion), assuring a majority of the current court for the sex discrimination holding.
5. Plaintiffs' attorneys Foley and Evan Wolfson (of the Lambda Legal Defense and Education Fund, Inc.), co-counsel in the case, are optimistic that the state will be unable to justify its discrimination. See Evan Wolfson, "Crossing the Threshold: Equal Marriage Rights for Lesbians and Gay Men and the Intra-Community Critique," 21 *New York University Review of Law and Social Change* 567 (1994–1995).

219

6. Loving v. Virginia, 388 U.S. 1 (U.S. Supreme Court, 1967), discussed in chapters 5 and 6.

7. Zablocki v. Redhail, 434 U.S. 374 (U.S. Supreme Court, 1978), discussed in chapter 5.

8. Turner v. Safley, 482 U.S. 78 (U.S. Supreme Court, 1987), discussed in chapter 5.

Chapter 2. A History of Same-Sex Marriage

1. For an account of We'wha's life, see Will Roscoe, *The Zuni Man-Woman* (Albuquerque, NM: University of New Mexico Press, 1991).

2. For an account of Ifeyinwa's life, see Ifi Amadiume, *Male Daughters, Female Husbands: Gender and Sex in an African Society* (London: Zed Books, 1987).

3. For an account of Sergius and Bacchus, see John Boswell, *Same-Sex Unions in Pre-Modern Europe,* 146–156 (New York: Villard Books, 1994).

4. See David F. Greenberg, *The Construction of Homosexuality,* 130 (Chicago: University of Chicago Press, 1988).

5. Jacob Neusner, *Sifra: An Analytical Translation,* volume 3, p. 74 (Atlanta: Scholars Press, 1988), translating chapter 193 of "Parashat Ahare Mot Parashah." I am endebted to Yair Chamudat for bringing this material to my attention.

6. The account in text is drawn from David M. Halperin, *One Hundred Years of Homosexuality,* 81 (New York: Routledge, 1990).

7. This is the translation according to Jeffrey H. Tigay, *The Evolution of the Gilgamesh Epic* (Philadelphia: University of Pennsylvania Press, 1982).

8. See Greenberg, *Construction of Homosexuality,* 124–125.

9. Ibid. Several of the statutes are translated in Martha T. Roth, *Law Collections from Mesopotamia and Asia Minor* (Atlanta: Scholars Press, 1995).

10. Ephraim Neufeld, *The Hittite Laws,* 10 (London: Luzac, 1951).

11. This is the reading of John Boswell, *Christianity, Social Tolerance, and Homosexuality,* 20–21 and note 39 (Chicago: University of Chicago Press, 1980), who disputes the reading preferred by Neufeld, *Hittite Laws,* 10–11: "If a slave gives the bride-price to a free youth and takes him to dwell in his household as husband [of his daughter], no-one shall surrender him." The bracketed portion is an interpolation by Neufeld, who admits as much. Neufeld (p. 151) also reports that earlier scholars had interpreted § 36 as a state sanction for "homosexual" relations among slaves and that "such a relationship among free men did not require any special legal provisions." Boswell (pp. 20–21) rejects Neufeld's speculations as a strained effort by a modern historian to read his own prejudices into another culture's text. Boswell's reading, in turn, is rejected by Roth, *Mesopotamia and Asia Minor,* 222.

12. Quotations in the text are from *On Homosexuality: Lysis, Phaedrus, and Symposium* (Buffalo, NY: Prometheus Books, 1991, translated by Benjamin Jowett, with selected retranslation, notes, and introduction by Eugene O'Connor). Plato's views about sex are complicated by his *Laws*, which is ambivalent about same-sex attraction. See Eva Cantarella, *Bisexuality in the Ancient World*, 61–63 (New Haven, CT: Yale University Press, 1992, translated by Cormac Ó Cuilleanáin), and Gregory Vlastos, *Platonic Studies*, 40–41 (Princeton, NJ: Princeton University Press, 1981).

13. Kenneth J. Dover, *Greek Homosexuality*, 89–91 (London: Duckworth, 1978), argues for "common ingredients" between different-sex marriages and Greek same-sex relationships. For the latter he describes a formal "courtship" by the dominant party (the husband/man) toward the receptive party (the wife/boy), including the expectation that the receptive party will respond to advances coyly. As was often the case in a traditional marriage, the family was involved in the receptive party's decision on whether to accept the dominant party's advances. Both types of relationships met with social disapproval if sexual relations occurred outside of the accepted courtship-to-wedding-vow relationship.

14. Strabo, *The Geography* 10.4.21. H. L. Jones's translation, *The Geography of Strabo*, volume 5, 155–159 (London: W. Heinemann, 1917–1933), renders this as "peculiar customs." Boswell, *Same-Sex Unions*, 89 and note 175, renders the Greek more literally as "peculiar laws." In the text I follow Boswell's translation of the relevant passages.

15. Boswell, *Same-Sex Unions*, 189–190. See L. R. de Pogey-Castries, *Histoire de L'Amour Grec dans L'Antiquité*, 42–46 (Paris: Stendahl, 1930); Bernard Sergent, *Homosexuality in Greek Myth* (Boston: Beacon Press, 1986, translated by Arthur Goldhammer); and Mark Golden, "Slavery and Homosexuality at Athens," 38 *Phoenix* 308, 319 note 49 (1984).

16. Cantarella, *Bisexuality in the Ancient World*, 81–83.

17. Contrary to earlier belief, it is now clear that republican Rome did not prohibit same-sex relationships. See Cantarella, *Bisexuality in the Ancient World*, 106–114; Saara Lilja, *Homosexuality in Republican and Augustan Rome*, 130–131 (Helsinki: Societas Scientarium Fennica, 1983); and Paul Veyne, "Homosexuality in Ancient Rome," in Phillipe Ariès and André Béjin, editors, *Western Sexuality* (Oxford: B. Blackwell, 1985, translated by Anthony Foster).

18. Gaius Suetonius Tranquillus, *The Twelve Caesars*, 223 (Sporus), 224 (the freedman) (London: Penguin, 1957, translated by Robert Graves). Book 15 of Tacitus's *Annals* reports Nero's marriage to the freedman Pythagorus. See *The Complete Works of Tacitus*, 376 (New York: Modern Library, 1942, translated by Alfred John Church and William Jackson Brodribb and edited by Moses Hadas).

19. Dio Cassius, *Epitome*, book 62; Earnest Cary's translation, *Dio's Roman History*, volume 8, pp. 135–137 (London: W. Heinemann, 1914–1927). According to Dio, the Greeks celebrated "even to the extent of praying that legitimate children might be born of them" (*Epitome*, book 62.13; Cary translation, 159). Dio was not amused. Nero asked one of his associates if he approved of the marriage to Sporus. The associate replied, "You do well, Caesar, to keep the company of such wives. Would that your father had had the same ambition and lived with a similar consort!" (*Epitome*, book 62.28; Cary translation, 135–137). Dio liked that response. See also Edward Gibbon, *The Decline and Fall of the Roman Empire,* chapter 4 (London: Penguin, 1952, edited and abridged by Dero A. Saunders).

20. Elagabalus married Hierocles, but not before some nice palace intrigue. Zoticus was desired by the emperor because "in particular he greatly surpassed all others in the size of his private parts." Hierocles bribed the cup bearers to drug Zoticus to induce impotence. Hierocles thereby won the hand of the emperor (Dio Cassius, *Epitome*, book 80; Cary translation, volume 9, pp. 465–471).

21. Lampridius, *Antoninus Elagabalus*, book 11; David Magie's translation, *Scriptores Historiae Auguste*, volume 2, p. 129 (London: W. Heinemann, 1922–1932). Lampridius's account of Elagabalus's same-sex marriage is in book 10; Magie's translation is on pp. 125–129.

22. See Royston Lambert, *Beloved and God: The Story of Hadrian and Antinous* (New York: Viking, 1984) and Marguerite Yourcenar, *Memoirs of Hadrian* (New York: Farrar, Straus, 1954).

23. Juvenal, *Satires*, book 2; G. G. Ramsey's translation, *Juvenal and Persius*, 132–135 (Cambridge: Harvard University Press, 1950). The reference is to the marriage of Gracchus.

24. Martial, *Epigrams*, book 7.42; Walter C. A. Ker's translation, 347–349 (Cambridge: Harvard University Press, 1950).

25. Translated in Boswell, *Same-Sex Unions*, 82.

26. The text is from the Theodosian Code 9.vii.3 and is translated in Greenberg, *Construction of Homosexuality*, 229. Cantarella, *Bisexuality in the Ancient World*, 175–176, argues that the statute only penalized passive anal sex.

27. The ancient sources in the text are discussed in Michel Foucault, *The Care of the Self*, 72–80 (New York: Vintage, 1986, translated by Robert Hurley, volume 3 of Foucault's *The History of Sexuality*).

28. See Peter Brown, *The Body and Society: Men, Women and Sexual Renunciation in Early Christianity* (New York: Columbia University Press, 1988).

29. *The Visigothic Code*, title V, § VI (Boston: Boston Book Co., 1910, edited and translated by Samuel P. Scott).

30. See the sources collected in Boswell, *Christianity, Social Tolerance and Homosexuality*, 186–194.

31. They are reported in William N. Eskridge, Jr., "A History of Same-Sex Marriage," 79 *Virginia Law Review* 1419 (1993), which has as an appendix my translation of one of the services of "spiritual brotherhood." In a public speech and in a telephone conversation with me in the early 1990s, the late John Boswell confessed that a priest gave him the critical leads for his book on *Same-Sex Unions*. Father Alexei was that priest.

32. For example, Pavel Florenskij, *La Colonna e il Fondamento della Verita*, 521–525 (Milan: Rosconi editore, 1974, translated into Italian by Pietro Modesto, introduction by Elemire Zolla). Boswell, *Same-Sex Unions*, 283–344, appends translations of a variety of liturgical ceremonies resembling the one in the text.

33. *Ritualae Graecorum Complectens Ritus et Ordines Divinae Liturgicae*, 707 (Milan: Ruscioni Editore, 1974, originally edited and translated by R. P. Jacobi Goar).

34. Boswell, *Same-Sex Unions*, chapters 5 and 6.

35. John Boswell, "Homosexuality and the Religious Life: A Historical Approach," in Jeannine Grammick, editor, *Homosexuality in the Priesthood and the Religious Life*, 3, 11 (New York: Crossroad, 1989), and John Boswell, "1500 Years of Blessing Gay and Lesbian Relationships: It's Nothing New to the Church" (videotape of lecture to the Washington, DC, chapter of Integrity, a gay and lesbian Episcopal group).

36. Boswell, *Same-Sex Unions*, 191. See pp. 192–198 for Boswell's doubts about other interpretations of the same-sex union ceremonies.

37. Brent D. Shaw, Book Review, *New Republic*, July 18, 1994, p. 33, is a scholarly critique of Boswell, *Same-Sex Unions*. Ralph Hexter responds to Shaw and Shaw responds to Hexter in *New Republic*, October 3, 1994, p. 39. Reviews by scholars more favorable to Boswell include Marina Warner, "More Than Friendship," *New York Times*, § 7 (Book Review Supplement), August 28, 1994, p. 7; Wendy Doniger, "Making Brothers," *Los Angeles Times* (Book Review Supplement), July 31, 1994, p. 1. I found all of these reviews informative and thoughtful. Although Shaw's review may be contentious (as Hexter claims), its main charge, that Boswell overreads or misreads some or many of his sources, strikes me as just. It is a charge that has been repeatedly and persuasively made against Boswell's earlier work; see, for example, Bruce Williams, "Homosexuality and Christianity: A Review Discussion," 46 *The Thomist* 609 (1982).

38. Alvar Cabeza de Vaca also witnessed unions between same-sex couples, stating in *Narrative of the Expeditions and Shipwrecks of Cabeza de Vaca* (1542) that he "saw a man married to another man." Juan de Torquemada, in the *Monarchia Indiana* (1615), described a common custom whereby "parents [gave] a boy to their young son, to have him for a woman and to use him as a woman; from that also began the law that if anyone approached the

boy, they were ordered to pay for it, punishing them with the same penalties as those breaking the condition of a marriage." These original sources are collected in Francisco Guerra, *The Pre-Columbian Mind* (New York: Seminar Press, 1971). See also the documents collected in Jonathan N. Katz, *Gay American History*, 281–334 (New York: Meridian, 1992, revised edition).

39. See Charles Callender and Lee M. Kochems, "Men and Not-Men: Male Gender-Mixing Statuses and Homosexuality," in Evelyn Blackwood, editor, *The Many Faces of Homosexuality: Anthropological Approaches to Homosexual Behavior*, 165 (New York: Harrington Park Press, 1986).

40. George Devereux, "Institutionalized Homosexuality of the Mohave Indians," 9 *Human Biology* 498, 513–515 (1937).

41. Other leading monographs include Charles Callender and Lee M. Kochems, "The North American *Berdache*," 24 *Current Anthropology* 443 (1983); Donald G. Forgey, "The Institution of *Berdache* Among the North American Plains Indians," 11 *Journal of Sex Research* 1 (1975); W. W. Hill, "The Status of the Hermaphrodite and Transvestite in Najavo Culture," 37 *American Anthropologist* 273 (1935); Nancy O. Lurie, "Winnebago *Berdache*," 55 *American Anthropologist* 708 (1953); Elsie C. Parsons, "The Zuni La'Mana," 18 *American Anthropologist* 521 (1916); James S. Thayer, "The Berdache of the Northern Plains," 36 *Journal of Anthropological Research* 287 (1980); and Harriet Whitehead, "The Bow and the Burden Strap: A New Look at Institutionalized Homosexuality in Native North America," in Sherry B. Ortner and Harriet Whitehead, editors, *Sexual Meanings: The Cultural Construction of Gender and Sexuality*, 80 (New York: Cambridge University Press, 1981).

42. Walter L. Williams, *The Spirit and the Flesh: Sexual Diversity in American Indian Culture* (Boston: Beacon Press, 1986). A second edition was brought out in 1992, but my citations are to the first edition.

43. Ibid., 246–247; Evelyn Blackwood, "Sexuality and Gender in Certain Native American Tribes: The Case of Cross-Gender Females," 10 *Signs* 27 (1984).

44. Clellan S. Ford and Frank A. Beach, *Patterns of Sexual Behavior*, 130–131 (New York: Harper & Row, 1951).

45. See Waldemar Bogoras, *The Chuckchee* (New York: AMS Press, 1975, reprint of an earlier edition); Greenberg, *Construction of Homosexuality*, 58–60; Serena Nanda, *Neither Man Nor Woman: The Hijras of India* (Belmont, CA: Wadsworth, 1990); and Robert I. Levy, "The Community Function of Tahitian Male Transvestism," 44 *Anthropological Quarterly* 12 (1971). See also Greenberg, *Construction of Homosexuality*, 60–61, where the *berdache* tradition is also attributed to the Dinka and Nuer of Sudan, the Konso and Amhara of Ethiopia, the Ottoro of Nubia, the Fanti of Ghana, the Thonga

of Zimbabwe, the Tanala and Bara of Madagascar, the Wolof of Senegal, and various tribes in Uganda.

46. See Greenberg, *Construction of Homosexuality*, 260, and Stephen O. Murray, *Oceanic Homosexualities*, 111, 130 (New York: Garland, 1992).

47. See Paul Gordon Schalow, "Introduction" to Ihara Saikaku, *The Great Mirror of Male Love* (Stanford, CA: Stanford University Press, 1990).

48. E. E. Evans-Pritchard, "Sexual Inversion Among the Azande," 72 *American Anthropologist* 1428–1430 (1970).

49. For example, Walter Cline, *Notes of the People of Siwah and el Garah in the Libyan Desert* (Menasha, WI: George Banta, 1936, edited by Leslie Spier).

50. See Bret Hinsch, *Passions of the Cut Sleeve: The Male Homosexual Tradition in China* (Berkeley, CA: University of California Press, 1990), and James Mc-Gough, "Deviant Marriage Patterns in Chinese Society," in Arthur Kleinman and Tsung-Ti Lin, editors, *Normal and Abnormal Behavior in Chinese Culture*, 171 (Boston: D. Reidel, 1990).

51. McGough, "Deviant Marriage Patterns," 187–188. See also Hinsch, *Passions of the Cut Sleeve*, 129; Jonathan D. Spence, *The Memory Palace of Matteo Ricci*, 226–231 (New York: Viking, 1984); and Vivien W. Ng, "Homosexuality and the State in Late Imperial China," in Martin B. Duberman et al., editors, *Hidden from History: Reclaiming the Gay and Lesbian Past*, 76 (New York: Penguin, 1989).

52. Andrea Sankar, "Sisters and Brothers, Lovers and Enemies: Marriage Resistance in Southern Kwangtung," in *The Many Faces of Homosexuality*, 69.

53. For example, Hinsch, *Passions of the Cut Sleeve*, 176–177.

54. See Judith Gay, "'Mummies and Babies' and Friends and Lovers in Lesotho," in *The Many Faces of Homosexuality*, 97.

55. For example, John Blacking, "Fictitious Kinship Amongst Girls of the Venda of the Northern Transvaal," 59 *Man* 155 (1959).

56. Gilbert H. Herdt, *Guardians of the Flutes: Idioms of Masculinity* (Chicago: University of Chicago Press, 2d edition, 1994), and Gilbert H. Herdt, "Ritualized Homosexual Behavior in the Male Cults of Melanesia, 1862–1983," in Gilbert Herdt, editor, *Ritualized Homosexuality in Melanesia*, 1 (Berkeley, CA: University of California Press, 1984).

57. Shirley Lindenbaum, "Variations on a Sociosexual Theme in Melanesia," in *Ritualized Homosexuality*, 337, 343 (first quotation in text), 345 (second quotation).

58. See Melville Herskovits, "A Note on 'Woman Marriage' in Dahomey," 10 *Africa* 335 (1937), and Eileen Jensen Krige, "Note on the Phalaborwa and Their Morula Complex," 11 *Bantu Studies* 357 (1937).

59. E. E. Evans-Pritchard, *Kinship and Marriage Among the Nuer*, 108–109 (Oxford, UK: Clarendon Press, 1951).

60. Eileen Jensen Krige, "Woman-Marriage, with Special Reference to the Lovedu: Its Significance for the Definition of Marriage," 44 *Africa* 11 (first quotation in text), 29 (second quotation) (1974).

61. Denise O'Brien, "Female Husbands in Southern Bantu Societies," in Alice Schlegel, editor, *Sexual Stratification: A Cross-Cultural View*, 109 (New York: Columbia University Press, 1977).

62. Ibid., 110. For other studies supporting the observation in text, see Amadiume, *Male Daughters, Female Husbands*; Laura Bohannan, "Dahomean Marriage: A Reevaluation," in Paul Bohannan and John Middleton, editors, *Marriage, Family, and Residence*, 85 (Garden City, NY: Natural History Press, 1968), reprinted from 19 *Africa* 273 (1949); H. Huber, "'Woman Marriage' in Some East African Societies," 63/64 *Anthropos* 745 (1969); Krige, "Woman Marriage"; and Regina S. Oboler, "Is the Female Husband a Man? Woman/Woman Marriage Among the Nandi of Kenya," 19 *Ethnology* 69 (1980).

63. See Boswell, *Christianity, Social Tolerance and Homosexuality*, 269–332; Greenberg, *Construction of Homosexuality*, 268–292, 301–346; Judith Brown, "Lesbian Sexuality in Medieval and Early Modern Europe," in *Hidden from History*, 67, 72.

64. See Vern L. Bullough and Bonnie Bullough, *Cross Dressing, Sex, and Gender* (Philadelphia: University of Pennsylvania Press, 1993); H. R. Trevor-Roper, *The European Witch-Craze of the Sixteenth and Seventeenth Centuries and Other Essays*, 90 (New York: Harper & Row, 1969); and Vern L. Bullough and James Brundage, editors, *Sexual Practices and the Medieval Church*, 206 (Buffalo, NY: Prometheus Books, 1982).

65. *Huon of Bordeaux* (London: G. Allen, 1895, translated by Sir John Bourchier and Lord Berners).

66. In addition to the sources in note 64 above, see Guido Ruggiero, *The Boundaries of Eros: Sex Crime and Sexuality in Renaissance Venice* (New York: Oxford University Press, 1985); this is a case study of state repression of same-sex intimacy in Venice.

67. Compare Michel de Montaigne, *Journal de Voyage en Italie par la Suisse et l'Allemagne en 1580 et 1581*, 231, 481 note 515 (Paris: Société des Belles Lettres, 1946, edited by Charles Dedeyan), with Spence, *Matteo Ricci*, 226.

68. See Williams, *Spirit and the Flesh*, 175.

69. See Spence, *Matteo Ricci*, 227–232.

70. See Bullough and Bullough, *Cross Dressing*, 94–112.

71. Ibid., 97–98 (see also 100–103, 134–138, 164–168). One eighteenth-century passing woman married three different wives, each of whom was persuaded she was actually a man.

72. See Katz, *Gay American History*, 209–279 (an entire section entitled "Passing Women: 1780–1920"); The San Francisco Lesbian and Gay History Proj-

ect, "'She Even Chewed Tobacco': A Pictorial Narrative of Passing Women in America," in *Hidden from History*, 183–194. For examples of marriages between women and passing women, see Katz, *Gay American History*, 225–226, 232–238, 240–242, 248–249, 250–251, 254–279.

73. Bullough and Bullough, *Cross Dressing*, 164.

74. Reprinted in Katz, *Gay American History*, 250.

75. Ibid., 251.

76. Lillian Faderman, *Surpassing the Love of Men: Romantic Friendship and Love Between Women from the Renaissance to the Present* (New York: Morrow, 1981).

77. See Elizabeth Mavor, *The Ladies of Llangollen: A Study in Romantic Friendship* (London: Joseph, 1971).

78. Faderman, *Surpassing the Love of Men*, 190–230. See also Letitia Rupp, "'Imagine My Surprise': Women's Relationships in Mid-Twentieth Century America," in *Hidden from History*, 395.

79. See B. R. Burg, *Sodomy and the Perception of Evil: English Sea Rovers in the Seventeenth-Century Caribbean* (New York: New York University Press, 1995, 2d edition) (pair bonding among pirates were male unions); Williams, *Spirit and the Flesh*, 162, 169–174 (cowboy sidekicks formed "male marriages"); Joshua Flynt, "Homosexuality Among Tramps," in Havelock Ellis, editor, *Studies in the Psychology of Sex*, 359 (London: W. Heinemann, Medical Books, 1946); and T. Dunbar Moodie, "Migrancy and Male Sexuality in the South African Gold Mines," in *Hidden from History*, 411 ("mine marriages").

80. Quoted in Robert K. Martin, "Knights-Errant and Gothic Seducers: The Representation of Male Friendship in Mid-Nineteenth Century America," in *Hidden from History*, 169.

81. For example, Martin B. Duberman, "Writhing Bedfellows in Antebellum South Carolina: Historical Interpretation and the Politics of Evidence," in *Hidden from History*, 153.

82. On Whitman's sexuality, see Justin Kaplan, *Walt Whitman: A Life* (New York: Simon & Schuster, 1980).

83. W. C. Rivers, *Walt Whitman's Abnormality* (London: George Allen, 1913), excerpted and supplemented with contemporary correspondence in Martin B. Duberman, *About Time: Exploring the Gay Past,* 106, 109 (New York: Meridian, 1991, revised edition).

84. See Faderman, *Surpassing the Love of Men*, 239–253, 297–313.

85. See Kent Gerard and Gert Hekma, editors, *The Pursuit of Sodomy: Male Homosexuality in Renaissance and Enlightenment Europe* (New York: Harrington Park Press, 1989), and Robert P. MacCubbin, editor, *'Tis Nature's Fault: Unauthorized Sexuality During the Enlightenment* (New York: Cambridge University Press, 1987).

86. Dirk J. Noordam, "Sodomy in the Dutch Republic, 1600–1725," in *The Pursuit of Sodomy*, 207, 212–213, 217.

87. See George Chauncey, Jr., *Gay New York: Gender, Urban Culture, and the Making of the Gay Male World, 1890–1940* (New York: Basic Books, 1994); Lillian Faderman, *Odd Girls and Twilight Lovers: A History of Lesbian Life in Twentieth-Century America* (New York: Columbia University Press, 1991); Allan Bérubé, "Lesbians and Gay Men in Early San Francisco" (unpublished paper on file with the San Francisco Gay History Project); and Ina Russell, editor, *Jeb and Dash: A Diary of Gay Life, 1918–1945* (Boston: Faber & Faber, 1993).

88. Russell, *Jeb and Dash*, 33. Jeb Alexander is a pseudonym adopted by the editor.

89. Faderman, *Odd Girls and Twilight Lovers*, 73. See also Eric Garber, "A Spectacle in Color: The Lesbian and Gay Subculture of Jazz Age Harlem," in *Hidden from History*, 318.

90. Exemplary of this emerging literature is Elizabeth Lapovsky Kennedy and Madeline D. Davis, *Boots of Leather, Slippers of Gold: A History of a Lesbian Community* (New York: Penguin, 1993).

91. The best documented example is Donald Vining, whose published diaries describe in detail his efforts at relationship: *A Gay Diary: 1933–1946* (New York: Pepys Press, 1979); *A Gay Diary: 1946–1954* (New York: Pepys Press, 1980); *A Gay Diary: 1954–1967* (New York: Pepys Press, 1981); *A Gay Diary: 1967–1975* (New York: Pepys Press, 1983).

92. See E. W. Saunders, "Reformers' Choice: Marriage License or Just License?" *One, Inc.*, volume 1, issue 8, pp. 10–12 (August 1953).

93. Donald W. Cory and John LeRoy, "Homosexual Marriage," 29 *Sexology* 660, 661 (1963). Cory is a pseudonym, and LeRoy probably is also.

94. The legal story of this hysteria is documented in William N. Eskridge, Jr., *Gaylaw*, chapter 2 (Cambridge, MA: Harvard University Press, forthcoming 1997).

95. The leading investigations are Alan P. Bell and Martin S. Weinberg, *Homosexualities: A Study of Diversity Among Men and Women* (New York: Simon & Schuster, 1978), which finds "close-coupled" relationships to be the happiest; Philip Blumstein and Pepper Schwartz, *American Couples: Money, Work, Sex* (New York: Morrow, 1983), a study of lesbian, gay, and straight couples that finds lesbian couples to be the most stable and least materialistic; Joseph Harry and William B. DeVall, *The Social Organization of Gay Males*, 80–100 (New York: Praeger, 1978), which includes a section on "Marriages Between Gay Males"; and Mary Mendola, *The Mendola Report: A New Look at Gay Couples*, 48–53 (New York: Crown, 1980), which is a nonempirical survey of lesbian and gay couples, most

of whom considered themselves "married," that is, in a relationship involving "commitment between two people."

96. "Looking Over Lesbians," *Partners Newsletter for Gay and Lesbian Couples*,
November/December, 1991. The Northstar Project in Minnesota found
that 64% of the lesbians and 31% of the gay men surveyed lived with
their partners. Northstar Project, *Out and Counted: A Survey of the Twin
Cities Gay and Lesbian Community*, 12 (Minneapolis, MN: Northstar,
1991). Surveys of gay men (August 1994 issue) and lesbians (August 1995
issue) by *The Advocate* reported similar findings.

97. This dialogue is reported in Don Kelley, "Homosexuals Should Get
Rights," *Los Angeles Collegian* [the student newspaper of Los Angeles City
College], March 3, 1971, p. 2. For a contemporary report on this couple
see Kay Tobin and Randy Wicker, *The Gay Crusaders*, 135–155 (New
York: Arno Press, 1975, 2d edition).

98. See letter from the Reverend Troy D. Perry, founder of MCC, to the
Honorable Shellie Bowers, August 8, 1991. The Service of Holy Union
attached to the letter is included in the appendix to this book.

99. Resolutions of the General Assembly of the Unitarian Universalist Association, "Gay and Lesbian Services of Union" (1984).

100. See Gustav Niebuhr, "Episcopalians Soften Stance on Sexuality," *New
York Times*, August 25, 1994, § A, p. 13. As adopted, the document
skirted the issue of same-sex marriage and included a statement (added
to appease conservatives) that homosexual activity is "a denial of God's
plan."

101. See "Presbyterians Vote for Unity," *Christian Century*, June 29–July 6,
1994, pp. 633–634. The Presbyterians had already forbidden their ministers to perform same-sex marriage ceremonies.

102. The report is described in Peter Steinfels, "Lutherans Balk on a Sex
Policy," *New York Times*, November 26, 1993, § A, p. 21.

103. See Peter Steinfels, "Methodists Again Say No to Homosexuality," *New
York Times*, May 13, 1992, § A, p. 19.

104. Pope John Paul II, "Letter to Families," February 2, 1994, reprinted in
Origins, March 3, 1994, p. 637 (Catholic News Service), not only reiter-
ates the Church's refusal to recognize same-sex unions but calls on
Catholics to oppose legal recognition of same-sex marriages on the
grounds that they are "a serious threat to the family and society" and
"inappropriately conferring an institutional value on deviant behavior"
(Letter, p. 20).

105. Letter from John J. McNeill to the Honorable Shellie Bowers, no date
[1991].

106. See "Two Churches Ousted by Baptists' Vote," *New York Times*, June 11,
1992, § A, p. 16.

107. Baker v. Nelson, 191 N.W.2d 185 (Minnesota Supreme Court, 1971), appeal dismissed, 409 U.S. 810 (U.S. Supreme Court, 1972).

108. Leading judicial decisions rejecting arguments for same-sex marriage are Jones v. Hallahan, 501 S.W.2d 588 (Kentucky Court of Appeals, 1973); Singer v. Hara, 522 P.2d 1187 (Washington Court of Appeals, 1974), review denied, 84 Wash. 2d 1008 (Washington Supreme Court, 1974); Adams v. Howerton, 486 F. Supp. 1119 (U.S. District Court for the Central District of California, 1980), affirmed on other grounds, 673 F.2d 1036 (U.S. Court of Appeals for the Ninth Circuit, 1982). Other decisions by judges and state attorneys general are listed in chapters 3 (note 24) and 5 (note 18).

109. Baehr v. Lewin, 852 P.2d 44 (Hawaii Supreme Court, 1993), clarified in response to the state's motion for reconsideration, 852 P.2d 74 (Hawaii Supreme Court, 1993).

110. The story of the Dixon amendment is told in Dean v. District of Columbia, 653 A.2d 307 (District of Columbia Court of Appeals, 1995) (opinion of Ferren, J., concurring in part).

111. See Deborah M. Henson, "A Comparative Analysis of Same-Sex Partnership Protections: Recommendations for American Reform," 7 *International Journal of Law and the Family* 282 (1993).

112. Danish Act Number 372, June 7, 1989 (Registered Partnership Act); Danish Act Number 373, June 7, 1989 (amending the Danish marriage, inheritance, penal, and tax laws to conform to the Registered Partnership Act). See Linda Nielsen, "Family Rights and the 'Registered Partnership' in Denmark," 4 *International Journal of Law and the Family* 297 (1990), as well as Henning Bech, "Report From a Rotten State: 'Marriage' and 'Homosexuality' in 'Denmark,'" in Ken Plummer, editor, *Modern Homosexualities*, 134 (London: Routledge, 1992).

113. Resolution on Equal Rights for Homosexuals and Lesbians in the EC, paragraph 14, p. 40 of the 1994 *Official Journal of the European Communities* (February 28, 1994).

Chapter 3. The Debate Within the Lesbian and Gay Community

1. E. W. Saunders, "Reformers' Choice: Marriage License or Just License?" *One, Inc.*, volume 1, issue 8, pp. 10–12 (August 1953).

2. "2 Girls Held After Marriage to Each Other," November 1947 (newspaper article in the file "Marriage and Relationships" at the Lesbian Herstory Archives, Brooklyn, New York).

3. Donald Webster Cory, *The Homosexual in America: A Subjective Approach*, 135 (New York: Greenberg, 1951). The quotation in text opens chap-

ter 13, "Love Is a Wonderful Thing." For other contemporary examples of homosexual men's predilection for one-night stands, see Gore Vidal, *The City and the Pillar*, 277 (New York: Dutton, 1948), and Donald Vining, *A Gay Diary, 1946–1954* (New York: Pepys Press, 1980), in which the author engages in nightly cruising even though involved in a long-term relationship.

4. Cory, *Homosexual in America*, 137–138.

5. See A. A. Deenen et al., "Intimacy and Sexuality in Gay Male Couples," 23 *Archives of Sexual Behavior* 421, 429 (1994).

6. "Gay Revolution Comes Out," *The Rat*, August 12–26, 1969, p. 7 (interview with members of the Gay Liberation Front in counterculture newspaper). See also Ralph Hall, "The Church, State & Homosexuality: A Radical Analysis," *Gay Power*, number 14 (no date; probably 1970), which includes this statement: "Homosexual marriages submitting to the guidelines of so-called conventional rites must be classed as reactionary." On gay radicalism generally, see Donn Teal, *Gay Radicals* (New York: Stein & Day, 1971), and Kay Tobin and Randy Wicker, *The Gay Crusaders* (New York: Arno Press, 1975, 2d edition).

7. See John Rechy, *The Sexual Outlaw* (New York: Grove Press, 1977). Rechy attacked gay marriage as emulation of heterosexual society and idealized male hustlers as the "shock troops of the sexual revolution."

8. "An Approach to Liberation," *Gay Liberation: A Red Butterfly Publication*, p. 12 (no date; probably 1970).

9. Important statements of the feminist critique are Shulamith Firestone, *The Dialectic of Sex: The Case for Feminist Revolution* (New York: Morrow, 1970), and Sheila Cronan, "Marriage," in Anne Koedt et al., editors, *Radical Feminism*, 213–221 (New York: Quadrangle, 1973). See also the essays collected in Herma Hill Kay, *Cases and Materials on Sex-Based Discrimination*, 239–246 (St. Paul: West, 1988, 3d edition), as well as the retrospective account in Alice Echols, *Daring to Be Bad: Radical Feminism in America 1967–1975* (Minneapolis: University of Minnesota Press, 1989).

10. Demanded by the National Coalition of Gay Organizations (State Demand Number 8) in February 1972. Federal Demand Number 4 was "Elimination of tax inequities victimizing single persons and same-sex couples."

11. Baker v. Nelson, 191 N.W.2d 185 (Minnesota Supreme Court, 1971), appeal dismissed, 409 U.S. 810 (U.S. Supreme Court, 1972).

12. See "Lesbians Ask Court to Permit Marriage," *Louisville Chronicle*, November 11, 1970. The Kentucky Court of Appeals upheld this action in Jones v. Hallahan, 501 S.W.2d 588 (Kentucky Court of Appeals, 1973), the second published decision denying a same-sex couple their marriage license.

13. Quoted in Eric Pianin, "Hearing Held on Women's Bid to Wed," *Louisville Times*, November 12, 1970.

14. See Grace Lichtenstein, "Homosexual Weddings Stir Controversy," *New York Times*, April 27, 1975, § B, p. 61; "Colorado Gays Marry," *The Gay Blade*, volume 6, issue 5, p. 1 (May 1975).

15. Quoted in Lichtenstein, "Homosexual Weddings," p. 61.

16. All the couples lost. The only reported decision is Adams v. Howerton, 486 F. Supp. 1119 (U.S. District Court for the Central District of California, 1982), affirmed, 673 F.2d 1036 (U.S. Court of Appeals for the Ninth Circuit, 1983).

17. See "Maryland Challenges Gay Marriage," *The Gay Blade*, volume 6, issue 8, p. 1 (August 1975).

18. The story of the Dixon amendment is told in Dean v. District of Columbia, 653 A.2d 307 (District of Columbia Court of Appeals, 1995) (opinion of Ferren, J., concurring in part). On the gay community's and Kameny's position, see Cheryl Kimmons, "The Case for Gay Marriage," *The Blade*, volume 7, issue 6, p. 6 (June 1976).

19. Their story is told in "Marriage Fight Due: Wisconsin Black Women Slate Christmas Wedding," *Mother*, volume 1, number 7, p. 1 (December 1971).

20. 1971 California Statutes at Large, chapter 1748, § 26.

21. See "Gay Couple Files Suit After Los Angeles Denies Marriage License," *Los Angeles Times*, March 16, 1977, § 2, p. 6.

22. 1977 California Statutes, chapter 339, §§ 1–2. For the debate and vote, see "Senate Approves Measure Banning Gay Marriages," *Los Angeles Times*, August 12, 1977, p. 33; "California Assembly Approves Bill Banning Gay Marriages," *Los Angeles Times*, August 14, 1977.

23. For negative responses from state attorneys general, see 190 Opinions of the Attorney General of Alabama 30 (1983), Opinions of the Attorney General of Arkansas (April 26, 1995), 1975 Opinions of the Attorney General of Colorado (1975), 93 Opinions of the Attorney General of Idaho 11 (1993), 77 Opinions of the Attorney General of Kansas (August 4, 1977), 92 Opinions of the Attorney General of Louisiana 699(A) (1992), 84 Opinions of the Attorney General of Maine 28 (1984), 1978 Opinions of the Attorney General of Mississippi 684 (1978), 1977 Opinions of the Attorney General of Nebraska 170 (1977), 1976 Opinions of the Attorney General of South Carolina 423 (1976), 88 Opinions of the Attorney General of Tennessee 43 (1988), 1977–1978 Opinions of the Attorney General of Virginia 154 (1977).

24. A chronological array of decisions rejecting same-sex couples' petition for equal marriage rights is as follows: Baker v. Nelson, 191 N.W.2d 185 (Minnesota Supreme Court, 1971), appeal dismissed, 409 U.S. 810 (U.S. Supreme Court, 1972); Jones v. Hallahan, 501 S.W.2d 588 (Kentucky Court of Appeals, 1973); Singer v. Hara, 522 P.2d 1187 (Washington Court of Appeals, 1974), review denied, 84 Wash. 2d 1008 (Washington Supreme

Court, 1974); Adams v. Howerton, 486 F. Supp. 1119 (U.S. District Court for the Central District of California, 1980), affirmed on other grounds, 673 F.2d 1036 (U.S. Court of Appeals for the Ninth Circuit, 1982); Slayton v. State, 633 S.W.2d 934 (Texas Court of Appeals, 1982); De Santo v. Barnsley, 476 A.2d 952 (Pennsylvania Superior Court, 1984); Cuevas v. Mills, No. 86–3244 (U.S. District Court for the District of Kansas, October 27, 1986) (unpublished opinion); In re Succession of Bacot, 502 So.2d 1118 (Louisiana Court of Appeals, 1987), writ denied, 503 So.2d 466 (Louisiana Supreme Court, 1987); Gajovski v. Gajovski, 610 N.E.2d 431 (Ohio Court of Appeals, 1991); Callender v. Corbett, No. 296666 (Arizona Superior Court, Pima County, April 13, 1994) (unpublished opinion); Dean v. District of Columbia, 653 A.2d 307 (District of Columbia Court of Appeals, 1995).

25. M.T. v. J.T., 355 A.2d 204 (New Jersey Superior Court, Appellate Division, 1976). This position was rejected in Frances B. v. Mark B., 78 Misc. 2d 112 (New York Supreme Court, 1974); Anonymous v. Anonymous, 325 N.Y.S.2d 499 (New York Supreme Court, 1971); In re Ladrach, 573 N.E.2d 828 (Ohio Probate Court, 1987). Those courts held that male-to-female transsexuals or transvestites are still men for purposes of marriage statutes.

26. Their stories are told through interviews in Suzanne Sherman, editor, *Lesbian and Gay Marriage: Private Commitments, Public Ceremonies*, 35–41, 85–95 (Philadelphia: Temple University Press, 1992).

27. For examples of queer boomer dismissiveness of the marriage option, see Dennis Altman, *Coming Out in the Seventies* (Sydney: Wild & Woolley, 1979); E. M. Ettore, *Lesbians, Women, and Society* (Boston: Routledge & Kegan Paul, 1980); Guy Hocquenghem, *Homosexual Desire* (Durham, NC: Duke University Press, 1993, 2d edition, translated by Danielle Dangoor).

28. For early soundings, see Philip Blumstein and Pepper Schwartz, *American Couples: Money, Work, Sex* (New York: Morrow, 1983) and Brad Green, "Gay 'Marriages': Delivering a Message," *The Blade*, volume 13, issue 5, § A, p. 1 (March 5, 1982), which cites evidence that "Gay couples are coming out of the closet" in the early 1980s.

29. See Deenen et al., "Intimacy and Sexuality in Gay Male Couples" (Generation X gay men are more likely to settle down into close-coupled relationships than gay baby boomers).

30. See Craig A. Bowman and Blake M. Cornish, "A More Perfect Union: A Legal and Social Analysis of Domestic Partnership Ordinances," 92 *Columbia Law Review* 1164 (1992) (student note), and Robert L. Eblin, "Domestic Partnership Recognition in the Workplace: Equitable Employee Benefits for Gay Couples (and Others)," 51 *Ohio State Law Journal* 1067 (1990) (student note).

31. "San Francisco Mayor Says No to Gay Marriage," *The Blade*, volume 14, issue 4, p. 9 (January 26, 1983).

32. The ultimate policy is set forth in City of Berkeley Domestic Partnership Information Sheet (January 1, 1987).

33. Daniel Weintraub and Bettina Boxall, "Ballot Fallout Expected from Wilson's Veto," *Los Angeles Times*, September 13, 1994, p. 3.

34. Braschi v. Stahl Associates, 74 N.Y.2d 201 (New York Court of Appeals, 1989).

35. See Alison D. v. Virginia M., 572 N.E.2d 27 (New York Court of Appeals, 1991), which refused to allow mother's former same-sex partner, who had bonded with her child, to have spouselike visitation rights to see the child (consider the excellent dissent of Judge Judith Kaye), and In re Cooper, 592 N.Y.S.2d 797 (New York Supreme Court, Appellate Division, 1993), appeal dismissed without opinion, 82 N.Y.2d 801 (New York Court of Appeals, 1993), in which a domestic partner was refused "spousal" inheritance rights. See also Coon v. Joseph, 237 Cal. Rptr. 873 (California Court of Appeals, First District, 1987), a case in which it was ruled that same-sex couples are not entitled to the same rights as married couples to sue for emotional distress resulting from injuries to a partner.

36. Danish Registered Partnership Act, Danish Act 372 of June 7, 1989.

37. Thomas B. Stoddard, "Why Gay People Should Seek the Right to Marry," *OUT/LOOK, National Lesbian and Gay Quarterly*, issue 6, p. 8 (Fall 1989), reprinted in Sherman, *Lesbian and Gay Marriage*, 13–19.

38. Paula L. Ettelbrick, "Since When Is Marriage a Path to Liberation?" *OUT/LOOK, National Gay and Lesbian Quarterly*, issue 6, p. 8 (Fall 1989), reprinted in Sherman, *Lesbian and Gay Marriage*, 20–26.

39. In addition to the works discussed in the text, see Richard D. Mohr, *A More Perfect Union: Why Straight America Must Stand Up for Gay Rights*, chapter 3 (Boston: Beacon Press, 1994); Andrew Sullivan, *Virtually Normal: An Argument About Homosexuality*, chapters 3 and 5 (New York: Knopf, 1995); "Symposium: The Family in the 1990s: An Exploration of Lesbian and Gay Rights," 1 *Law & Sexuality: A Review of Lesbian and Gay Legal Issues* 1–96 (1991), which includes articles by Harlon L. Dalton, Nitya Duclos, and Mary C. Dunlap, in addition to the article by Nan D. Hunter, cited in note 40 below; "Noose or Knot? The Debate Over Lesbian Marriage," *OUT/WEEK: New York's Lesbian and Gay News Magazine*, September 18, 1989, pp. 38–43 (articles by Sarah Petitt, Ashley McNeely, and Catherine Saalfield); Marc A. Fajer, "Can Two Real Men Eat Quiche Together? Storytelling, Gender-Role Stereotypes, and Legal Protection for Lesbians and Gay Men," 46 *University of Miami Law Review* 511 (1992); Steven K. Homer, "Against Marriage," 29 *Harvard Civil Rights–Civil Liberties Law Review* 505 (1994) (student note); Ruthann Robson and S. E. Valentine,

"Lov(h)ers: Lesbians as Intimate Partners and Lesbian Legal Theory," 63 *Temple Law Review* 511 (1990); and Andrew Sullivan, "A (Conservative) Case for Gay Marriage," *New Republic*, August 28, 1993, pp. 20, 22.

40. Nan D. Hunter, "Marriage, Law, and Gender: A Feminist Inquiry," 1 *Law and Sexuality: A Review of Lesbian and Gay Legal Issues* 9, 12 (1991).

41. Nancy D. Polikoff, "We Will Get What We Ask For: Why Legalizing Gay and Lesbian Marriage Will Not 'Dismantle the Legal Structure of Gender in Every Marriage,'" 79 *Virginia Law Review* 1535 (1993). Responding, in turn, to Polikoff is Evan Wolfson, "Crossing the Threshold: Equal Marriage Rights for Lesbians and Gay Men, and the Intra-community Critique," 21 *New York University Review of Law and Social Change* 567 (1994–1995).

42. Jack Baker's reasons why he and Mike McConnell sued for same-sex marriage emphasized that "homosexuals are entitled to the same rights enjoyed by heterosexuals." Letter from Jack Baker to Donn Teal (October 21, 1970), excerpted in Teal, *Gay Militants*, 283–284.

43. Wisconsin Statutes § 765.001 (West 1993).

44. The ADA provides that a public entity may not discriminate against a qualified individual with a mental or physical disability. 42 U.S.C. §§ 12102, 12132 (1995 Supplement); see 28 C.F.R. § 35.104 (1995), which defines disability. AIDS is a disability under the regulations. 28 C.F.R. § 35.104(1)(B)(ii) (1995).

45. Virginia Code § 18.2–66 (1988).

46. Burns Indiana Statutes § 31–7–1–2 (Michie 1987).

47. A history of that dropping away is developed in William N. Eskridge, Jr., *Gaylaw,* chapters 1–3 (Cambridge, MA: Harvard University Press, forthcoming 1997). Drafts of these chapters are available upon request.

48. See 10 U.S.C. § 654(b) (1995 Supplement), which codifies "don't ask, don't tell." See United States Navy v. Meinhold, 34 F.2d 1469 (U.S. Court of Appeals for the Ninth Circuit, 1994), which interprets previous regulations as not excluding Navy personnel simply because of their homosexual status.

49. Adrienne Rich, "Compulsory Heterosexuality and Lesbian Existence (1980)," in A. Rich, *Blood, Bread, and Poetry: Selected Prose 1979–1985,* pp. 23–75 (New York: Norton, 1986).

50. For example, Official Code of Georgia § 19–3–6 (Michie 1991) ("Marriage is encouraged by the law").

51. For other lists, see Hayden Curry and Denis Clifford, *Legal Guide for Lesbian and Gay Couples* (Berkeley, CA: Nolo Press, 1994, 8th edition), and Nitya Duclos, "Some Complicating Thoughts on Same-Sex Marriage," 1 *Law and Sexuality: A Review of Lesbian and Gay Legal Issues* 31, 52–53 (1991).

52. District of Columbia Code §§ 16–910 to 16–916 (1981); id. § 3–213.1 (support action brought by state).

53. Id. § 20–303(a) ("spouse" is first in line for appointment after personal representatives named in a will, while "lover" is last in line, included in the category "any other person," after any "relation" of the decedent and the decedent's largest creditor).
54. Id. § 21–2043(c).
55. Id. § 21–2210(a).
56. Id. § 21–541.
57. Id. § 21–522.
58. Id. § 21–546.
59. Id. § 16–2701.
60. Id. §§ 1–622.7(b) & 1–623.7(b) (Supp. 1991).
61. Id. § 1–624.10.
62. Id. § 16–1001; see generally id. §§ 16–1006 to 16–1036 (Supp. 1991).
63. Id. § 24–483(a), (c) (1981).
64. Id. § 14–306.
65. Id. § 45–216.
66. Id. § 15–502.
67. Id. § 2–2813.
68. Id. § 2–1502; see also id. § 2–1507 (custody of remainder of body vests in spouse).
69. Id. §§ 19–301 to 19–305 (surviving spouse usually receives 50% or all of the estate).
70. Id. § 19–101.
71. Id. §§ 16–2921 to 16–2925 & 19–102.
72. See 8 U.S.C. § 1151(b)(2)(A)(i) (1994).
73. Id. § 1430(a), (b), (d).
74. 42 U.S.C. §§ 401–403 (1988).
75. 38 U.S.C. §§ 1310–1318 (1994).
76. Barbara J. Cox, "Alternative Families: Obtaining Traditional Family Benefits Through Litigation, Legislation, and Collective Bargaining," 2 *Wisconsin Women's Law Journal* 1 (1986), develops some of the ways by which cohabiting couples can create some of the same benefits of marriage.
77. See In re Kowalski, 478 N.W.2d 790 (Minnesota Court of Appeals, 1991); Karen Thompson and Julie Andrzekewski, *Why Can't Sharon Kowalski Come Home?* (San Francisco: Spinsters, 1988).
78. District of Columbia Code § 22–301 (1981).
79. Id. § 16–904.
80. Id. § 16–916.
81. Id. §§ 16–910 (division of property), 16–911 to -913 (alimony).
82. For example, 42 U.S.C. § 1382 (1994).
83. For example, District of Columbia Code § 1–608.1 (1981) (antinepotism rule); id. § 21–2068 (conflict-of-interest rule).

84. The following text is strongly influenced by my reading of Milton C. Regan, Jr., *Family Law and the Pursuit of Intimacy* (New York: New York University Press, 1993), and the sources discussed therein.

85. Plato, *Symposium*, line 192b-d, in *On Homosexuality: Lysis, Phaedrus, and Symposium*, 124 (Buffalo, NY: Prometheus Books, 1991, translated by Benjamin Jowett, with selected retranslation by Eugene O'Connor).

86. Alan P. Bell and Martin S. Weinberg, *Homosexualities: A Study of Diversity Among Men and Women* (New York: Simon & Schuster, 1978).

87. See, for example, Lawrence A. Kurdek and J. Patrick Schmitt, "Relationship Quality of Gay Men in Closed or Open Relationships," in John P. De Cecco, editor, *Gay Relationships*, 217 (New York: Harrington Park Press, 1988).

88. See Philip Blumstein and Pepper Schwartz, *American Couples: Money, Work, Sex* (New York: Morrow, 1983), an empirical study finding that lesbian couples enjoy stable and rewarding relationships, even more so than heterosexual or gay male couples; Susan E. Johnson, *Staying Power: Long-Term Lesbian Couples* (Tallahassee, FL: Naiad Press, 1990), a nonempirical study that found great satisfaction among 108 lesbian couples; David McWhirter and Andrew Mattison, *The Male Couple* (Englewood Cliffs, NJ: Prentice-Hall, 1984), a similar nonempirical study of gay male couples; and Lawrence A. Kurdek and J. Patrick Schmitt, "Relationship Quality of Partners in Heterosexual, Married, Heterosexual Cohabiting, and Gay and Lesbian Relationships," 51 *Journal of Personality and Social Psychology* 711 (1986), an empirical survey finding equal levels of satisfaction among committed gay, lesbian, and straight couples and less satisfaction among cohabiting couples.

89. Larry Kramer, *Faggots* (New York: Plume, 1978). See also Andrew Holleran, *Dancer from the Dance* (New York: Morrow, 1978); John Rechy, *City of Night* (New York: Grove Press, 1963); and Edmund White, *States of Desire: Travels in Gay America* (New York: Plume, 1991).

90. A near caricature of this attitude, associated with a bitter rejection of same-sex marriage, can be found in John Rechy, *The Sexual Outlaw* (New York: Grove Press, 1977).

91. See, for example, Edward O. Laumann et al., *The Social Organization of Sexuality: Sexual Practices in the United States*, 313–316 (Chicago: University of Chicago Press, 1994), which reports that fewer gay men than straight men have live-in partners; the authors speculate that lack of social and formal recognition of gay relationships contributes to this phenomenon.

92. See Deenen et al., "Intimacy and Sexuality in Gay Male Couples," 429, which speculates that gay men coming of age in the 1980s value committed and monogamous relationships more than do older gay men.

93. Autobiographical works by Paul Monette are *Borrowed Time: An AIDS Memoir* (New York: Harcourt Brace Jovanovich, 1988) and *Becoming a*

Man: Half a Life Story (New York: Harcourt Brace Jovanovich, 1992). A powerfully romantic work of fiction is *Halfway Home* (New York: Crown, 1991). Monette died of complications associated with AIDS in 1994.

94. Ettelbrick, "Since When Is Marriage a Path to Liberation?" 20. Ettelbrick credits a "bit of T-shirt philosophy" for the introductory crack. For a similar kind of argument, see the three lesbian feminist essays in "Noose or Knot? The Debate over Lesbian Marriage," *OUT/WEEK: New York's Lesbian and Gay News Magazine*, September 18, 1989, pp. 38–43 (essays by Sarah Petitt, Ashley McNeely, and Catherine Saalfield).

95. See Polikoff, "We Will Get What We Ask For," 1538–1540.

96. 387 U.S. 1 (1967).

97. See Robin West, "Equality Theory, Marital Rape, and the Promise of the Fourteenth Amendment," 42 *Florida Law Review* 45 (1990); Anne C. Dailey, "To Have and To Hold: The Marital Rape Exemption and the Fourteenth Amendment," 99 *Harvard Law Review* 1255 (1986) (student note); Jaye Sitton, "Old Wine in New Bottles: The 'Marital' Rape Allowance," 72 *North Carolina Law Review* 261 (1993) (student comment).

98. Ettelbrick, "Since When Is Marriage a Path to Liberation?" 21.

99. See also Barbara Findlen, "Is Marriage The Answer? Domestic Partnership Activists Don't Think So," *Ms.*, May/June 1995, p. 86.

100. Janet Lever, "Sexual Revelations," *The Advocate*, August 1994, pp. 17, 24. The August 1995 issue of *The Advocate* reported similar results among lesbians. See also "Readers Favor Legal Marriage," *Partners Magazine for Gay and Lesbian Couples*, July/August 1990, p. 1, which reveals overwhelming support among respondents for marriage. The *Partners* National Survey of Lesbian and Gay Couples is discussed in Elizabeth Rhodes, "New Ties That Bind: Same-Sex Couples Challenge the System to Gain Legal Recognition of Their Commitments to Each Other," *Seattle Times*, July 21, 1991, § K, p. 1.

101. Quoted in Findlen, "Is Marriage The Answer?" 91.

102. Ettelbrick, "Since When Is Marriage a Path to Liberation?" 22.

103. Ibid., 23.

104. See Mary Mendola, *The Mendola Report: A New Look at Gay Couples* (New York: Crown, 1980) and Letitia Anne Peplau, "Research on Homosexual Couples: An Overview," in De Cecco, editor, *Gay Relationships*, 33–40. See also Joseph Harry and W. De Vall, *The Social Organization of Gay Males* (New York: Praeger, 1978); Sylvia A. Law, "Homosexuality and the Social Meaning of Gender," 1988 *Wisconsin Law Review* 187; and Claudia A. Lewis, "From This Day Forward: A Feminine Moral Discourse on Homosexual Marriage," 97 *Yale Law Journal* 1783 (1988) (student note).

105. Kath Weston, *Families We Choose: Lesbians, Gays, Kinship* (New York: Columbia University Press, 1991).

106. See Laura Benkov, *Reinventing the Family: The Emerging Story of Lesbian and Gay Parents* (New York: Crown, 1994); Frederick W. Bozett and Marvin B. Sussman, editors, *Homosexuality and Family Relations* (New York: Harrington Park Press, 1990); Marla J. Hollandsworth, "Gay Men Creating Families through Surro-Gay Arrangements: A Paradigm for Reproductive Freedom," 3 *The American University Journal of Gender and the Law* 183 (1995); and Nancy D. Polikoff, "This Child Does Have Two Mothers: Redefining Parenthood to Meet the Needs of Children in Lesbian-Mother and Other Nontraditional Families," 78 *Georgetown Law Journal* 459 (1990).

107. Ettelbrick, "Since When Is Marriage a Path to Liberation?" 24. Also see Robson and Valentine, "Lov(h)ers," 538 (citing Ettelbrick and other authors).

108. See Wolfson, "Crossing the Threshold," 582–585.

109. The facts in the account that follows are taken from Judge Coleman's opinion in Bottoms v. Bottoms, 444 S.E.2d 276 (Virginia Court of Appeals, 1994), reversed, 457 S.E.2d 102 (Virginia Supreme Court, 1995), and from a law review article by Sharon Bottoms's attorney in the case. See Stephen B. Pershing, "'Entreat Me Not to leave Thee': *Bottoms v. Bottoms* and the Custody Rights of Gay and Lesbian Parents," 3 *William and Mary Bill of Rights Journal* 289 (1994).

Chapter 4. Mainstream Objections to Same-Sex Marriage

1. *Black's Law Dictionary*, 876 (Minneapolis: West Publishing Co., 1979, 5th edition) (quotation in text). See also *Oxford English Dictionary* (New York: Oxford University Press, 1971); *Webster's Ninth New Collegiate Dictionary*, 729 (Springfield, MA: Merriam-Webster, 1989) ("marriage" is "the institution whereby men and women are joined in a special kind of social and legal dependence for the purpose of founding and maintaining a family"); *Webster's Third International Dictionary* (Springfield, MA: Merriam-Webster, 1986).

2. *The American Heritage Dictionary, Second Collegiate Edition*, 768 (Boston: Houghton Mifflin, 1985); see also *Oxford English Dictionary*, whose secondary definition of marriage includes "intimate union."

3. For an example in print, see Donald Webster Cory and John LeRoy, "Homosexual Marriage," 29 *Sexology* 660 (1963).

4. See, for example, J. L. Walker and N. F. White, "The Varieties of Therapeudic Experience: Conjoint Therapy in a Homosexual Marriage," *Canada's Mental Health*, volume 23, issue 2, pp. 3–5 (1975).

5. 10 U.S.C. § 654(b) (1995 Supplement). The law was picking up the term from Department of Defense Directive 1332.1 (the pre-1994 military's

exclusionary regulation), which cited "homosexual marriage" as a ground for discharge from the armed forces. 32 C.F.R. part 41, appendix A, § H.1.c (1994).

6. Jones v. Hallahan, 501 S.W.2d 588, 589 (Kentucky Court of Appeals, 1973). Other state courts have quoted and followed *Hallahan's* definition of marriage and its argument that the Constitution cannot change the definition of marriage. See Singer v. Hara, 522 P.2d 1187 (Washington Court of Appeals, 1974), review denied, 84 Wash. 2d 1008 (Washington Supreme Court, 1974).

7. Baker v. Nelson, 191 N.W.2d 185, 186 (Minnesota Supreme Court, 1971), appeal dismissed, 409 U.S. 810 (U.S. Supreme Court, 1972).

8. Dean v. District of Columbia, No. CA 90–13892 (District of Columbia Superior Court, December 30, 1991), affirmed on other grounds, 653 A.2d 307 (District of Columbia Court of Appeals, 1995).

9. Pope John Paul II, "Letter to Families," February 2, 1994, p. 20, reprinted in *Origins,* March 3, 1994, p. 637 (Catholic News Service). On the immediate background of this letter, see Alan Cowell, "Pope Deplores Gay Marriage," *New York Times,* February 23, 1994, § A, p. 2. On the Church history behind the letter, see Peter O. Brown, *The Body and Society: Men, Women and Sexual Renunciation in Early Christianity* (New York: Columbia University Press, 1988).

10. Pope John Paul II, "Letter to Families," 20.

11. The leading works are Germain Grisez, *Living a Christian Life* (Quincy, IL: Franciscan Press, 1993, volume 2 of *The Way of the Lord Jesus*); "The Homosexual Movement: A Response by the Ramsey Colloquium," *First Things,* Number 41, March 1994, p. 16; John Finnis, "Law, Morality, and 'Sexual Orientation,'" 69 *Notre Dame Law Review* 1049 (1994).

12. Finnis, "Law, Morality, and 'Sexual Orientation,'" 1054–1063. This account of Plato and Aristotle is disputed by Martha Nussbaum's testimony in the trial surrounding the constitutional challenge to Colorado's antigay initiative.

13. Steven Macedo, "Homosexuality and the Conservative Mind," *Georgetown Law Journal* (in press).

14. See California Statutes 1957, chapter 2121, § 1, which provided that unions entered before 1958 and recognized by tribal law as marriages were valid marriages in that state.

15. M.T. v. J.T., 355 A.2d 204 (New Jersey Superior Court, Appellate Division, 1976).

16. See, for example, Gajovski v. Gajovski, 610 N.E.2d 431 (Ohio Court of Appeals, 1991); Frances B. v. Mark B., 78 Misc. 2d 112 (New York Supreme Court, 1974).

17. For marriages of people who are genitally female and chromosomally male to men, see John Money and Anke A. Ehrhardt, *Man and Woman Boy and*

Girl, 111 (Baltimore: Johns Hopkins University Press, 1972); John Money and Patricia Tucker, *Sexual Signatures*, 55 (Boston: Little, Brown, 1975); and John Money et al., "Fetal Feminization Induced by Androgen Insensitivity in the Testicular Feminizing Syndrome: Effect on Marriage and Maternalism," 123 *Johns Hopkins Medical Journal* 105 (1968), a survey of ten women, four of whom were married (and happily so). For marriages of people who are genitally male and chromosomally female to women, see John Money, *Venuses Penuses*, 161 (Buffalo, NY: Prometheus Books, 1986), an extensive case study of a chromosomal female happily married to a woman; and Roberta Cowell, *Roberta Cowell's Story* (London: W. Heinemann, 1954), an autobiography.

18. See John Money and Ernesto Pollitt, "Cytogenetic and Psychosexual Ambiguity: Klinefelter's Syndrome and Transvestism Compared," 11 *Archives of General Psychiatry* 589 (1964), on the XXY pattern; Raul C. Schiavi et al., "Sex Chromosome Anomalies, Hormones, and Sexuality," 45 *Archives of General Psychiatry* 19 (1988), on the XYY and XXY patterns; and Elizabeth McCauley et al., "Psychosocial Adjustment of Adult Women with Turner Syndrome," 29 *Clinical Genetics* 284 (1986), on the XO and other chromosomal pattern variations.

19. For accounts of the debate, see Alan Barnard and Anthony Good, *Research Practices in the Study of Kinship*, 89–91 (London: Academic Press, 1984); Edmund R. Leach, *Social Anthropology*, 176–203 (New York: Oxford University Press, 1982); E. Kathleen Gough, "The Nayars and the Definition of Marriage," 89 *Journal of the Royal Anthropological Institute* 23–24, 32–33 (1959); and Gloria A. Marshall, "Marriage: A Comparative Analysis," 10 *International Encyclopedia of the Social Sciences*, 8–19 (New York: Macmillan, 1968).

20. *Notes and Queries on Anthropology*, 110 (London: Royal Anthropological Institute, 1951, 6th edition).

21. Edmund R. Leach, "Polyandry, Inheritance and the Definition of Marriage," 53 *Man* 182, 183 (1955).

22. Gough, "Nayars and the Definition of Marriage," 32.

23. Leach, *Social Anthropology*, 182–183. See Barnard and Good, *Study of Kinship*, 89–91; R. Needham, "Remarks on the Analysis of Kinship and Marriage," in R. Needham, editor, *Rethinking Kinship and Marriage*, 5–8 (London: Tavistock, 1971).

24. Eileen J. Krige, "Woman-Marriage, with Special Reference to the Lovedu: Its Significance for the Definition of Marriage," 44 *Africa* 11 (1974).

25. Baehr v. Lewin, 852 P.2d 44, 56 (Hawaii Supreme Court, 1993) (opinion of Levinson, J.). Justice Levinson's opinion found that the claimants had presented a valid claim of sex discrimination but rejected their right-to-marry claim. See chapters 5 and 6 for an explication of the distinction.

Moral and religious thinkers make the same kind of claim as the one in the text (e.g., Pope John Paul II, "Letter to Families," 20).

26. St. Augustine, Bishop of Hippo, *De Bono Conjugali*, in *Treatises on Marriage and Other Subjects* (New York: Fathers of the Church, 1955).

27. Finnis, "Law, Morality, and 'Sexual Orientation,'" 1065; see also p. 1066 for a discussion that is even more metaphysical in its conception that the "sexual union can *actualize* and allow them to *experience* their *real common good—their marriage* with the two goods, parenthood and friendship" (emphasis in original).

28. Grisez, *Living a Christian Life*, 636, condemns as immoral a married couple's intercourse "if spouses unable to engage in [vaginal] intercourse due to the husband's impotence masturbate each other to orgasm, if a couple trying to prevent the transmission of disease use a condom, or if either or both spouses do something in order to impede conception."

29. See, for example, David P. McWhirter et al., *Homosexuality/Heterosexuality: Concepts of Sexual Orientation*, parts IV and V (New York: Oxford University Press, 1990).

30. See, for example, Richard A. Posner, *Sex and Reason* (Cambridge, MA: Harvard University Press, 1992).

31. Dean v. District of Columbia, No. CA 90–13892 (District of Columbia Superior Court, December 30, 1991), affirmed on other grounds, 653 A.2d 307 (District of Columbia Court of Appeals, 1995).

32. Adams v. Howerton, 486 F. Supp. 1119, 1123 (U.S. District Court for the Central District of California, 1982), affirmed on other grounds, 673 F.2d 1036 (U.S. Court of Appeals for the Ninth Circuit, 1983).

33. "Thou shalt not lie with mankind as with womankind: it *is* abomination" (Leviticus 18:22); see also 20:13 ("If a man lies with a male as with a woman, both of them have committed an abomination"). Gay-friendly readers have interpreted this and other passages to be nothing more than references to "unclean" practices, for example, Daniel A. Helminiak, *What the Bible Really Says About Homosexuality*, 43–54 (San Francisco: Alamo Square Press, 1994), but a more accurate reconstruction emphasizes the Old Testament's anxiety about male anal intercourse; see Lewis John Eron, "Homosexuality and Judaism," in Arlene Swidler, editor, *Homosexuality and World Religions*, 103, 112–114 (Valley Forge, PA: Trinity Press International, 1993), and the Israelites' reaction to Egyptian practices, including same-sex marriages. See Jacob Neusner, *Sifra: An Analytical Translation*, volume 3, p. 74 (Atlanta: Scholars Press, 1988), which is quoted in chapter 2.

34. Traditional antihomosexual interpretations of St. Paul's Rom. 1:26–27, 1 Cor. 6:9–10, and 1 Tim. 1:10 (which some scholars think was not written by St. Paul) are disputed in Derrick Sherwin Bailey, *Homosexuality and the Western Christian Tradition* (Hamden, CT: Archon Books, 1955),

whose arguments are pursued further by John Boswell, *Christianity, Social Tolerance, and Homosexuality: Gay People in Western Europe from the Beginning of the Christian Era to the Fourteenth Century* (Chicago: University of Chicago Press, 1980), and by Helminiak, *What the Bible Really Says*, 61–96.

35. Denise Carmody and John Carmody, "Homosexuality and Roman Catholicism," in *Homosexuality and World Religions*, 135.

36. William N. Eskridge, Jr., "A History of Same-Sex Marriage," 79 *Virginia Law Review* 1419, 1449–1452 (1993). An appendix to that article (pp. 1512–1513) is my translation of one of the "spiritual brotherhood" rituals.

37. John Boswell, *Same-Sex Unions in Premodern Europe* (New York: Villard Books, 1994).

38. The responses were collected and filed as Appendices 12–22 to the "Memorandum on the History of Same-Sex Marriage," which I drafted for the plaintiffs in Dean v. District of Columbia, No. CA90–13892 (District of Columbia Superior Court, filed September 4, 1991).

39. Rabbi Yoel H. Kahn, "The *Kedushah* of Homosexual Relationships" (address at the Central Conference of American Rabbis, May 26, 1989), included in this book's appendix. See also letter from Michael D. Garbus, Vice President of Religious Affairs, Bet Mishpachah, to Judge Shellie Bowers, District of Columbia Superior Court (August 21, 1991).

40. Letter from the Reverend John H. Mack, Minister, First Congregational United Church of Christ, to Judge Shellie Bowers, District of Columbia Superior Court (July 31, 1991), included in the appendix.

41. Letter from the Reverend William H. Carey, Pastor, Lighthouse Apostolic Church, to Judge Shellie Bowers, District of Columbia Superior Court (August 1, 1991), included in the appendix.

42. Letter from Father James P. Mallon, Dignity, to Judge Shellie Bowers, District of Columbia Superior Court (July 29, 1991), included in the appendix.

43. Letter from Father John McNeill to Judge Shellie Bowers, District of Columbia Superior Court (undated).

44. Antonio A. Feliz, *Out of the Bishop's Closet*, 81–83, 93–94 (San Francisco: Alamo Square Press, 1992, 2d edition).

45. For example, letter from Peggy Monroe, Oversight Committee, University Friends Meeting, to Judge Shellie Bowers, District of Columbia Superior Court (August 2, 1991).

46. Letter from the Reverend Carla B. Gorrell, Minister, Westminster Presbyterian Church, to Judge Shellie Bowers, District of Columbia Superior Court (August 5, 1991), included in the appendix.

47. Letter from the Reverend Richard E. Stetler, Minister, Capitol Hill United Methodist Church, to Judge Shellie Bowers, District of Columbia Superior Court (August 13, 1991), included in the appendix.

48. Joan Sexton, "Learning from Gays," *Commonweal*, June 17, 1994, p. 28.

49. Harvey Mansfield, "Saving Liberalism from Liberals," *Harvard Crimson*, November 8, 1993, discussed in Macedo, "Homosexuality and the Conservative Mind." See also Harry Jaffa, *Original Intent and the Framers of the Constitution: A Disputed Question*, 364–367 (Washington, DC: Regnery Gateway, 1993), which states that if homosexual behavior is not "unnatural, nothing is unnatural."

50. See Pope John Paul II, "Letter to Families," 20; "Response by the Ramsey Colloquium"; Finnis, "Law, Morality, and 'Sexual Orientation,'" 1051–1053.

51. Hadley Arkes, "Closet Straight," *National Review*, July 5, 1993, p. 43.

52. Richard A. Posner, *Sex and Reason*, 311 (Cambridge, MA: Harvard University Press, 1992).

53. For example, James D. Wilson, "Gays Under Fire," *Newsweek*, September 14, 1992, pp. 34, 37. (In the *Newsweek* poll, 58% disapproved of legally recognized "gay marriage" and 35% approved).

54. See G. Sidney Buchanan, "Same-Sex Marriage: The Linchpin Issue," 10 *University of Dayton Law Review* 541 (1985).

55. Zablocki v. Redhail, 434 U.S. 374 (U.S. Supreme Court, 1978), discussed in chapter 5.

56. Turner v. Safley, 482 U.S. 78 (U.S. Supreme Court, 1987), discussed in chapter 5.

57. A 1991 poll found the public divided 45% to 44% against different-race marriages. A 1990 poll of whites found 65% opposed to a close relative's marrying an African American. A 1992 poll found 58% opposed to same-sex marriage. A 1991 poll found that only one in five respondents believed that different-race marriages should be illegal. These interesting polls are collected in James Trosino's useful student note, "American Wedding: Same-Sex Marriage and the Miscegenation Analogy," 73 *Boston University Law Review* 93, 93 and notes 2, 3, and 6 (1993).

58. See, for example, Alan P. Bell and Martin A. Weinberg, *Homosexualities: A Study of Diversity Among Men and Women* (New York: Simon & Schuster, 1978); Philip Blumstein and Pepper Schwartz, *American Couples: Money, Work, and Sex* (New York: Morrow, 1983); David P. McWhirter and A. M. Mattison, *The Male Couple* (Englewood Cliffs, NJ: Prentice-Hall, 1984); S. M. Duffy and C. E. Rosbult, "Satisfaction and Commitment in Homosexual and Heterosexual Relationships," 12 *Journal of Homosexuality* 1 (1986); and Lawrence A. Kurdek and J. Patrick Schmitt, "Relationship Quality of Partners in Heterosexual Married, Heterosexual Cohabiting, Gay, and Lesbian Relationships," 51 *Journal of Personality and Social Psychology* 711 (1986).

59. Letitia Anne Peplau and Susan D. Cochran, "Sex Differences in Values Concerning Love Relationships," paper presented at the Annual Meeting of the

American Psychological Association, September 1980, described in Letitia Anne Peplau and Susan D. Cochran, "A Relationship Perspective on Homosexuality," in McWhirter et al., *Homosexuality/Heterosexuality*, 321, 333–334.

60. See Laura Benkov, *Reinventing the Family: The Emerging Story of Lesbian and Gay Parents*, 108–143 (New York: Crown, 1994); Frederick W. Bozett, editor, *Homosexuality and the Family* (New York: Haworth, 1989); Marla J. Hollandsworth, "Gay Men Creating Families Through Surro-Gay Arrangements: A Paradigm for Reproductive Freedom," 3 *The American University Journal of Gender and the Law* 183 (1995); Sharon Elizabeth Rush, "Breaking with Tradition: Surrogacy and Gay Fathers," in Diana T. Meyers et al., eds., *Kindred Matters: Rethinking the Philosophy of the Family*, 102 (Ithaca, NY: Cornell University Press, 1993); E. Donald Shapiro and Lisa Schultz, "Single-Sex Families: The Impact of Birth Innovations Upon Traditional Family Notions," 24 *Journal of Family Law* 271 (1985–1986); and Randy Shilts, "Gay People Make Babies Too," *The Advocate*, October 22, 1975, p. 25.

61. The Editors of the Harvard Law Review, *Sexual Orientation and the Law*, 119 (Cambridge, MA: Harvard University Press, 1989). The cite for the figure quoted in the text was a secondhand report of a panel of family law experts at an ABA meeting. This is not a very good cite.

62. Quoted in Benkov, *Reinventing the Family*, 143.

63. See Duffy and Rusbult, "Satisfaction and Commitment," and Peplau and Cochran, "A Relationship Perspective on Homosexuality," 335–336.

64. Peplau and Cochran, "A Relationship Perspective on Homosexuality," 335–336.

65. On the disadvantages for lesbian mothers of not being able to marry another woman, see Saralie Bisnovich Pennington, "Children of Lesbian Mothers," in Frederick W. Bozett, editor, *Gay and Lesbian Parents*, 58, 68–69 (New York: Praeger, 1987).

66. Important empirical studies include Susan Golombok et al., "Children in Lesbian and Single Parent Households: Psychosexual and Psychiatric Appraisal," 24 *Journal of Child Psychology and Psychiatry* 551 (1983); David J. Kleber et al., "The Impact of Parental Homosexuality in Child Custody Cases: A Review of the Literature," 14 *Bulletin of the American Academy of Psychology and Law* 81 (1986); and Mary E. Hotvedt and Jane Barclay Mandel, "Children of Lesbian Mothers," in William Paul et al. editors, *Homosexuality: Social, Psychological, and Biological Issues* 275, 282 (Beverly Hills, CA: Sage Publications, 1982). Reviews of the empirical literature are contained in Charlotte J. Patterson, "Children of Lesbians and Single-Parent Households: Psychosexual and Psychiatric Appraisals," 63 *Child Development* 1025 (1992); Nancy D. Polikoff, "This Child Does Have Two Mothers: Redefining Parenthood to Meet the Needs of Children in

Lesbian-Mother and Other Nontraditional Families," 78 *Georgetown Law Journal*, 459, 561–566 (1990): Alisa Steckel, "Psychosexual Development of Children of Lesbian Mothers," in *Gay and Lesbian Parents*, 75.

67. See Richard Green et al., "Lesbian Mothers and Their Children: A Comparison with Solo Parent Heterosexual Mothers and Their Children," 15 *Archives of Sexual Behavior* 167 (1986); Golombok et al., "Children in Lesbian and Single Parent Households," 562–567. See also Rhonda R. Rivera, "Legal Issues in Gay and Lesbian Parenting," in *Gay and Lesbian Parents*, 199, 226 note 79 (which reports an unpublished study comparing children in households having two lesbian parents with those in households having a single female parent, whether straight or lesbian).

68. See Polikoff, "This Child Does Have Two Mothers," 459.

69. This story is taken from Benkov, *Reinventing the Family*, 214–227. The legal disposition is In re Kristen Janine Pearlman, No. 87–24926 (Circuit Court for the 17th Judicial Circuit, Broward County, Florida, March 31, 1989).

70. Quoted in Benkov, *Reinventing the Family*, 220.

71. Ibid., 221.

72. Ibid., 226–227.

73. "I wanted to break off visitation because Janine is not the 'female' gay," Rose said. "She's the 'dyke' gay. And Kristen was getting to that impressionable age." Ibid., 219.

74. Andrew Sullivan, "Here Comes the Groom: A (Conservative) Case for Gay Marriage," *New Republic*, August 28, 1989, pp. 20, 22.

75. Posner, *Sex and Reason*, 311.

76. Ibid. Judge Posner says further (p. 312) that the state would be "in the dishonest position of propagating a false picture of the reality of homosexuals' lives" by presenting us as capable of marital happiness. I have responded to this argument in William N. Eskridge, Jr., "A Social Constructionist Critique of Posner's *Sex and Reason*: Steps Toward a Gaylegal Agenda," 102 *Yale Law Journal* 333, 346–347, 352–365 (1992).

77. Posner, *Sex and Reason*, 313.

78. See Sam Howe Verhovek, "Texas Capital Ends Benefits for Partners," *New York Times*, May 9, 1994, p. 8.

79. Thoughtful studies include The Bureau of National Affairs, *Recognizing Nontraditional Families* (Washington, DC: Bureau of National Affairs, 1991); Stanford University Committee on Faculty and Staff Benefits, *Report of the Subcommittee on Domestic Partners' Benefits* (Palo Alto, CA: Stanford University, 1991); and Hewitt Associates, *Domestic Partners and Employee Benefits* (Lincolnshire, IL: Hewitt Associates, 1991). These and other internal studies are usefully discussed in Darren Spedale, *The Domestic Partner Dilemma: Extending Benefits to Domestic Partners of Employees* (Durham, NC: Senior Thesis, Duke University, 1993).

80. See Spedale, *Domestic Partner Dilemma*, 36–39.

81. See Elizabeth Murphy, *The Rise of Employer-Provided Benefits for Domestic Partners* (West Hollywood, CA: City of West Hollywood, 1992), and Jennifer Steinhauser, "Increasingly, Employers Offer Benefits to All Partners," *New York Times*, August 20, 1994, p. 25.

82. The lifetime cost for treating a person with AIDS was less than $100,000 in the early 1990s, according to Fred Hellinger, "Forecasting the Medical Care Costs of the HIV Epidemic: 1990–1994," *Inquiry*, Fall 1991, p. 213, and probably somewhat higher now because there is projected to be a longer survival period. Nonetheless, treating AIDS is, on the whole, much cheaper than treating cancer, serious heart disease, and premature babies.

83. The argument that follows is taken from William N. Eskridge, Jr., and Brian D. Weimer, "The Economics Epidemic in an AIDS Perspective," 61 *University of Chicago Law Review* 733, 768–769 (1994), and is generally accepted in Tomas J. Philipson and Richard A. Posner, *Private Choices and Public Health: The AIDS Epidemic in an Economic Perspective*, 148, 179–180 (Cambridge, MA: Harvard University Press, 1993).

84. Benny Henriksson and Hasse Ytterburg, "Sweden: The Power of the Moral(istic) Left," in David L. Kirp and Ronald Bayer, editors, *AIDS and the Industrialized Democracies: Passions, Politics, and Policies*, 317, 321–322 (New York: Rutgers University Press, 1992).

85. Naim v. Naim, 350 U.S. 891 (U.S. Supreme Court, 1955), remanding case to the Virginia Supreme Court, which on remand did nothing, 90 S.E.2d 849 (Virginia Supreme Court, 1956), appeal dismissed for lack of a substantial federal question, 350 U.S. 985 (U.S. Supreme Court, 1956).

Chapter 5. The Constitutional Case: The Right to Marry

1. See Earl M. Maltz, "Constitutional Protection for the Right to Marry: A Dissenting View," 60 *George Washington Law Review* 949 (1992).

2. Buck v. Bell, 274 U.S. 200 (U.S. Supreme Court, 1927).

3. This is the case where Justice Holmes made his celebrated crack, "Three generations of imbeciles are enough." The decision is criticized, and the crack takes on sinister meaning, in Stephen Jay Gould, "Carrie Buck's Daughter," 2 *Constitutional Commentary* 331 (1985).

4. Skinner v. Oklahoma, 316 U.S. 535, 541 (U.S. Supreme Court, 1942).

5. Palko v. Connecticut, 302 U.S. 319 (U.S. Supreme Court, 1937).

6. Meyer v. Nebraska, 262 U.S. 390 (U.S. Supreme Court, 1923), which invalidated state restrictions on teaching in any language other than English. See also Pierce v. Society of Sisters, 268 U.S. 510 (U.S. Supreme Court, 1925), which struck down law requiring all children to attend private schools as interfering with parents' rights to manage their children's education; Maynard v. Hill, 125 U.S. 190 (U.S. Supreme Court, 1888), which

stated that marriage is "the most important relation in life" and is the "foundation of the family and of society, without which there would be neither civilization nor progress."

7. Poe v. Ullman, 367 U.S. 497, 541 (U.S. Supreme Court, 1961) (Harlan, J., dissenting), which quotes Corfield v. Coryell, Fed. Cas. No. 3,230, 4 Wash. C.C. 371, 380 (U.S. Circuit Court for the Eastern District of Pennsylvania, 1823) (Justice Bushrod Washington); and Calder v. Bull, 3 U.S. 385, 388 (U.S. Supreme Court, 1799). Although written in dissent, Justice Harlan's approach has been considered authoritative. See Planned Parenthood of Southeastern Pennsylvania v. Casey, 112 S. Ct. 2791 (U.S. Supreme Court, 1992) (joint opinion).

8. Griswold v. Connecticut, 381 U.S. 479, 487 (U.S. Supreme Court, 1965).

9. *Poe*, 367 U.S. at 553 (Harlan, J., dissenting).

10. Loving v. Virginia, 388 U.S. 1, 12 (U.S. Supreme Court, 1967).

11. Zablocki v. Redhail, 434 U.S. 374 (U.S. Supreme Court, 1978).

12. Id. at 385, quoting Cleveland Board of Education v. LaFleur, 414 U.S. 632, 639–640 (U.S. Supreme Court, 1974). Only Justice William Rehnquist dissented from the Court's judgment, but Justice Lewis Powell objected to the Court's expansion of the right to marry beyond the *Loving* context.

13. Id. at 386.

14. Id. at 387 note 12, 388.

15. "State regulation has included bans on incest, bigamy, and homosexuality, as well as the various preconditions to marriage, such as blood tests. . . . A 'compelling state purpose inquiry' would cast doubt on the network of restrictions that the States have fashioned to govern marriage and divorce." *Zablocki*, 434 U.S. at 399 (Powell, J., concurring in the judgment).

16. Turner v. Safley, 482 U.S. 78, 95 (U.S. Supreme Court, 1987).

17. Justice O'Connor distinguished Butler v. Wilson, 415 U.S. 953 (U.S. Supreme Court, 1974), summarily affirming Johnson v. Rockefeller, 365 F. Supp. 377 (U.S. District Court for the Southern District of New York, 1973) (a three-judge court), which had upheld a "prohibition on marriage only for inmates sentenced to life imprisonment; and, importantly, denial of the right was part of the punishment for crime."

18. Leading judicial decisions rejecting a right to marry for same-sex couples are Baehr v. Lewin, 852 P.2d 44 (Hawaii Supreme Court, 1993); Jones v. Hallahan, 501 S.W.2d 588 (Kentucky Court of Appeals, 1973); Baker v. Nelson, 191 N.W.2d 185 (Minnesota Supreme Court, 1971), appeal dismissed, 409 U.S. 810 (U.S. Supreme Court, 1972); Singer v. Hara, 522 P.2d 1187 (Washington Court of Appeals, 1974), review denied, 84 Wash. 2d 1008 (Washington Supreme Court, 1974); and Adams v. Howerton, 486 F. Supp. 1119 (U.S. District Court, Central District of California, 1980), affirmed on other grounds, 673 F.2d 1036 (U.S. Court of App247eals for the Ninth Circuit, 1982).

Other decisions finding their jurisdictions' marriage statutes to constitute valid prohibitions of same-sex marriage include Callender v. Corbett, No. 296666 (Arizona Superior Court, Pima County, April 13, 1994); Ross v. Denver Department of Health & Hospitals, 883 P.2d 516 (Colorado Court of Appeals, 1994); Dean v. District of Columbia, 653 A.2d 307 (District of Columbia Court of Appeals, 1995); Van Dyck v. Van Dyck, 425 S.E.2d 853 (Georgia Supreme Court, 1993); Cuevas v. Mills, No. 86–3244 (U.S. District Court for the District of Kansas, October 27, 1986) (applying Kansas law); In re Succession of Bacot, 502 So. 2d 1118 (Louisiana Court of Appeals, 1987), writ denied, 503 So. 2d 466 (Louisiana Supreme Court, 1987); Jacobson v. Jacobson, 314 N.W.2d 78 (North Dakota Supreme Court, 1981); Gajovski v. Gajovski, 610 N.E. 2d 431 (Ohio Court of Appeals, 1991); De Santo v. Barnsley, 476 A.2d 952 (Pennsylvania Superior Court, 1984); In re Estate of Cooper, 564 N.Y.S.2d 684 (New York Surrogate Court, 1990), affirmed, 592 N.Y.S.2d 797 (New York Supreme Court, Appellate Division, 2d Department, 1993), appeal dismissed, 624 N.E.2d (New York Court of Appeals, 1993); Anonymous v. Anonymous, 325 N.Y.S.2d 499 (New York Supreme Court, 1971); United States v. Williams, No. 90–5731 (U.S. Court of Appeals for the Fourth Circuit, 1991) (applying South Carolina law); and Slayton v. State, 633 S.W.2d 934 (Texas Court of Civil Appeals, 1982).

In addition to the Hawaii attorney general (whose opinion was solicited and rendered in connection with the *Baehr* case), the attorneys general of other states have issued opinions that their states' marriage laws prohibit same-sex marriage and can constitutionally do so. They include 190 Opinions of the Attorney General of Alabama 30 (1983); Opinions of the Attorney General of Arkansas (April 26, 1995); 1975 Opinions of the Attorney General of Colorado (1975); 1993 Opinions of the Attorney General of Idaho 119 (1993); 77 Opinions of the Attorney General of Kansas (August 4, 1977); Opinions of the Attorney General of Louisiana (December 23, 1992); Opinions of the Attorney General of Maine (October 30, 1984); Opinions of the Attorney General of Mississippi (July 10, 1978); 1976 Opinions of the Attorney General of South Carolina (August 12, 1976); 88 Opinions of the Attorney General of Tennessee 43 (1988).

19. Baker v. Nelson, 191 N.W.2d 185, 187 (Minnesota Supreme Court, 1971), appeal dismissed, 409 U.S. 810 (U.S. Supreme Court, 1972).
20. Id. at 186.
21. Jones v. Hallahan, 501 S.W.2d 588, 589 (Kentucky Court of Appeals, 1973). See also Singer v. Hara, 522 P.2d 1187 (Washington Court of Appeals, 1974) review denied, 84 Wash. 2d 1008 (Washington Supreme Court, 1974).
22. Baehr v. Lewin, 852 P.2d 44, 56 (Hawaii Supreme Court, 1993) (opinion of Levinson, J.).

23. *Zablocki*, 434 U.S. at 387 note 12.

24. Id. at 388.

25. *Poe*, 367 U.S. at 553 (Harlan, J., dissenting), quoted in *Griswold*, 381 U.S. at 498–499 (Goldberg, J., concurring).

26. Eisenstadt v. Baird, 405 U.S. 438, 453 (U.S. Supreme Court, 1972).

27. Stanley v. Georgia, 394 U.S. 557 (U.S. Supreme Court, 1969).

28. See Richard A. Posner, "The Uncertain Protection of Privacy by the Supreme Court," 1979 *Supreme Court Review* 173, 198, and Harry H. Wellington, "Common Law Rules and Constitutional Double Standards: Some Notes on Adjudication," 83 *Yale Law Journal* 221, 296 (1973).

29. Bowers v. Hardwick, 478 U.S. 186 (U.S. Supreme Court, 1986).

30. For cases stating or holding that *Griswold* protects against consensual sodomy prosecutions when the couple is married, see Lovisi v. Slayton, 539 F.2d 349 (U.S. Court of Appeals for the Fourth Circuit, 1976); State v. Poe, 252 S.E.2d 843 (North Carolina Court of Appeals, 1979), appeal dismissed, 259 S.E.2d 304 (North Carolina Supreme Court, 1980); and State v. Santos, 413 A.2d 58 (Supreme Court of Rhode Island, 1980). On the other hand, forcible sodomy has been prosecuted even when the couple is married. See, for example, People v. Liberta, 474 N.E.2d 567 (New York Court of Appeals, 1984).

31. The decision has been criticized as inaccurate history, by Anne B. Goldstein, "History, Homosexuality, and Political Values: Searching for the Hidden Determinants of *Bowers v. Hardwick*," 97 *Yale Law Journal* 1073, 1081–1091 (1988); as reinforcing archaic gender roles, by Sylvia A. Law, "Homosexuality and the Social Meaning of Gender," 1988 *Wisconsin Law Review* 187, 230; as undermining self-governance, by Frank I. Michelman, "Law's Republic," 97 *Yale Law Journal* 1493, 1494–1499 (1987); as ill informed, by Richard A. Posner, *Sex and Reason*, 341–350 (Cambridge, MA: Harvard University Press, 1992); as transparently reflecting personal anti-homosexual attitudes, by Thomas B. Stoddard, "*Bowers v. Hardwick*: Precedent by Personal Predilection," 54 *University of Chicago Law Review* 648, 655–656 (1987) (essay); as inconsistent with precedent, by Laurence H. Tribe, *American Constitutional Law* 1425–1429 (Mineola, NY: Foundation Press, 1988, 2d edition); and as generally slippery, by Janet E. Halley, "Reasoning About Sodomy: Act and Identity in and After *Bowers v. Hardwick*," 79 *Virginia Law Review* 1721, 1741–1742 (1993).

No other Supreme Court decision in recent memory has generated such a large volume of uniformly negative reviews. All the leading commentators have urged the Court to overrule *Bowers*, on grounds ranging from the due process privacy right, Jed Rubenfeld, "The Right of Privacy," 102 *Harvard Law Review* 737, 799–802 (1989); to equal protection gender discrimination, Law, "Social Meaning of Gender"; Andrew Koppelman,

"The Miscegenation Analogy: Sodomy Law as Sex Discrimination," 98 *Yale Law Journal* 145, 147 (1988) (student note); to freedom of expression, David Cole and William N. Eskridge, Jr., "From Hand-Holding to Sodomy: First Amendment Protection of Homosexual (Expressive) Conduct," 29 *Harvard Civil Rights–Civil Liberties Law Review* 319, 325–330 (1994); to cruel and unusual punishment, Kendall Thomas, "Beyond the Privacy Principle," 92 *Columbia Law Review* 1431, 1461 (1992).

32. Charles Fried, *Order and Law,* 81–84 (New York: Simon & Schuster, 1991). On Fried's role in *Poe,* see David J. Garrow, *Liberty and Sexuality: The Right to Privacy and the Making of Roe* v. Wade, 190 (New York: Macmillan, 1994).

33. See John M. Finnis, "Law, Morality, and 'Sexual Orientation,'" 69 *Notre Dame Law Review* 1049, 1050–1053 (1994).

34. See, for example, Alfred C. Kinsey et al., *Sexual Behavior in the American Male,* 393 (Philadelphia: Saunders, 1948), in which it is reported that 59% of American males in the 1940s had engaged in oral sex and 37% in anal sex; Morton Hunt, *Sexual Behavior in the 1970s,* 199, 204 (Chicago: Playboy Press, 1974), which reports that 90% of married couples under age 25 in the 1970s engaged in oral sex and that nearly 25% of married couples under age 35 engaged in anal sex; and Philip Blumstein and Pepper Schwartz, *American Couples: Money, Work, Sex,* 236 (New York: Morrow, 1983), which states that over 70% of heterosexual couples in the early 1980s engaged in oral sex.

35. See Vern L. Bullough, *Science in the Bedroom,* 138–143 (New York: Basic Books, 1994), which cites instructional descriptions of sodomy in manuals written by authors who believed heterosexual intercourse the only permissible form, for example, Theodore van de Velde, *Ideal Marriage: Its Physiology and Technique* (New York: Covici Friede, 1930).

36. Ruthann Robson, *Lesbian (Out)law: Survival Under the Rule of Law,* 47–59 (Ithaca, NY: Firebrand Books, 1992), chapter 3, "Crimes of Lesbian Sex."

37. Janet S. St. Lawrence et al., "Differences in Gay Men's AIDS Risk Knowledge and Behavior Patterns in High and Low AIDS Prevalence Cities," 104 *Public Health Reports* 391 (1989), found that 51% of the sexual activities practiced by gay men in high-AIDS-incidence cities involved just mutual masturbation or body rubbing, 26% involved oral intercourse of some kind, and 23% involved anal intercourse (10% with a condom). A great deal more anal intercourse (almost 50% of the activities) was found in low-AIDS-incidence cities.

38. See People v. Onofre, 415 N.E.2d 936 (New York Court of Appeals, 1980), and Commonwealth v. Bonadio, 415 A.2d 47 (Pennsylvania Supreme Court, 1980).

39. City of Dallas v. England, 846 S.W.2d 956 (Texas Court of Criminal Appeals, 1992, writ of error to the Texas Supreme Court dismissed on juris-

dictional grounds, 1993); Michigan Organization for Human Rights v. Kelley, No. 88–815820 CZ (Michigan Circuit Court, July 9, 1990), invalidating state law, with Attorney General declining to appeal; Gryczan v. Montana, No. BDV-93–1869 (First District, Lewis and Clark County, June 28, 1994), preliminary injunction.

40. Commonwealth v. Wasson, 842 S.W.2d 487 (Kentucky Supreme Court, 1992).

41. See Defendants' Response to Plaintiffs' First Request for Answers to Interrogatories, pp. 6–10 (December 17, 1993), outlined in Evan Wolfson (co-counsel for plaintiffs), "Crossing the Threshold: Equal Marriage Rights for Lesbians and Gay Men, and the Intra-Community Critique," 21 *New York University Review of Law and Social Change* 567 (1994). The main academic works suggesting possible state interests are Posner, *Sex and Reason*, 311–313, and G. Sidney Buchanan, "Same-Sex Marriage: The Linchpin Issue," 10 *Dayton University Law Review* 541 (1985).

42. This was the interpretation of former justice Tom C. Clark, who joined the Court's opinion in *Griswold* and retired soon thereafter. See Clark, "Religion, Morality, and Abortion: A Constitutional Appraisal," 2 *Loyola of Los Angeles Law Review* 1, 9 (1969).

43. Golombok et al., "Children in Lesbian and Single Parent Households," 562–567.

44. Ibid., 570.

45. See Richard Green et al., "Lesbian Mothers and Their Children: A Comparison with Solo Parent Heterosexual Mothers and Their Children," 15 *Archives of Sexual Behavior* 167 (1986), as well as Rhonda R. Rivera, "Legal Issues in Gay and Lesbian Parenting," in Frederick W. Bozett, editor, *Gay and Lesbian Parents*, 199, 226 note 79 (New York: Praeger, 1987) (reporting an unpublished study comparing children in households having two lesbian parents with those in households having a single female parent, either straight or lesbian).

46. Jennifer Gerarda Brown, "Competitive Federalism and the Legislative Incentives to Recognize Same-Sex Marriages," 68 *Southern California Law Review* 745 (1995).

47. For informative commentary, see Barbara J. Cox, "Same-Sex Marriage and Choice-of-Law: If We Marry in Hawaii, Are We Still Married When We Return Home?" 1994 *Wisconsin Law Review* 1033; Joseph W. Hovermill, "A Conflict of Laws and Morals: The Choice of Law Implications of Hawaii's Recognition of Same-Sex Marriages," 53 *Maryland Law Review* 450 (1994).

48. City of Cleburne v. Cleburne Living Center, 473 U.S. 432 (U. S. Supreme Court, 1985), quoting United States Department of Agriculture v. Moreno,

413 U.S. 528 (U. S. Supreme Court, 1973). See also Coates v. Cincinnati, 402 U.S. 611, 615 (U.S. Supreme Court, 1971).

49. See T.F.P. v. Leavitt, 840 F. Supp. 110 (U.S. District Court for the District of Utah, 1993), which holds that the ADA, 42 U.S.C. § 12132, preempts state prohibition against marriages by people with AIDS.

50. *Zablocki*, 434 U.S. at 387 note 12, 388.

51. A slice of the empirical evidence, relating to adolescent decision making in sexually risky activity, is surveyed in William N. Eskridge, Jr. and Brian D. Weimer, "The Economics Epidemic in an AIDS Perspective," 61 *University of Chicago Law Review* 733 (1994).

52. Reynolds v. United States, 98 U.S. 145, 164–165 (U.S. Supreme Court, 1878).

53. Cleveland v. United States, 329 U.S. 14, 19 (U.S. Supreme Court, 1946), the prosecution of a Mormon polygamist for bringing one of his wives across state lines "for immoral purposes," therefore in violation of the Mann Act.

54. See *Turner*, 482 U.S. 78. Much of the argument that follows is indebted to Posner, *Sex and Reason*, 253–260, which also contains useful references to secondary sources.

55. Board of Directors of Rotary International v. Rotary Club of Duarte, 481 U.S. 537 (U.S. Supreme Court, 1987), and Roberts v. United States Jaycees, 468 U.S. 609 (U.S. Supreme Court 1984).

56. I do not consider other, less common, variations on the two-person partnership marriage. For example, could two lesbians and two male sperm donors form a four-person marriage?

57. See Carolyn S. Bratt, "Incest Statutes and the Fundamental Right of Marriage: Is Oedipus Free to Marry?" 18 *Family Law Quarterly* 257 (1984), and Robert Drinan, "The *Loving* Decision and the Freedom to Marry," 29 *Ohio State Law Journal* 358 (1968). Beyond Salisbury v. List, 501 F. Supp. 105 (U.S. District Court for the District of Colorado, 1980), which recognizes that the state has compelling interests to regulate consanguinity, and Israel v. Allen, 577 P.2d 762 (Colorado Supreme Court, 1978), which invalidates prohibition of marriage by adoptive siblings, the case law is not thoughtful.

58. The arguments in this paragraph and the next are drawn from Herbert Maisch, *Incest* (London: Deutsch, 1973, translated by Colin Bearne), and Bratt, "Is Oedipus Free to Marry?" an excellent discussion of the literature, one that concludes that most restrictions do not satisfy *Zablocki*.

59. The scientific evidence is assembled and analyzed in Bratt, "Is Oedipus Free to Marry?"

60. The discussion in the text is based on Maisch, *Incest*.

61. See, for example, State v. Buck, 757 P.2d 861 (Oregon Court of Appeals 1988) and State v. Kaiser, 663 P.2d 839 (Washington Court of Appeals, 1983), both of which concern a man and his stepdaughter.
62. Israel v. Allen, 577 P.2d 762 (Colorado Supreme Court, 1978).

Chapter 6. The Constitutional Case: Discrimination

1. Loving v. Virginia, 388 U.S. 1 (1967).
2. On the history of antimiscegenation laws, see Derrick A. Bell, Jr., *Race, Racism, and American Law*, 64–108 (Boston: Little, Brown, 1992, 3d edition); Robert J. Sickels, *Race, Marriage, and the Law* (Albuquerque, NM: University of New Mexico Press, 1972); Harvey M. Appelbaum, "Miscegenation Statutes: A Constitutional and Social Problem," 53 *Georgetown Law Journal* 49 (1964); A. Leon Higginbotham and Barbara K. Kopytoff, "Racial Purity and Interracial Sex in the Law of Colonial and Antebellum Virginia," 77 *Georgetown Law Journal* 1967 (1989); James Trosino, "American Wedding: Same-Sex Marriage and the Miscegenation Analogy," 73 *Boston University Law Review* 93 (1993) (student note); and Walter J. Wadlington, "The *Loving* Case: Virginia's Anti-Miscegenation Statute," 52 *Virginia Law Review* 1189 (1966).
3. William Waller Hening, compiler, *Statutes at Large, Being a Collection of the Laws of Virginia from the First Session of the Legislature in the Year 1619*, volume 2, pp. 86–87 (New York: R. & W. & G. Bartow, 1823).
4. Quoted in Higginbotham & Kopytoff, "Racial Purity and Interracial Sex," 2019.
5. *Congressional Globe*, 39th Congress, 1st Session, part 1, 322 (1866) (Senator Lyman Trumbull, Republican, Illinois). See Alfred Avins, "Anti-Miscegenation Laws and the Fourteenth Amendment: The Original Intent," 52 *Virginia Law Review* 1224 (1966).
6. *Congressional Globe*, 37th Congress, 2d Session, part 2, appendix, 84 (1863).
7. *The People Shall Judge: Readings in the Formulation of American Policy*, 784, 786 (Chicago: College of the University of Chicago, 1949, edited by the Social Science Staff), which excerpts the Constitution and Ritual of the Knights of the White Camellia (1869). A fascinating treatment of the "purity of blood" argument, and its practical difficulties in implementation, is Eva Saks, "Representing Miscegenation Law," 8 *Raritan*, Fall 1988, p. 39.
8. See F. James Davis, *Who Is Black?* (University Park, PA: Pennsylvania State University Press, 1991); Herbert Hovenkamp, "Social Science and Segregation Before *Brown*," 1985 *Duke Law Journal* 624; Paul A. Lombardo, "Miscegenation, Eugenics, and Racism: Historical Footnotes to *Loving v. Virginia*," 21 *University of California at Davis Law Review* 421 (1988); and Saks, "Representing Miscegenation Law."

9. Scott v. Georgia, 39 Ga. 321, 324 (Supreme Court of Georgia, 1869).

10. Id. at 326. See also Green v. State, 58 Ala. 190, 195 (Alabama Supreme Court, 1877), which stated that neither whites nor blacks can benefit from intermarriage, because "he [God] has made the two races distinct"; Lonas v. State, 50 Tenn. 287, 299–300 (Tennessee Supreme Court, 1871), which upheld antimiscegenation law, "[t]o prevent violence and bloodshed which would arise from such cohabitation, distasteful to our people, and unfit to produce the human race in any of the types in which it was created."

11. State v. Jackson, 80 Mo. 175, 179 (Missouri Supreme Court, 1883).

12. Pace v. Alabama, 106 U.S. 583 (U.S. Supreme Court, 1883).

13. Plessy v. Ferguson, 163 U.S. 537 (U.S. Supreme Court, 1896), which said the Fourteenth Amendment "could not have been intended to abolish distinctions based upon color, or to enforce social, as distinguished from political equality, or a commingling of the two races upon terms unsatisfactory to either." In dissent, Justice John Marshall Harlan objected to segregation as legal backing for a social "caste" system.

14. An Act to Preserve Racial Integrity, Virginia Acts 1924, chapter 371, approved March 20, 1924, codified at § 5099a of the *Virginia Code of 1936* (Charlottesville, VA: Michie, 1936).

15. Id. § 5, *1936 Code* § 5099a(5).

16. Id. § 1, *1936 Code* § 5099a(1).

17. Id. § 4, *1936 Code* § 5099a(4).

18. Id. § 2, *1936 Code* § 5099a(2).

19. *1936 Code* § 4546.

20. Gunnar Myrdal, *An American Dilemma: The Negro Problem and Modern Democracy*, 606 (New York: Harper, 1944).

21. Perez v. Lippold, 198 P.2d 17 (California Supreme Court, 1948).

22. Naim v. Naim, 87 S.E.2d 749 (Virginia Supreme Court, 1955), remanded, 350 U.S. 891 (U.S. Supreme Court, 1956), reaffirming original opinion, 90 S.E.2d 849 (Virginia Supreme Court, 1956), appeal dismissed, 350 U.S. 985 (U.S. Supreme Court, 1956).

23. McLaughlin v. Florida, 379 U.S. 184, 188, 192–193 (U.S. Supreme Court, 1964).

24. Quoted in *Loving*, 388 U.S. at 3.

25. *Naim*, 87 S.E.2d at 756.

26. Id. at 11–12.

27. Kingsley Davis, "Intermarriage in Caste Societies," 43 *American Anthropologist* 376, 389 (1941).

28. Singer v. Hara, 522 P.2d 1187 (Washington Court of Appeals, 1974), review denied, 84 Wash. 2d 1008 (Washington Supreme Court, 1974).

29. Sylvia A. Law, "Homosexuality and the Social Meaning of Gender," 1988 *Wisconsin Law Review* 187; Andrew Koppelman, "Why Discrimination

Against Lesbians and Gay Men Is Sex Discrimination," 69 *New York University Law Review* 197 (1994). See also Andrew Koppelman, "The Miscegenation Analogy: Sodomy Law as Sex Discrimination," 98 *Yale Law Journal* 145 (1988) (student note), and Claudia A. Lewis, "From This Day Forward: A Feminine Moral Discourse on Homosexual Marriage," 97 *Yale Law Journal* 1783 (1988) (student note).

30. Baehr v. Lewin, 852 P.2d 52 (Hawaii Supreme Court, 1993) (Levinson, J., for a plurality), reaffirmed by a majority of the court in response to the state's motion for reconsideration, 852 P.2d 74 (Hawaii Supreme Court, 1993).

31. Hawaii Constitution, Article I, § 5.

32. *Singer*, 522 P.2d at 1192 (distinguishing *Loving* in this way).

33. Id. at 1194.

34. Act of June 22, 1994, § 1, Hawaii Session Laws 217. Compare *Singer*, 522 P.2d at 1192 note 8: "[I]f the state legislature were to change the definition of marriage to include the legal union of members of the same sex but also provide that marriage licenses and the accompanying protections of the marriage laws could only be extended to male couples, then it is likely that the state marriage laws would be in conflict with the ERA for failure to provide equal benefits to female couples."

35. District of Columbia Human Rights Act, District of Columbia Code § 1–2501 *et seq.* (1994). See Dean v. District of Columbia, 653 A.2d 307 (District of Columbia Court of Appeals 1995) (opinion of Ferren, J., for the majority on the Human Rights Act issues), which assumes, consistent with the District's concession, that the Human Rights Act's prohibitions apply to the District and its laws.

36. Craig v. Boren, 429 U.S. 190, 197 (U.S. Supreme Court, 1976).

37. Mississippi University for Women v. Hogan, 458 U.S. 718, 725 (U.S. Supreme Court, 1982). For other examples, see Orr v. Orr, 440 U.S. 268 (U.S. Supreme Court, 1979), which invalidated a law permitting alimony to be assessed only against husbands and not against wives, and Weinberger v. Wiesenfeld, 420 U.S. 636 (U.S. Supreme Court, 1975), which invalidated the Social Security rule giving lesser survivors' benefits to widowers than to widows.

38. J.E.B. v. Alabama ex rel. T.B., 114 S. Ct. 1419, 1425 note 6 (U.S. Supreme Court, 1994), and Harris v. Forklift Systems, Inc., 114 S. Ct. 367, 373 (U.S. Supreme Court, 1994) (Ginsburg, J., concurring).

39. *Craig*, 429 U.S. at 198–199, quoting Schlesinger v. Ballard, 419 U.S. 498 (U.S. Supreme Court, 1975), first quotation, and Weinberger v. Wiesenfeld, 420 U.S. 636 (U.S. Supreme Court, 1975), second quotation.

40. The argument that follows is initially drawn from Law, "Homosexuality and the Social Meaning of Gender," and Koppelman, "Why Discrimination Against Gays and Lesbians Is Sex Discrimination."

41. Randolph Trumbach, "The Birth of the Queen: Sodomy and the Emergence of Gender Equality in Modern Culture, 1660–1750," in Martin B. Duberman et al., editors, *Hidden from History: Reclaiming the Gay and Lesbian Past*, 129 (New York: Meridian, 1989).

42. The account that follows is inspired by and borrows from George Chauncey, Jr., *Gay New York: Gender, Urban Culture, and the Making of the Gay Male World, 1890–1940* (New York: Basic Books, 1994), and Carroll Smith-Rosenberg, *Disorderly Conduct: Visions of Gender in Victorian America* (New York: Oxford University Press, 1985). This account will be tied to a history of legal developments in William N. Eskridge, Jr., *Gaylaw,* chapter 1 (Cambridge, MA: Harvard University Press, forthcoming 1997).

43. See Suzanne Pharr, *Homophobia: A Weapon of Sexism* (Little Rock, AR: Chardon Press, 1988).

44. See Jessica Benjamin, *The Bonds of Love: Psychoanalysis, Feminism, and the Problem of Domination* (New York: Pantheon, 1988); Nancy Chodorow, *The Reproduction of Mothering* (Berkeley: University of California Press, 1978); Dorothy Dinnerstein, *The Mermaid and the Minotaur: Sexual Arrangements and Human Malaise* (New York: Harper & Row, 1976), and Paul Hoch, *White Hero, Black Beast: Racism, Sexism, and the Mask of Masculinity* (London: Photo Press, 1979).

45. Stephen F. Morin and Ellen M. Garfinkle, "Male Homophobia," 34 *Journal of Social Issues*, Winter 1978, pp. 29, 31. For similar findings, see Mary R. Laner and Roy H. Laner, "Sexual Preference or Personal Style? Why Lesbians Are Disliked," 5 *Journal of Homosexuality* 339 (1980), and Mary R. Laner and Roy H. Laner, "Personal Style or Sexual Preference? Why Gay Men Are Disliked," 9 *International Review of Modern Society* 215 (1979). Koppelman, "Why Discrimination Against Lesbians and Gay Men Is Sex Discrimination," 238 note 157, lists other sources to the same effect.

46. A. P. MacDonald and Richard G. Games, "Some Characteristics of Those Who Hold Positive and Negative Attitudes Toward Homosexuals," 1 *Journal of Homosexuality* 9, 19 (1979).

47. Kathryn N. Black and Michael R. Stevenson, "The Relationship of Self-Reported Sex-Role Characteristics and Attitudes Toward Homosexuality," in John P. DeCecco, editor, *Bashers, Baiters and Bigots: Homophobia in American Society*, 83 (New York: Harrington Park Press, 1985).

48. Albert D. Klassen et al., *Sex and Morality in the U.S.: An Empirical Inquiry under the Auspices of the Kinsey Institute*, chapter 10 (Middletown, CT: Wesleyan University Press, 1989).

49. Ibid., 241, quoting A. P. MacDonald et al., "Attitudes Toward Homosexuality: Preservation of Sex Morality or the Double Standard?" 40 *Journal of Consulting and Clinical Psychology* 161 (1972).

50. See Gay Law Students Association v. Pacific Telephone & Telegraph, 595 P.2d 592 (California Supreme Court, 1979); Commonwealth of Kentucky v. Wasson, 842 S.W.2d 487 (Kentucky Supreme Court, 1992); see also Gay Rights Coalition v. Georgetown University, 536 A.2d 1 (District of Columbia Court of Appeals, en banc, 1987), which interpreted the District's Human Rights Act, a "super-statute."

51. Watkins v. United States, 847 F.2d 1329 (U.S. Court of Appeals for the Ninth Circuit, 1988), affirmed on other grounds [estoppel], 875 F.2d 699 (U.S. Court of Appeals for the Ninth Circuit, en banc, 1989).

52. Washington v. Davis, 426 U.S. 229 (U.S. Supreme Court, 1976).

53. Id. at 242, citing *McLaughlin*.

54. Id. at 240.

55. Yick Wo v. Hopkins, 118 U.S. 356 (U.S. Supreme Court, 1886).

56. *Davis*, 426 U.S. at 239 (emphasis added); accord, *Loving*, 388 U.S. at 9–10.

57. *Loving*, 388 U.S. at 9–10 (deliberations surrounding Fourteenth Amendment "inconclusive"); *McLaughlin*, 379 U.S. 184 (similar).

58. See *Craig*, 429 U.S. 190; Frontiero v. Richardson, 411 U.S. 677 (U.S. Supreme Court, 1973) (plurality opinion of Brennan, J.); Gerald Gunther, "The Supreme Court, 1971 Term—Foreword: In Search of Evolving Doctrine on a Changing Court: A Model for a Newer Equal Protection," 86 *Harvard Law Review* 1 (1972).

59. Ruth Bader Ginsburg, "Sexual Equality under the Fourteenth and Equal Rights Amendments," 1979 *Washington University Law Quarterly* 161.

60. In addition to *Loving* (race) and *Craig* (sex), see Trimble v. Gordon, 430 U.S. 762 (U.S. Supreme Court, 1976), on nonmarital birth, and Korematsu v. United States, 323 U.S. 214 (U.S. Supreme Court, 1944), on race (although the Court upheld the challenged classification).

    The Supreme Court has also said that classifications based on citizenship or alienage are suspect classifications, Graham v. Richardson, 403 U.S. 365 (U.S. Supreme Court, 1971), but I read this line of cases as reflecting principles of federalism. Congress has primary authority for regulating immigration and citizenship, and the Court is alert to the concern that state regulations may interfere with this power and with national treaty obligations. See Toll v. Moreno, 458 U.S. 1 (U.S. Supreme Court, 1982). Hence, state classifications have frequently been invalidated, but congressional classifications have not.

61. See City of Cleburne v. Cleburne Living Center, 473 U.S. 432 (U.S. Supreme Court, 1985), involving disability; New York City Transit Authority v. Beazer, 440 U.S. 568 (U.S. Supreme Court, 1979), involving addiction; Massachusetts Board of Retirement v. Murgia, 427 U.S. 307 (U.S. Supreme Court, 1976), involving age; Independent School District v. Rodriguez, 411 U.S. 1 (U.S. Supreme Court, 1973), involving wealth; and

Dandridge v. Williams, 397 U.S. 471 (U.S. Supreme Court, 1970), involving wealth.

62. Frontiero v. Richardson, 411 U.S. 677, 686 (U.S. Supreme Court, 1973) (plurality opinion of Brennan, J.), quoted in *Cleburne*, 473 U.S. at 440; accord, Mathews v. Lucas, 427 U.S. 495, 505 (U.S. Supreme Court, 1976), on nonmarital birth.

63. *McLaughlin*, 379 U.S. at 192.

64. *Cleburne*, 473 U.S. at 440. See also Plyler v. Doe, 457 U.S. 202, 216 note 14 (U.S. Supreme Court, 1982), on how the invocation of such characteristics is a red flag that decision makers are responding to their own or others' "deep-seated prejudice."

65. *Murgia*, 427 U.S. at 313.

66. *Cleburne*, 473 U.S. at 442.

67. This story is told in William N. Eskridge, Jr., "Gadamer/Statutory Interpretation," 90 *Columbia Law Review* 609 (1990), and will be developed in greater detail in Eskridge, *Gaylaw*, chapters 2 and 3.

68. The Supreme Court so held in Boutilier v. Immigration and Naturalization Service, 387 U.S. 118 (U.S. Supreme Court, 1967).

69. Useful collections of evidence include Linda D. Garnets and Douglas C. Kimmel, editors, *Psychological Perspectives on Lesbian and Gay Male Experiences* (New York: Columbia University Press, 1993), and John C. Gonsiorek, "The Empirical Basis for the Demise of the Illness Model of Homosexuality," in James D. Weinrich and J. Gonsiorek, editors, *Homosexuality: Research Implications for Public Policy,* 115 (Newbury Park, CA: Sage Publications, 1991).

70. Resolution of the APA, December 15, 1973. An excellent history of the debate and the shift in evidence can be found in Ronald Bayer, *Homosexuality and American Psychiatry: The Politics of Diagnosis* (Princeton, NJ: Princeton University Press, 1987, new edition).

71. 135 *Congressional Record* S5040–S5042 (daily edition, May 9, 1989).

72. This claim is explored and persuasively critiqued in Janet Halley, "The Politics of the Closet: Towards Equal Protection for Gay, Lesbian, and Bisexual Identity," 36 *University of California at Los Angeles Law Review* 915 (1989).

73. *Watkins*, 847 F.2d at 1347.

74. The studies are sympathetically described and reviewed in Simon LeVay and Dean H. Hamer, "Evidence for a Biological Influence in Male Homosexuality," *Scientific American*, May 1994, pp. 44–49, and more critically in William Byne, "The Biological Evidence Challenged," *Scientific American*, May 1994, pp. 50–55.

75. See Alan P. Bell, Martin S. Weinberg, and Sue Kiefer Hammersmith, *Sexual Preference: Its Development in Men and Women* (Bloomington, IN: Indiana University Press, 1981); Richard Green, *The "Sissy Boy" Syndrome and the*

Development of Homosexuality (New Haven, CT: Yale University Press, 1987); and Richard A. Posner, *Sex and Reason*, 101–108 (Cambridge, MA: Harvard University Press, 1992).

76. *Watkins*, 847 F.2d at 1347–1348.

77. *Frontiero*, 411 U.S. at 685–686 (plurality opinion of Brennan, J.).

78. *Murgia*, 427 U.S. at 313; see also Bowen v. Gilliard, 483 U.S. 587, 603 (U.S. Supreme Court, 1987), and Lyng v. Castillo, 477 U.S. 635, 638 (U.S. Supreme Court, 1986), on family status.

79. *Cleburne*, 473 U.S. at 443.

80. Standard sources for the history of antihomosexual persecution before World War II include Chauncey, *Gay New York*; Lillian Faderman, *Odd Girls and Twilight Lovers: A History of Lesbian Life in Twentieth-Century America* (New York: Penguin, 1991). For World War II, see Allan Bérubé, *Coming Out Under Fire: The History of Gay Men and Women in World War Two* (New York: Free Press, 1990). For the postwar period, see Barry D. Adam, *The Rise of a Gay and Lesbian Movement* (Boston: Twayne Publishers, 1987), and John D'Emilio, *Sexual Politics, Sexual Communities: The Making of a Homosexual Minority in the United States, 1940–1970* (Chicago: University of Chicago Press, 1983).

81. See Eskridge, *Gaylaw*, chapter 2.

82. See Hearings of the Senate Committee on Labor and Human Resources (No. 103–703), 103d Congress, 2d Session (1994).

Epilogue: Fear of Flaunting

1. See McConnell v. Anderson, 451 F.2d 193 (U.S. Court of Appeals for the Eighth Circuit, 1971), upholding the withdrawal of employment from a gay man after he applied for a marriage license, and Singer v. United States Civil Service Commission, 530 F.2d 247 (U.S. Court of Appeals for the Ninth Circuit, 1976), vacated, 429 U.S. 1034 (U.S. Supreme Court, 1977) (same).

2. See Price Waterhouse v. Ann Hopkins, 490 U.S. 228 (United States Supreme Court, 1989), which holds that a woman can sue for sex discrimination if unfavorable employment action is based upon feelings that she is too "mannish," and Mary Anne Case, "Disaggregating Gender from Sex and Sexual Orientation: The Effeminate Man in the Law and Feminist Jurisprudence," 105 *Yale Law Journal* 1 (1995), demonstrating that *Hopkins* requires a finding of sex discrimination if a man is fired for being too "effeminate."

3. See Richard A. Isay, *Being Homosexual: Gay Men and Their Development* (New York: Farrar, Straus & Giroux, 1989), and Michael Ruse, *Homosexuality: A Philosophical Inquiry* (Cambridge, MA: Basil Blackwell, 1988). For a

historical survey, see Kenneth Lewes, *The Psychoanalytic Theory of Male Homosexuality* (New York: Simon & Schuster, 1988).

4. John Rawls, *A Theory of Justice* (Cambridge, MA: Harvard University Press, 1971).

5. Plessy v. Ferguson, 163 U.S. 537 (U.S. Supreme Court, 1896) (Harlan, J., dissenting).

6. Antonin Scalia, "The Rule of Law as a Law of Rules," 56 *University of Chicago Law Review* 1775 (1989).

COURT CASES

Federal Cases

Reynolds v. United States, 98 U.S. 145 (U.S. Supreme Court, 1878). The Court upheld a prosecution of a polygamist. The Court implicitly rejected a right to marry more than one spouse at a time.

Pace v. Alabama, 106 U.S. 583 (U.S. Supreme Court, 1883). The Court upheld a state law barring different-race marriage. The Court rejected the argument that the law's discrimination on the basis of race violated the equal protection clause of the Fourteenth Amendment.

Skinner v. Oklahoma, 316 U.S. 535 (U.S. Supreme Court, 1942). The Court invalidated Oklahoma's law requiring sterilization of certain criminals (e.g., thieves) and not others (e.g., embezzlers) as a violation of the equal protection clause of the Fourteenth Amendment.

Poe v. Ullman, 367 U.S. 497 (U.S. Supreme Court, 1961). The Court dismissed constitutional challenges to Connecticut's law prohibiting the sale and use of contraceptives. The Court found the controversy insufficiently "ripe" to adjudicate, but Justice Harlan wrote an influential dissent that argued that the law violated the due process clause of the Fourteenth Amendment. Justice Harlan's approach was recognized as the classic articulation of the "right to privacy" in *Planned Parenthood of Southeastern Pennsylvania v. Casey*, 112 S. Ct. 2791 (U.S. Supreme Court, 1992) (Joint Opinion).

McLaughlin v. Florida, 379 U.S. 184 (U.S. Supreme Court, 1964). The Court invalidated a law barring different-race couples from cohabiting; the law violated the equal protection clause. The decision implicitly overruled *Pace v. Alabama*.

Griswold v. Connecticut, 381 U.S. 479 (U.S. Supreme Court, 1965). The Court invalidated Connecticut's anticontraception law as a violation of a "right to privacy" found in the "penumbras" of the Bill of Rights. The right to privacy was to prove robust; the penumbral analysis was not.

Loving v. Virginia, 388 U.S. 1 (U.S. Supreme Court, 1967). The Court invalidated
Virginia's prohibition of different-race marriage as a violation of both the equal
protection and due process clauses. The decision explicitly overruled *Pace v.
Alabama*. In defense of its antimiscegenation law, Virginia cited the disapproval
of different-race marriage by religious and moral traditions, an argument the
Court rejected. This decision initiated the "right to marry" line of cases.

Craig v. Boren, 429 U.S. 190 (U.S. Supreme Court, 1976). The Court invalidated a state law setting different age requirements for males and females
purchasing low-alcohol beer. Notwithstanding the failure of the federal
Equal Rights Amendment to be ratified, the Court held that classifications
based on sex should be subjected to heightened judicial scrutiny under the
auspices of the equal protection clause.

Zablocki v. Redhail, 434 U.S. 374 (U.S. Supreme Court, 1978). The Court invalidated Wisconsin's bar to remarriage when one partner has unpaid support
obligations from a previous marriage. Emphasizing the state's interference
with *Loving*'s right to marry, the Court held that the law violated the equal
protection clause.

Adams v. Howerton, 486 F. Supp. 1119 (U.S. District Court for the Central District of California, 1980), affirmed on other grounds, 673 F.2d 1036 (U.S.
Court of Appeals for the Ninth Circuit, 1982). Relying on biblical tradition, the court refused to recognize a same-sex marriage under either state
or federal law.

Bowers v. Hardwick, 478 U.S. 186 (U.S. Supreme Court, 1986). The Court held
that Georgia's sodomy law did not violate the right to privacy, at least with
respect to "homosexual sodomy."

Turner v. Safley, 482 U.S. 78 (U.S. Supreme Court, 1987). The Court invalidated Missouri's almost complete bar to marriage by prison inmates. Although the Court deferred to state rules regulating prisoners, it held that
denial of the right to marry requires more rigorous justification because the
unitive and legal features of marriage are so fundamental in our polity.

Watkins v. United States, 847 F.2d 1329 (U.S. Court of Appeals for the Ninth
Circuit, 1988), affirmed on narrower grounds, 875 F.2d 699 (U.S. Court of
Appeals for the Ninth Circuit, sitting en banc, 1989). The court invalidated
the discharge of a gay serviceman as a violation of the equal protection
clause. The opinion of the panel is the most thorough justification for sub-
jecting classifications based on sexual orientation to heightened scrutiny,
similar to the scrutiny required for classifications based on sex.

State Cases

Perez v. Lippold, 198 P.2d 17 (California Supreme Court, 1948). The court invalidated the state law barring different-race marriage as a violation of the

equal protection clause. This was the first reported case invalidating an antimiscegenation law.

Naim v. Naim, 87 S.E.2d 749 (Virginia Supreme Court, 1955), remanded, 350 U.S. 891 (U.S. Supreme Court, 1955), reaffirming original holding, 90 S.E.2d 849 (Virginia Supreme Court, 1956), appeal dismissed, 350 U.S. 985 (U.S. Supreme Court, 1956). The court upheld the state law barring different–race marriage. The Supreme Court remanded in light of its anti-segregation decisions but the state court successfully stuck with its original holding and the Supreme Court backed down.

Anonymous v. Anonymous, 325 N.Y.S.2d 499 (New York Supreme Court, 1971). The court refused to recognize the marriage of a man and a male transvestite whom the first man had mistaken for a woman.

Baker v. Nelson, 191 N.W.2d 185 (Minnesota Supreme Court, 1971), appeal dismissed, 409 U.S. 810 (U.S. Supreme Court, 1972). This was the first re-ported case in which an American court confronted, and denied, a claim by a same-sex couple that they were entitled to the same marriage rights as different-sex couples. The court rejected the claims under both state law and the U.S. Constitution.

Jones v. Hallahan, 501 S.W.2d 588 (Kentucky Court of Appeals, 1973). The court upheld against federal constitutional attack Kentucky's denial of mar-riage rights to same-sex couples. The court held that marriage cannot in-clude same-sex couples as a matter of definition.

Singer v. Hara, 522 P.2d 1187 (Washington Court of Appeals, 1974), review denied, 84 Wash. 2d l008 (Washington Supreme Court, 1974). The court upheld against state and federal constitutional attack Washington's denial of marriage rights to same-sex couples. This was the first reported case to reject an argument that denying same–sex couples the right to marry is sex dis-crimination in violation of the state constitution's equal rights amendment.

M. T. v. J. T., 355 A.2d 204 (New Jersey Superior Court, Appellate Division, l976). The court held that a male-to-female transsexual could marry a male; the court counted the transsexual as a female, hence preserving marriage as inherently man-woman.

Israel v. Allen, 577 P.2d 762 (Colorado Supreme Court, 1978). The court in-validated the state's prohibition of marriage by adoptive siblings as a viola-tion of the due process clause.

De Santo v. Barnsley, 476 A.2d 952 (Pennsylvania Superior Court, 1984). The court held that common-law marriage cannot include same-sex couples for the same reasons they are excluded from statutory marriage.

Coon v. Joseph, 237 Cal. Rptr. 873 (California Court of Appeals, First District, 1987). The court held that same-sex couples are not entitled to the same rights as married couples to sue for emotional distress resulting from injuries to one of the partners.

In re Ladrach, 573 N.E.2d 828 (Ohio Probate Court, 1987). The court held that a male-to-female transsexual cannot marry a male because that would amount to a prohibited same-sex marriage.

In re Succession of Bacot, 502 So.2d 1118 (Louisiana Court of Appeals, 1987), writ denied, 503 So. 2d 466 (Louisiana Supreme Court, 1987). In response to claims that the decedent's male lover must be limited to one-tenth of the estate because he was living in "concubinage" with the decedent, the court held that two men cannot live in concubinage for the same definitional reason they cannot marry.

Braschi v. Stahl Associates, 74 N.Y.2d 201 (New York Court of Appeals, 1989). The court held that New York statutory law allows a committed same-sex partner to inherit rights to a rent-controlled apartment upon the death of the other partner. The statute allowed rights to any close "family member" living with the deceased, and the court found that same-sex couples could be "family."

Alison D. v. Virginia M., 572 N.E.2d 27 (New York Court of Appeals, 1991). Declining to expand upon *Braschi*, the court refused to require visitation rights to a child for the same-sex partner of the child's biological mother.

In re Kowalski, 478 N.W.2d 790 (Minnesota Court of Appeals, 1991). The court held that a same-sex partner can be appointed guardian for an incapacitated partner. The prior guardian had been the father of the incapacitated partner.

Gajovski v. Gajovski, 610 N.E.2d 431 (Ohio Court of Appeals, 1991). In response to a petition to terminate his alimony payments to a former wife because she was living in "concubinage," the court held that a woman could not live in concubinage with another woman for the same definitional reasons she could not marry another woman.

Commonwealth v. Wasson, 842 S.W.2d 487 (Kentucky Supreme Court, 1992). The court held that the state's sodomy law violates both the right to privacy and the equal protection clause of the state constitution. This is the first state court to hold that a statute classifying on the basis of sexual orientation is a discrimination that is subject to strict judicial scrutiny.

Baehr v. Lewin, 852 P.2d 44 (Hawaii Supreme Court, 1993), clarified in response to the state's motion for reconsideration, 852 P.2d 74 (Hawaii Supreme Court, 1993). The court held that the state's denial of marriage rights to same-sex couples is discriminatory under the state constitution's equal rights amendment and remanded the case for trial to determine whether the discrimination could be justified by a compelling state interest.

Callender v. Corbett, No. 296666 (Arizona Superior Court, Pima County, April 13, 1994). The court upheld against state and federal constitutional attack the state's denial of marriage rights to same-sex couples.

Dean v. District of Columbia, 653 A.2d 307 (District of Columbia Court of Appeals, 1995). The court interpreted the District's marriage law to deny marriage rights to same-sex couples and further interpreted the District's human rights law (which prohibits any sex or sexual orientation discrimination) to permit discrimination against same-sex couples. A divided court rejected federal constitutional attacks on the law.

Bottoms v. Bottoms, 457 S.E.2d 102 (Virginia Supreme Court, 1995). The court held that a lesbian mother involved in a committed same-sex relationship is presumptively unfit to have custody of her biological child. The court ordered custody of the child to be vested in the mother of the biological mother (i.e., the child's biological grandmother).

REFERENCES

Adam, Barry D. *The Rise of a Gay and Lesbian Movement.* Boston: Twayne Publishers, 1987.

Altman, Dennis. *Coming Out in the Seventies.* Sydney: Wild & Woolley, 1979.

Amadiume, Ifi. *Male Daughters, Female Husbands: Gender and Sex in an African Society.* London: Zed Books, 1987.

"An Approach to Liberation." *Gay Liberation: A Red Butterfly Publication* (no date), p. 12.

Appelbaum, Harvey M. "Miscegenation Statutes: A Constitutional and Social Problem." *Georgetown Law Journal,* vol. 53 (1964).

Arkes, Hadley. "Closet Straight." *National Review,* July 5, 1993.

Avins, Alfred. "Anti-Miscegenation Laws and the Fourteenth Amendment: The Original Intent." *Virginia Law Review,* vol. 52 (1966).

Bailey, Derrick Sherwin. *Homosexuality and the Western Christian Tradition.* Hamden, CT: Archon Books, 1955.

Barnard, Alan, and Anthony Good. *Research Practices in the Study of Kinship.* London: Academic Press, 1984.

Bayer, Ronald. *Homosexuality and American Psychiatry: The Politics of Diagnosis.* Rev. ed. Princeton, NJ: Princeton University Press, 1987.

Bech, Henning. "Report from a Rotten State: 'Marriage' and 'Homosexuality' in 'Denmark.'" In *Modern Homosexualities,* edited by Ken Plummer. London: Routledge, 1992.

Bell, Alan P., and Martin A. Weinberg. *Homosexualities: A Study of Diversity Among Men and Women.* New York: Simon & Schuster, 1978.

Bell, Alan P., et al. *Sexual Preference: Its Development in Men and Women.* Bloomington, IN: Indiana University Press, 1981.

Bell, Derrick A., Jr. *Race, Racism, and American Law.* 3d ed. Boston: Little, Brown, 1992.

Benjamin, Jessica. *The Bonds of Love: Psychoanalysis, Feminism, and the Problem of Domination.* New York: Pantheon, 1988.

Benkov, Laura. *Reinventing the Family: The Emerging Story of Lesbian and Gay Parents.* New York: Crown, 1994.

Bérubé, Allan. *Coming Out Under Fire: The History of Gay Men and Women in World War Two.* New York: Free Press, 1990.

———. "Lesbians and Gay Men in Early San Francisco." Unpublished paper on file with the San Francisco Gay History Project.

Black, Kathryn N., and Michael R. Stevenson. "The Relationship of Self-Reported Sex-Role Characteristics and Attitudes Toward Homosexuality." In *Bashers, Baiters and Bigots: Homophobia in American Society*, edited by John P. DeCecco. New York: Harrington Park Press, 1985.

Blacking, John. "Fictitious Kinship Amongst Girls of the Venda of the Northern Transvaal." *Man*, vol. 59 (1959).

Blackwood, Evelyn. "Sexuality and Gender in Certain Native American Tribes: The Case of Cross-Gender Females." *Signs*, vol. 10 (1984).

Blumstein, Philip, and Pepper Schwartz. *American Couples: Money, Work, Sex.* New York: Morrow, 1983.

Bogoras, Waldemar. *The Chuckchee.* New York: AMS Press, 1975.

Bohannan, Laura. "Dahomean Marriage: A Reevaluation." In *Marriage, Family, and Residence*, edited by Paul Bohannan and John Middleton. Garden City, NY: Natural History Press, 1968. Reprinted from *Africa*, vol. 19 (1949).

Boswell, John. *Christianity, Social Tolerance, and Homosexuality: Gay People in Western Europe from the Beginning of the Christian Era to the Fourteenth Century.* Chicago: University of Chicago Press, 1980.

———. "Homosexuality and the Religious Life: A Historical Approach." In *Homosexuality in the Priesthood and the Religious Life*, edited by Jeannine Grammick. New York: Crossroad, 1989.

———. *Same-Sex Unions in Premodern Europe.* New York: Villard Books, 1994.

———. "1500 Years of Blessing Gay and Lesbian Relationships: It's Nothing New to the Church" (videotape of lecture to the Washington, DC, chapter of Integrity, a gay and lesbian Episcopal group).

Bowman, Craig A., and Blake M. Cornish. "A More Perfect Union: A Legal and Social Analysis of Domestic Partnership Ordinances." *Columbia Law Review*, vol. 92 (1992).

Bozett, Frederick W., ed. *Homosexuality and the Family.* New York: Haworth, 1989.

Bozett, Frederick W., and Marvin B. Sussman, eds. *Homosexuality and Family Relations.* New York: Harrington Park Press, 1990.

Bratt, Carolyn S. "Incest Statutes and the Fundamental Right of Marriage: Is Oedipus Free to Marry?" *Family Law Quarterly*, vol. 18 (1984).

Brown, Jennifer Gerarda. "Competitive Federalism and the Legislative Incentives to Recognize Same-Sex Marriages." *Southern California Law Review*, vol. 68 (1995).

Brown, Judith. "Lesbian Sexuality in Medieval and Early Modern Europe." In *Hidden from History: Reclaiming the Gay and Lesbian Past*, edited by Martin B. Duberman et al. New York: Penguin Books, 1989.

Brown, Peter O. *The Body and Society: Men, Women and Sexual Renunciation in Early Christianity*. New York: Columbia University Press, 1988.

Buchanan, G. Sidney. "Same-Sex Marriage: The Linchpin Issue." *University of Dayton Law Review*, vol. 10 (1985).

Bullough, Vern L. *Science in the Bedroom*. New York: Basic Books, 1994.

Bullough, Vern L., and James Brundage, eds. *Sexual Practices and the Medieval Church*. Buffalo, NY: Prometheus Books, 1982.

Bullough, Vern L., and Bonnie Bullough. *Cross Dressing, Sex, and Gender*. Philadelphia: University of Pennsylvania Press, 1993.

Bureau of National Affairs. *Recognizing Nontraditional Families*. Washington, DC: Bureau of National Affairs, 1991.

Burg, B. R. *Sodomy and the Perception of Evil: English Sea Rovers in the Seventeenth-Century Caribbean*. 2d ed. New York: New York University Press, 1995.

Byne, William. "The Biological Evidence Challenged." *Scientific American*, May 1994.

"California Assembly Approves Bill Banning Gay Marriages." *Los Angeles Times*, August 14, 1977.

Callender, Charles, and Lee M. Kochems. "The North American *Berdache*." *Current Anthropology*, vol. 24 (1983).

———. "Men and Not-Men: Male Gender-Mixing Statuses and Homosexuality." In *The Many Faces of Homosexuality: Anthropological Approaches to Homosexual Behavior*, edited by Evelyn Blackwood. New York: Harrington Park Press, 1986.

Cantarella, Eva. *Bisexuality in the Ancient World*. Translated by Cormac Ó Cuilleanáin. New Haven, CT: Yale University Press, 1992.

Carmody, Denise, and John Carmody. "Homosexuality and Roman Catholicism." In *Homosexuality and World Religions*, edited by Arlene Swidler. Valley Forge, PA: Trinity Press International, 1993.

Case, Mary Anne. "Disaggregating Gender from Sex and Sexual Orientation: The Effeminate Man in the Law and Feminist Jurisprudence." *Yale Law Journal*, vol. 105 (1995).

Chauncey, George, Jr. *Gay New York: Gender, Urban Culture, and the Making of the Gay Male World, 1890–1940*. New York: Basic Books, 1994.

Chodorow, Nancy. *The Reproduction of Mothering.* Berkeley: University of California Press, 1978.

Clark, T. C. "Religion, Morality, and Abortion: A Constitutional Appraisal." *Loyola of Los Angeles Law Review,* vol. 2 (1969).

Cline, Walter. *Notes of the People of Siwah and el Garah in the Libyan Desert.* Edited by Leslie Spier. Menasha, WI: George Banta, 1936.

Cole, David, and William N. Eskridge, Jr. "From Hand-Holding to Sodomy: First Amendment Protection of Homosexual (Expressive) Conduct." *Harvard Civil Rights–Civil Liberties Law Review,* vol. 29 (1994).

"Colorado Gays Marry." *The Gay Blade,* vol. 6 (May 1975).

Cory, Donald Webster. *The Homosexual in America: A Subjective Approach.* New York: Greenberg, 1951.

Cory, Donald Webster, and John LeRoy. "Homosexual Marriage." *Sexology,* vol. 29 (1963).

Cowell, Alan. "Pope Deplores Gay Marriage." *New York Times,* February 23, 1994, sec. A, p. 2.

Cowell, Roberta. *Roberta Cowell's Story.* London: Heinemann, 1954.

Cox, Barbara J. "Alternative Families: Obtaining Traditional Family Benefits Through Litigation, Legislation, and Collective Bargaining." *Wisconsin Women's Law Journal,* vol. 2 (1986).

———. "Same-Sex Marriage and Choice-of-Law: If We Marry in Hawaii, Are We Still Married When We Return Home?" *Wisconsin Law Review,* 1994.

Cronan, Sheila. "Marriage." In *Radical Feminism,* edited by Anne Koedt et al. New York: Quadrangle Books, 1973.

Curry, Hayden, and Denis Clifford. *Legal Guide for Lesbian and Gay Couples.* 8th ed. Berkeley, CA: Volo Press, 1994.

Dailey, Anne C. "To Have and to Hold: The Marital Rape Exemption and the Fourteenth Amendment." *Harvard Law Review,* vol. 99 (1986).

Davis, F. James. *Who Is Black?* University Park, PA: Pennsylvania State University Press, 1991.

Davis, Kingsley. "Intermarriage in Caste Societies." *American Anthropologist,* vol. 43 (1941).

Deenen, A. A., et al. "Intimacy and Sexuality in Gay Male Couples." *Archives of Sexual Behavior,* vol. 23 (1994).

D'Emilio, John. *Sexual Politics, Sexual Communities: The Making of a Homosexual Minority in the United States, 1940–1970.* Chicago: University of Chicago Press, 1983.

de Pogey-Castries, L. R. *Histoire de L'Amour Grec dans L'Antiquité.* Paris: Stendahl, 1930.

Devereux, George. "Institutionalized Homosexuality of the Mohave Indians." *Human Biology,* vol. 9 (1937).

Dinnerstein, Dorothy. *The Mermaid and the Minotaur: Sexual Arrangements and Human Malaise*. New York: Harper & Row, 1976.

Dio Cassius. *Epitome* (book 62). In *Dio's Roman History*, translated by Earnest Cary. London: W. Heinemann, 1914–1927.

Doniger, Wendy. "Making Brothers." *Los Angeles Times*, July 31, 1994, Book Review Supplement, p. 1.

Dover, Kenneth J. *Greek Homosexuality*. London: Duckworth, 1978.

Drinan, Robert. "The *Loving* Decision and the Freedom to Marry." *Ohio State Law Journal*, vol. 29 (1968).

Duberman, Martin B. *About Time: Exploring the Gay Past*. Rev. ed. New York: Meridian, 1991.

———. "Writhing Bedfellows in Antebellum South Carolina: Historical Interpretation and the Politics of Evidence." In *Hidden from History: Reclaiming the Gay and Lesbian Past*, edited by Martin B. Duberman et al. New York: Penguin Books, 1989.

Duclos, Nitya. "Some Complicating Thoughts on Same-Sex Marriage." *Law and Sexuality: A Review of Lesbian and Gay Legal Issues*, vol. 1 (1991).

Duffy, S. M., and C. E. Rosbult. "Satisfaction and Commitment in Homosexual and Heterosexual Relationships." *Journal of Homosexuality*, vol. 12 (1986).

Eblin, Robert L. "Domestic Partnership Recognition in the Workplace: Equitable Employee Benefits for Gay Couples (and Others)." *Ohio State Law Journal*, vol. 51 (1990).

Echols, Alice. *Daring to Be Bad: Radical Feminism in America 1967–1975*. Minneapolis: University of Minnesota Press, 1989.

Editors of the Harvard Law Review. *Sexual Orientation and the Law*. Cambridge, MA: Harvard University Press, 1989.

Eron, Lewis John. "Homosexuality and Judaism." In *Homosexuality and World Religions*, edited by Arlene Swidler. Valley Forge, PA: Trinity Press International, 1993.

Eskridge, William N., Jr. "Gadamer/Statutory Interpretation." *Columbia Law Review*, vol. 90 (1990).

———. "A Social Constructionist Critique of Posner's *Sex and Reason*: Steps Toward a Gaylegal Agenda." *Yale Law Journal*, vol. 102 (1992).

———. "A History of Same-Sex Marriage." *Virginia Law Review*, vol. 79 (1993).

———. *Gaylaw*. Cambridge, MA: Harvard University Press, in press.

Eskridge, William N., Jr., and Brian D. Weimer. "The Economics Epidemic in an AIDS Perspective." *University of Chicago Law Review*, vol. 61 (1994).

Ettelbrick, Paula L. "Since When Is Marriage a Path to Liberation?" *OUT/LOOK, National Gay and Lesbian Quarterly*, issue 6 (fall 1989).

Ettore, E. M. *Lesbians, Women, and Society*. Boston: Routledge & Kegan Paul, 1980.

Evans-Pritchard, E. E. *Kinship and Marriage Among the Nuer.* Oxford, UK: Clarendon Press, 1951.

———. "Sexual Inversion Among the Azande." *American Anthropologist,* vol. 72 (1970).

Faderman, Lillian. *Surpassing the Love of Men: Romantic Friendship and Love Between Women from the Renaissance to the Present.* New York: Morrow, 1981.

———. *Odd Girls and Twilight Lovers: A History of Lesbian Life in Twentieth-Century America.* New York: Columbia University Press, 1991.

Fajer, Marc A. "Can Two Real Men Eat Quiche Together? Storytelling, Gender-Role Stereotypes, and Legal Protection for Lesbians and Gay Men." *University of Miami Law Review,* vol. 46 (1992).

Feliz, Antonio A. *Out of the Bishop's Closet.* 2d ed. San Francisco: Alamo Square Press, 1992.

Findlen, Barbara. "Is Marriage the Answer? Domestic Partnership Activists Don't Think So." *Ms.,* May/June 1995.

Finnis, John M. "Law, Morality, and 'Sexual Orientation.'" *Notre Dame Law Review,* vol. 69 (1994).

Firestone, Shulamith. *The Dialectic of Sex: The Case for Feminist Revolution.* New York: Morrow, 1970.

Florenskij, Pavel. *La Colonna e il Fondamento della Verita.* Translated into Italian by Pietro Modesto, with an introduction by Elemire Zolla. Milan: Ruscioni Editore, 1974.

Flynt, Joshua. "Homosexuality Among Tramps." In *Studies in the Psychology of Sex,* edited by Havelock Ellis. London: W. Heinemann, Medical Books, 1946.

Ford, Clellan S., and Frank A. Beach. *Patterns of Sexual Behavior.* New York: Harper & Row, 1951.

Forgey, Donald G. "The Institution of Berdache Among the North American Plains Indians." *Journal of Sex Research,* vol. 11 (1975).

Foucault, Michel. *The History of Sexuality.* Vol. 3, *The Care of the Self.* Translated by Robert Hurley. New York: Vintage Books, 1986.

Fried, Charles. *Order and Law.* New York: Simon & Schuster, 1991.

Gaius Suetonius Tranquillus. *The Twelve Caesars.* Translated by Robert Graves. London: Penguin Books, 1957.

Garber, Eric. "A Spectacle in Color: The Lesbian and Gay Subculture of Jazz Age Harlem." In *Hidden from History: Reclaiming the Gay and Lesbian Past,* edited by Martin B. Duberman et al. New York: Penguin Books, 1989.

Garnets, Linda D., and Douglas C. Kimmel, eds. *Psychological Perspectives on Lesbian and Gay Male Experiences.* New York: Columbia University Press, 1993.

Garrow, David J. *Liberty and Sexuality: The Right to Privacy and the Making of Roe v. Wade.* New York: Macmillan, 1994.

"Gay Couple Files Suit After Los Angeles Denies Marriage License." *Los Angeles Times*, March 16, 1977, sec. 2, p. 6.

Gay, Judith. "'Mummies and Babies' and Friends and Lovers in Lesotho." In *The Many Faces of Homosexuality: Anthropological Approaches to Homosexual Behavior*, edited by Evelyn Blackwood. New York: Harrington Park Press, 1986.

"Gay Revolution Comes Out." *The Rat*, August 12–26, 1969, p. 7.

Gerard, Kent, and Gert Hekma, eds. *The Pursuit of Sodomy: Male Homosexuality in Renaissance and Enlightenment Europe*. New York: Harrington Park Press, 1989.

Gibbon, Edward. *The Decline and Fall of the Roman Empire*. Edited and abridged by Dero A. Saunders. London: Penguin Books, 1952.

Ginsburg, Ruth Bader. "Sexual Equality Under the Fourteenth and Equal Rights Amendments." *Washington University Law Quarterly*, 1979.

Goar, R. P. Jacobi, ed. and trans. *Ritualae Graecorum Complectens Ritus et Ordines Divinae Liturgicae*. Milan: Ruscioni Editore, 1974.

Golden, Mark. "Slavery and Homosexuality at Athens." *Phoenix*, vol. 38 (1984).

Goldstein, Anne B. "History, Homosexuality, and Political Values: Searching for the Hidden Determinants of *Bowers v. Hardwick*." *Yale Law Journal*, vol. 97 (1988).

Golombok, Susan, et al. "Children in Lesbian and Single Parent Households: Psychosexual and Psychiatric Appraisal." *Journal of Child Psychology and Psychiatry*, vol. 24 (1983).

Gonsiorek, John C. "The Empirical Basis for the Demise of the Illness Model of Homosexuality." In *Homosexuality: Research Implications for Public Policy*, edited by James D. Weinrich and J. Gonsiorek. Newbury Park, CA: Sage, 1991.

Gough, E. Kathleen. "The Nayars and the Definition of Marriage." *Journal of the Royal Anthropological Institute*, vol. 89 (1959).

Gould, Stephen Jay. "Carrie Buck's Daughter." *Constitutional Commentary*, vol. 2 (1985).

Green, Brad. "Gay 'Marriages': Delivering a Message." *The Blade*, vol. 13 (March 5, 1982).

Green, Richard. *The "Sissy Boy" Syndrome and the Development of Homosexuality*. New Haven, CT: Yale University Press, 1987.

Green, Richard, et al. "Lesbian Mothers and Their Children: A Comparison with Solo Parent Heterosexual Mothers and Their Children." *Archives of Sexual Behavior*, vol. 15 (1986).

Greenberg, David F. *The Construction of Homosexuality*. Chicago: University of Chicago Press, 1988.

Grisez, Germain. *The Way of the Lord Jesus*. Vol. 2, *Living a Christian Life*. Quincy, IL: Franciscan Press, 1993.

Guerra, Francisco. *The Pre-Columbian Mind*. New York: Seminar Press, 1971.

Gunther, Gerald. "The Supreme Court, 1971 Term — Foreword: In Search of Evolving Doctrine on a Changing Court: A Model for a Newer Equal Protection." *Harvard Law Review*, vol. 86 (1972).

Hall, Ralph. "The Church, State & Homosexuality: A Radical Analysis." *Gay Power*, no. 14 [no date].

Halley, Janet. "The Politics of the Closet: Towards Equal Protection for Gay, Lesbian, and Bisexual Identity." *University of California at Los Angeles Law Review*, vol. 36 (1989).

———. "Reasoning About Sodomy: Act and Identity in and After *Bowers v. Hardwick*." *Virginia Law Review*, vol. 79 (1993).

Halperin, David M. *One Hundred Years of Homosexuality*. New York: Routledge, 1990.

Harry, Joseph, and William B. DeVall. *The Social Organization of Gay Males*. New York: Praeger, 1978.

Hellinger, Fred. "Forecasting the Medical Care Costs of the HIV Epidemic: 1990–1994." *Inquiry*, fall 1991.

Helminiak, Daniel A. *What the Bible Really Says About Homosexuality*. San Francisco: Alamo Square Press, 1994.

Hening, William Waller, comp. *Statutes at Large, Being a Collection of the Laws of Virginia from the First Session of the Legislature in the Year 1619*. Vol. 2. New York: R. & W. & G. Bartow, 1823.

Henriksson, Benny, and Hasse Ytterburg. "Sweden: The Power of the Moral(istic) Left." In *AIDS and the Industrialized Democracies: Passions, Politics, and Policies*, edited by David L. Kirp and Ronald Bayer. New York: Rutgers University Press, 1992.

Henson, Deborah M. "A Comparative Analysis of Same-Sex Partnership Protections: Recommendations for American Reform." *International Journal of Law and the Family*, vol. 7 (1993).

Herdt, Gilbert H. *Guardians of the Flutes: Idioms of Masculinity*. 2d ed. Chicago: University of Chicago Press, 1994.

———. "Ritualized Homosexual Behavior in the Male Cults of Melanesia, 1862–1983." In *Ritualized Homosexuality in Melanesia*, edited by Gilbert H. Herdt. Berkeley: University of California Press, 1984.

Herskovits, Melville. "A Note on 'Woman Marriage' in Dahomey." *Africa*, vol. 10 (1937).

Hewitt Associates. *Domestic Partners and Employee Benefits*. Lincolnshire, IL: Hewitt Associates, 1991.

Hexter, Ralph. Response to Brent D. Shaw. *New Republic*, October 3, 1994, p. 39.

Higginbotham, A. Leon, and Barbara K. Kopytoff. "Racial Purity and Interracial Sex in the Law of Colonial and Antebellum Virginia." *Georgetown Law Journal*, vol. 77 (1989).

Hill, W. W. "The Status of the Hermaphrodite and Transvestite in Najavo Culture." *American Anthropologist*, vol. 37 (1935).

Hinsch, Bret. *Passions of the Cut Sleeve: The Male Homosexual Tradition in China.* Berkeley: University of California Press, 1990.

Hoch, Paul. *White Hero, Black Beast: Racism, Sexism, and the Mask of Masculinity.* London: Photo Press, 1979.

Hocquenghem, Guy. *Homosexual Desire.* 2d ed. Translated by Danielle Dangoor. Durham, NC: Duke University Press, 1993.

Hollandsworth, Marla J. "Gay Men Creating Families through Surro-Gay Arrangements: A Paradigm for Reproductive Freedom." *The American University Journal of Gender and the Law*, vol. 3 (1995).

Holleran, Andrew. *Dancer from the Dance.* New York: Morrow, 1978.

Homer, Steven K. "Against Marriage." *Harvard Civil Rights–Civil Liberties Law Review*, vol. 29 (1994).

Hotvedt, Mary E., and Jane Barclay Mandel. "Children of Lesbian Mothers." In *Homosexuality: Social, Psychological, and Biological Issues*, edited by William Paul et al. Beverly Hills, CA: Sage, 1982.

Hovenkamp, Herbert. "Social Science and Segregation Before *Brown*." *Duke Law Journal* (1985).

Hovermill, Joseph W. "A Conflict of Laws and Morals: The Choice of Law Implications of Hawaii's Recognition of Same-Sex Marriages." *Maryland Law Review*, vol. 53 (1994).

Huber, H. "'Woman Marriage' in Some East African Societies." *Anthropos*, vols. 63/64 (1969).

Hunt, Morton. *Sexual Behavior in the 1970s.* Chicago: Playboy Press, 1974.

Hunter, Nan D. "Marriage, Law, and Gender: A Feminist Inquiry." *Law and Sexuality: A Review of Lesbian and Gay Legal Issues*, vol. 1 (1991).

Huon of Bordeaux. Translated by Sir John Bourchier and Lord Berners. London: G. Allen, 1895.

Isay, Richard A. *Being Homosexual: Gay Men and Their Development.* New York: Farrar, Straus & Giroux, 1989.

Jaffa, Harry. *Original Intent and the Framers of the Constitution: A Disputed Question.* Washington, DC: Regnery Gateway, 1993.

Johnson, Susan E. *Staying Power: Long-Term Lesbian Couples.* Tallahassee, FL: Naiad Press, 1990.

Juvenal. *Satires* (book 2). In *Juvenal and Persius*, translated by G. G. Ramsey. Cambridge, MA: Harvard University Press, 1950.

Kaplan, Justin. *Walt Whitman: A Life.* New York: Simon & Schuster, 1980.

Katz, Jonathan N. *Gay American History.* Rev. ed. New York: Meridian, 1992.

Kay, Herma Hill. *Cases and Materials on Sex-Based Discrimination.* 3d ed. St. Paul: West, 1988.

Kelley, Don. "Homosexuals Should Get Rights." *Los Angeles Collegian* [the student newspaper of Los Angeles City College], March 3, 1971, p. 2.

Kennedy, Elizabeth Lapovsky, and Madeline D. Davis. *Boots of Leather, Slippers of Gold: A History of a Lesbian Community.* New York: Penguin Books, 1993.

Kimmons, Cheryl. "The Case for Gay Marriage." *The Blade*, vol. 7 (June 1976).

Kinsey, Alfred C., et al. *Sexual Behavior in the American Male.* Philadelphia: Saunders, 1948.

Klassen, Albert D., et al. *Sex and Morality in the U.S.: An Empirical Inquiry Under the Auspices of the Kinsey Institute.* Middletown, CT: Wesleyan University Press, 1989.

Kleber, David J., et al. "The Impact of Parental Homosexuality in Child Custody Cases: A Review of the Literature." *Bulletin of the American Academy of Psychology and Law*, vol. 14 (1986).

Koppelman, Andrew. "The Miscegenation Analogy: Sodomy Law as Sex Discrimination." *Yale Law Journal*, vol. 98 (1988).

———. "Why Discrimination Against Lesbians and Gay Men Is Sex Discrimination." *New York University Law Review*, vol. 69 (1994).

Kramer, Larry. *Faggots.* New York: Plume, 1978.

Krige, Eileen Jensen. "Note on the Phalaborwa and Their Morula Complex." *Bantu Studies*, vol. 11 (1937).

———. "Woman-Marriage, with Special Reference to the Lovedu: Its Significance for the Definition of Marriage." *Africa*, vol. 44 (1974).

Kurdek, Lawrence A., and J. Patrick Schmitt. "Relationship Quality of Partners in Heterosexual Married, Heterosexual Cohabiting, Gay, and Lesbian Relationships." *Journal of Personality and Social Psychology*, vol. 51 (1986).

———. "Relationship Quality of Gay Men in Closed or Open Relationships." In *Gay Relationships*, edited by John P. De Cecco. New York: Harrington Park Press, 1988.

Lambert, Royston. *Beloved and God: The Story of Hadrian and Antinous.* New York: Viking, 1984.

Lampridius. *Antoninus Elagabalus* (book 11). In *Scriptores Historiae Auguste*, vol. 2, translated by David Magie. London: W. Heinemann, 1922–1932.

Laner, Mary R., and Roy H. Laner. "Personal Style or Sexual Preference? Why Gay Men Are Disliked." *International Review of Modern Society*, vol. 9 (1979).

———. "Sexual Preference or Personal Style? Why Lesbians Are Disliked." *Journal of Homosexuality*, vol. 5 (1980).

Laumann, Edward O., et al. *The Social Organization of Sexuality: Sexual Practices in the United States.* Chicago: University of Chicago Press, 1994.

Law, Sylvia A. "Homosexuality and the Social Meaning of Gender." *Wisconsin Law Review*, 1988.

Leach, Edmund R. "Polyandry, Inheritance and the Definition of Marriage." *Man*, vol. 53 (1955).

————. *Social Anthropology*. New York: Oxford University Press, 1982.

"Lesbians Ask Court to Permit Marriage." *Louisville Chronicle*, November 11, 1970.

LeVay, Simon, and Dean H. Hamer. "Evidence for a Biological Influence in Male Homosexuality." *Scientific American*, May 1994.

Lever, Janet. "Sexual Revelations." *The Advocate*, August 1994.

Levy, Robert I. "The Community Function of Tahitian Male Transvestism." *Anthropological Quarterly*, vol. 44 (1971).

Lewes, Kenneth. *The Psychoanalytic Theory of Male Homosexuality*. New York: Simon & Schuster, 1988.

Lewis, Claudia A. "From This Day Forward: A Feminine Moral Discourse on Homosexual Marriage." *Yale Law Journal*, vol. 97 (1988).

Lichtenstein, Grace. "Homosexual Weddings Stir Controversy." *New York Times*, April 27, 1975, sec. B, p. 61.

Lilja, Saara. *Homosexuality in Republican and Augustan Rome*. Helsinki: Societas Scientarium Fennica, 1983.

Lindenbaum, Shirley. "Variations on a Sociosexual Theme in Melanesia." In *Ritualized Homosexuality in Melanesia*, edited by Gilbert H. Herdt. Berkeley: University of California Press, 1984.

Lombardo, Paul A. "Miscegenation, Eugenics, and Racism: Historical Footnotes to *Loving v. Virginia*." *University of California at Davis Law Review*, vol. 21 (1988).

"Looking Over Lesbians." *Partners Newsletter for Gay and Lesbian Couples*, November/December, 1991.

Lurie, Nancy O. "Winnebago *Berdache*." *American Anthropologist*, vol. 55 (1953).

MacCubbin, Robert P., ed. *'Tis Nature's Fault: Unauthorized Sexuality During the Enlightenment*. New York: Cambridge University Press, 1987.

MacDonald, A. P., and Richard G. Games. "Some Characteristics of Those Who Hold Positive and Negative Attitudes Toward Homosexuals." *Journal of Homosexuality*, vol. 1 (1979).

MacDonald, A. P., et al. "Attitudes Toward Homosexuality: Preservation of Sex Morality or the Double Standard?" *Journal of Consulting and Clinical Psychology*, vol. 40 (1972).

Macedo, Steven. "Homosexuality and the Conservative Mind." *Georgetown Law Journal* (in press).

Maisch, Herbert. *Incest*. Translated by Colin Bearne. London: Deutsch, 1973.

Maltz, Earl M. "Constitutional Protection for the Right to Marry: A Dissenting View." *George Washington Law Review*, vol. 60 (1992).

Mansfield, Harvey. "Saving Liberalism from Liberals." *Harvard Crimson*, November 8, 1993.

"Marriage Fight Due: Wisconsin Black Women Slate Christmas Wedding." *Mother*, vol. 1 (December 1971).

Marshall, Gloria A. "Marriage: A Comparative Analysis." In *International Encyclopedia of the Social Sciences*. Vol. 10. New York: Macmillan, 1968.

Martial. *Epigrams* (book 7). Translated by Walter C. A. Ker. Cambridge, MA: Harvard University Press, 1950.

Martin, Robert K. "Knights-Errant and Gothic Seducers: The Representation of Male Friendship in Mid-Nineteenth-Century America." In *Hidden from History: Reclaiming the Gay and Lesbian Past*, edited by Martin B. Duberman et al. New York: Penguin Books, 1989.

"Maryland Challenges Gay Marriage." *The Gay Blade*, vol. 6 (August 1975).

Mavor, Elizabeth. *The Ladies of Llangollen: A Study in Romantic Friendship*. London: Joseph, 1971.

McCauley, Elizabeth, et al. "Psychosocial Adjustment of Adult Women with Turner Syndrome." *Clinical Genetics*, vol. 29 (1986).

McGough, James. "Deviant Marriage Patterns in Chinese Society." In *Normal and Abnormal Behavior in Chinese Culture*, edited by Arthur Kleinman and Tsung-Ti Lin. Boston: D. Reidel, 1990.

McWhirter, David, and Andrew Mattison. *The Male Couple*. Englewood Cliffs, NJ: Prentice-Hall, 1984.

McWhirter, David P., et al. *Homosexuality/Heterosexuality: Concepts of Sexual Orientation*. New York: Oxford University Press, 1990.

Mendola, Mary. *The Mendola Report: A New Look at Gay Couples*. New York: Crown, 1980.

Michelman, Frank I. "Law's Republic." *Yale Law Journal*, vol. 97 (1987).

Mohr, Richard D. *A More Perfect Union: Why Straight America Must Stand Up for Gay Rights*. Boston: Beacon Press, 1994.

Monette, Paul. *Borrowed Time: An AIDS Memoir*. New York: Harcourt Brace Jovanovich, 1988.

———. *Halfway Home*. New York: Crown, 1991.

———. *Becoming a Man: Half a Life Story*. New York: Harcourt Brace Jovanovich, 1992.

Money, John. *Venuses Penuses*. Buffalo, NY: Prometheus Books, 1986.

Money, John, and Anke A. Ehrhardt. *Man and Woman Boy and Girl*. Baltimore: Johns Hopkins University Press, 1972.

Money, John, and Ernesto Pollitt. "Cytogenetic and Psychosexual Ambiguity: Klinefelter's Syndrome and Transvestism Compared." *Archives of General Psychiatry*, vol. 11 (1964).

Money, John, and Patricia Tucker. *Sexual Signatures*. Boston: Little, Brown, 1975.

Money, John, et al. "Fetal Feminization Induced by Androgen Insensitivity in the Testicular Feminizing Syndrome: Effect on Marriage and Maternalism." *Johns Hopkins Medical Journal*, vol. 123 (1968).

Montaigne, Michel de. *Journal de Voyage en Italie par la Suisse et l'Allemagne en 1580 et 1581*. Edited by Charles Dedeyan. Paris: Société des Belles Lettres, 1946.

Moodie, T. Dunbar. "Migrancy and Male Sexuality in the South African Gold Mines." In *Hidden from History: Reclaiming the Gay and Lesbian Past*, edited by Martin B. Duberman et al. New York: Penguin Books, 1989.

Morin, Stephen F., and Ellen M. Garfinkle. "Male Homophobia." *Journal of Social Issues*, vol. 34 (winter 1978).

Murphy, Elizabeth. *The Rise of Employer-Provided Benefits for Domestic Partners*. West Hollywood, CA: City of West Hollywood, 1992.

Murray, Stephen O. *Oceanic Homosexualities*. New York: Garland, 1992.

Myrdal, Gunnar. *An American Dilemma: The Negro Problem and Modern Democracy*. New York: Harper, 1944.

Nanda, Serena. *Neither Man Nor Woman: The Hijras of India*. Belmont, CA: Wadsworth, 1990.

Needham, Rodney. "Remarks on the Analysis of Kinship and Marriage." In *Rethinking Kinship and Marriage*, edited by Rodney Needham. London: Tavistock, 1971.

Neufeld, Ephraim. *The Hittite Laws*. London: Luzac, 1951.

Neusner, Jacob. *Sifra: An Analytical Translation*. Vol. 3. Atlanta: Scholars Press, 1988.

Ng, Vivien W. "Homosexuality and the State in Late Imperial China." In *Hidden from History: Reclaiming the Gay and Lesbian Past*, edited by Martin B. Duberman et al. New York: Penguin, 1989.

Niebuhr, Gustav. "Episcopalians Soften Stance on Sexuality." *New York Times*, August 25, 1994, sec. A, p. 13.

Nielsen, Linda. "Family Rights and the 'Registered Partnership' in Denmark." *International Journal of Law and the Family*, vol. 4 (1990).

Noordam, Dirk J. "Sodomy in the Dutch Republic, 1600–1725." In *The Pursuit of Sodomy: Male Homosexuality in Renaissance and Enlightenment Europe*, edited by Kent Gerard and Gert Hekma. New York: Harrington Park Press, 1989.

"Noose or Knot? The Debate Over Lesbian Marriage." *OUT/WEEK: New York's Lesbian and Gay News Magazine*, September 18, 1989, pp. 38–43.

Northstar Project. *Out and Counted: A Survey of the Twin Cities Gay and Lesbian Community*. Minneapolis: Northstar, 1991.

Oboler, Regina S. "Is the Female Husband a Man? Woman/Woman Marriage Among the Nandi of Kenya." *Ethnology*, vol. 19 (1980).

O'Brien, Denise. "Female Husbands in Southern Bantu Societies." In *Sexual Stratification: A Cross-Cultural View*, edited by Alice Schlegel. New York: Columbia University Press, 1977.

Parsons, Elsie C. "The Zuni *La'Mana.*" *American Anthropologist*, vol. 18 (1916).

Patterson, Charlotte J. "Children of Lesbians and Single-Parent Households: Psychosexual and Psychiatric Appraisals." *Child Development*, vol. 63 (1992).

Pennington, Saralie Bisnovich. "Children of Lesbian Mothers." In *Gay and Lesbian Parents*, edited by Frederick W. Bozett. New York: Praeger, 1987.

Peplau, Letitia Anne. "Research on Homosexual Couples: An Overview." In *Gay Relationships*, edited by John P. De Cecco. New York: Harrington Park Press, 1988.

Peplau, Letitia Anne, and Susan D. Cochran. "Sex Differences in Values Concerning Love Relationships." Paper presented at the Annual Meeting of the American Psychological Association, September 1980.

Pershing, Stephen B. "'Entreat Me Not to leave Thee': *Bottoms v. Bottoms* and the Custody Rights of Gay and Lesbian Parents." *William and Mary Bill of Rights Journal*, vol. 3 (1994).

Pharr, Suzanne. *Homophobia: A Weapon of Sexism*. Little Rock, AR: Chardon Press, 1988.

Philipson, Tomas J., and Richard A. Posner. *Private Choices and Public Health: The AIDS Epidemic in an Economic Perspective*. Cambridge, MA: Harvard University Press, 1993.

Pianin, Eric. "Hearing Held on Women's Bid to Wed." *Louisville Times*, November 12, 1970.

Plato. *On Homosexuality: Lysis, Phaedrus, and Symposium*. Translated by Benjamin Jowett, with selected retranslation, notes, and introduction by Eugene O'Connor. Buffalo, NY: Prometheus Books, 1991

Polikoff, Nancy D. "This Child Does Have Two Mothers: Redefining Parenthood to Meet the Needs of Children in Lesbian-Mother and Other Non-traditional Families." *Georgetown Law Journal*, vol. 78 (1990).

———. "We Will Get What We Ask For: Why Legalizing Gay and Lesbian Marriage Will Not 'Dismantle the Legal Structure of Gender in Every Marriage.'" *Virginia Law Review*, vol. 79 (1993).

Pope John Paul II. "Letter to Families" (February 2, 1994). Reprinted in *Origins* (Catholic News Service), vol. 23, March 3, 1994, p. 637.

Posner, Richard A. "The Uncertain Protection of Privacy by the Supreme Court." *Supreme Court Review*, 1979.

———. *Sex and Reason*. Cambridge, MA: Harvard University Press, 1992.

"Presbyterians Vote for Unity." *Christian Century*, June 29–July 6, 1994, pp. 663–664.

Ramsey Colloquium. "The Homosexual Movement: A Response by the Ramsey Colloquium." *First Things*, no. 41 (March 1994).

Rawls, John. *A Theory of Justice.* Cambridge, MA: Harvard University Press, 1971.

"Readers Favor Legal Marriage." *Partners Magazine for Gay and Lesbian Couples*, July/August 1990.

Rechy, John. *City of Night.* New York: Grove Press, 1963.

————. *The Sexual Outlaw.* New York: Grove Press, 1977.

Regan, Milton C., Jr. *Family Law and the Pursuit of Intimacy.* New York: New York University Press, 1993.

Resolution on Equal Rights for Homosexuals and Lesbians in the European Community. *Official Journal of the European Communities*, February 28, 1994.

Rhodes, Elizabeth. "New Ties That Bind: Same-Sex Couples Challenge the System to Gain Legal Recognition of Their Commitments to Each Other." *Seattle Times*, July 21, 1991, sec. K, p. 1.

Rich, Adrienne. "Compulsory Heterosexuality and Lesbian Existence (1980)." In *Blood, Bread, and Poetry: Selected Prose 1979–1985.* New York: Norton, 1986.

Rivera, Rhonda R. "Legal Issues in Gay and Lesbian Parenting." In *Gay and Lesbian Parents*, edited by Frederick W. Bozett. New York: Praeger, 1987.

Rivers, W. C. *Walt Whitman's Abnormality.* London: George Allen, 1913.

Robson, Ruthann. *Lesbian (Out)law: Survival Under the Rule of Law.* Ithaca, NY: Firebrand Books, 1992.

Robson, Ruthann, and S. E. Valentine. "Lov(h)ers: Lesbians as Intimate Partners and Lesbian Legal Theory." *Temple Law Review*, vol. 63 (1990).

Roscoe, Will. *The Zuni Man-Woman.* Albuquerque, NM: University of New Mexico Press, 1991.

Roth, Martha T. *Law Collections from Mesopotamia and Asia Minor.* Atlanta: Scholars Press, 1995.

Royal Anthropological Institute. *Notes and Queries on Anthropology.* 6th ed. London: Royal Anthropological Institute, 1951.

Rubenfeld, Jed. "The Right of Privacy." *Harvard Law Review*, vol. 102 (1989).

Ruggiero, Guido. *The Boundaries of Eros: Sex Crime and Sexuality in Renaissance Venice.* New York: Oxford University Press, 1985.

Rupp, Letitia. "'Imagine My Surprise': Women's Relationships in Mid-Twentieth Century America." In *Hidden from History: Reclaiming the Gay and Lesbian Past*, edited by Martin B. Duberman et al. New York: Penguin Books, 1989.

Ruse, Michael. *Homosexuality: A Philosophical Inquiry.* Cambridge, MA: Basil Blackwell, 1988.

Rush, Sharon Elizabeth. "Breaking with Tradition: Surrogacy and Gay Fathers." In *Kindred Matters: Rethinking the Philosophy of the Family*, edited by Diana T. Meyers et al. Ithaca, NY: Cornell University Press, 1993.

Russell, Ina, ed. *Jeb and Dash: A Diary of Gay Life, 1918–1945*. Boston: Faber & Faber, 1993.

Saks, Eva. "Representing Miscegenation Law." *Raritan*, vol. 8 (fall 1988).

"San Francisco Mayor Says No to Gay Marriage." *The Blade*, vol. 14 (January 26, 1983).

San Francisco Lesbian and Gay History Project. "'She Even Chewed Tobacco': A Pictorial Narrative of Passing Women in America." In *Hidden from History: Reclaiming the Gay and Lesbian Past*, edited by Martin B. Duberman et al. New York: Penguin Books, 1989.

Sankar, Andrea. "Sisters and Brothers, Lovers and Enemies: Marriage Resistance in Southern Kwangtung." In *The Many Faces of Homosexuality: Anthropological Approaches to Homosexual Behavior*, edited by Evelyn Blackwood. New York: Harrington Park Press, 1986.

Saunders, E. W. "Reformers' Choice: Marriage License or Just License?" *One, Inc.*, vol. 1 (August 1953).

Scalia, Antonin. "The Rule of Law as a Law of Rules." *University of Chicago Law Review*, vol. 56 (1989).

Schalow, Paul Gordon. "Introduction" to *The Great Mirror of Male Love*, by Ihara Saikaku. Stanford, CA: Stanford University Press, 1990.

Schiavi, Raul C., et al. "Sex Chromosome Anomalies, Hormones, and Sexuality." *Archives of General Psychiatry*, vol. 45 (1988).

Scott, Samuel P., ed. and trans. *The Visigothic Code*. Boston: Boston Book Co., 1910.

"Senate Approves Measure Banning Gay Marriages." *Los Angeles Times*, August 12, 1977, p. 33.

Sergent, Bernard. *Homosexuality in Greek Myth*. Translated by Arthur Goldhammer. Boston: Beacon Press, 1986.

Sexton, Joan. "Learning from Gays." *Commonweal*, June 17, 1994.

Shapiro, E. Donald, and Lisa Schultz. "Single-Sex Families: The Impact of Birth Innovations upon Traditional Family Notions." *Journal of Family Law*, vol. 24 (1985–1986).

Shaw, Brent D. Review of *Same-Sex Unions*, by John Boswell. *New Republic*, July 18, 1994.

———. Response to Ralph Hexter. *New Republic*, October 3, 1994, p. 39.

Sherman, Suzanne, ed. *Lesbian and Gay Marriage: Private Commitments, Public Ceremonies*. Philadelphia: Temple University Press, 1992.

Shilts, Randy. "Gay People Make Babies Too." *The Advocate*, October 22, 1975.

Sickels, Robert J. *Race, Marriage, and the Law*. Albuquerque, NM: University of New Mexico Press, 1972.

Sitton, Jaye. "Old Wine in New Bottles: The 'Marital' Rape Allowance." *North Carolina Law Review*, vol. 72 (1993).

Smith-Rosenberg, Carroll. *Disorderly Conduct: Visions of Gender in Victorian America*. New York: Oxford University Press, 1985.

Social Science Staff of the College of the University of Chicago, eds. *The People Shall Judge: Readings in the Formulation of American Policy*. Chicago: College of the University of Chicago, 1949.

Spedale, Darren. "The Domestic Partner Dilemma: Extending Benefits to Domestic Partners of Employees." Senior thesis, Duke University, 1993.

Spence, Jonathan D. *The Memory Palace of Matteo Ricci*. New York: Viking, 1984.

Stanford University Committee on Faculty and Staff Benefits. *Report of the Subcommittee on Domestic Partners' Benefits*. Palo Alto, CA: Stanford University, 1991.

St. Augustine, Bishop of Hippo. *De Bono Conjugali*. In *Treatises on Marriage and Other Subjects*. New York: Fathers of the Church, 1955.

Steckel, Alisa. "Psychosexual Development of Children of Lesbian Mothers." In *Gay and Lesbian Parents*, edited by Frederick W. Bozett. New York: Praeger, 1987.

Steinfels, Peter. "Methodists Again Say No to Homosexuality." *New York Times*, May 13, 1992, sec. A, p. 19.

————. "Lutherans Balk on a Sex Policy." *New York Times*, November 26, 1993, sec. A, p. 21.

Steinhauser, Jennifer. "Increasingly, Employers Offer Benefits to All Partners." *New York Times*, August 20, 1994, p. 25.

St. Lawrence, Janet S., et al. "Differences in Gay Men's AIDS Risk Knowledge and Behavior Patterns in High and Low AIDS Prevalence Cities." *Public Health Reports*, vol. 104 (1989).

Stoddard, Thomas B. "*Bowers v. Hardwick*: Precedent by Personal Predilection." *University of Chicago Law Review*, vol. 54 (1987).

————. "Why Gay People Should Seek the Right to Marry." *OUT/LOOK, National Lesbian and Gay Quarterly*, issue 6 (fall 1989).

Strabo. *The Geography*. Translated by H. L. Jones. London: W. Heinemann, 1917–1933.

Sullivan, Andrew. "Here Comes the Groom: A (Conservative) Case for Gay Marriage." *New Republic,* August 28, 1989.

————. *Virtually Normal: An Argument About Homosexuality*. New York: Knopf, 1995.

"Symposium: The Family in the 1990s: An Exploration of Lesbian and Gay Rights." *Law & Sexuality: A Review of Lesbian and Gay Legal Issues*, vol. 1 (1991).

Tacitus. *The Complete Works of Tacitus*. Translated by Alfred John Church and William Jackson Brodribb and edited by Moses Hadas. New York: Modern Library, 1942.

Teal, Donn. *Gay Radicals*. New York: Stein & Day, 1971.

Thayer, James S. "The Berdache of the Northern Plains." *Journal of Anthropological Research*, vol. 36 (1980).

Thomas, Kendall. "Beyond the Privacy Principle." *Columbia Law Review*, vol. 92 (1992).

Thompson, Karen, and Julie Andrzekewski. *Why Can't Sharon Kowalski Come Home?* San Francisco: Spinsters, 1988.

Tigay, Jeffrey H. *The Evolution of the Gilgamesh Epic.* Philadelphia: University of Pennsylvania Press, 1982.

Tobin, Kay, and Randy Wicker. *The Gay Crusaders.* 2d ed. New York: Arno Press, 1975.

Trevor-Roper, H. R. *The European Witch-Craze of the Sixteenth and Seventeenth Centuries and Other Essays.* New York: Harper & Row, 1969.

Tribe, Laurence H. *American Constitutional Law.* 2d ed. Mineola, NY: Foundation Press, 1988.

Trosino, James. "American Wedding: Same-Sex Marriage and the Miscegenation Analogy." *Boston University Law Review*, vol. 73 (1993).

Trumbach, Randolph. "The Birth of the Queen: Sodomy and the Emergence of Gender Equality in Modern Culture, 1660–1750." In *Hidden from History: Reclaiming the Gay and Lesbian Past*, edited by Martin B. Duberman et al. New York: Meridian, 1989.

"Two Churches Ousted by Baptists' Vote." *New York Times*, June 11, 1992, sec. A, p. 16.

"Two Girls Held After Marriage to Each Other." November 1947 (newspaper article in the file on "Marriage and Relationships" at the Lesbian Herstory Archives, Brooklyn, New York).

van de Velde, Theodore. *Ideal Marriage: Its Physiology and Technique.* New York: Covici Friede, 1930.

Verhovek, Sam Howe. "Texas Capital Ends Benefits for Partners." *New York Times*, May 9, 1994, p. 8.

Veyne, Paul. "Homosexuality in Ancient Rome." In *Western Sexuality*, edited by Phillipe Ariès and André Bejin and translated by Anthony Foster. Oxford: B. Blackwell, 1985.

Vidal, Gore. *The City and the Pillar.* New York: Dutton, 1948.

Vining, Donald. *A Gay Diary: 1933–1946.* New York: Pepys Press, 1979.

———. *A Gay Diary, 1946–1954.* New York: Pepys Press, 1980.

———. *A Gay Diary: 1954–1967.* New York: Pepys Press, 1981.

———. *A Gay Diary: 1967–1975.* New York: Pepys Press, 1983.

Vlastos, Gregory. *Platonic Studies.* Princeton, NJ: Princeton University Press, 1981.

Wadlington, Walter J. "The *Loving* Case: Virginia's Anti-Miscegenation Statute." *Virginia Law Review*, vol. 52 (1966).

Walker, J. L., and N. F. White. "The Varieties of Therapeutic Experience: Conjoint Therapy in a Homosexual Marriage." *Canada's Mental Health*, vol. 23 (1975).

Warner, Marina. "More Than Friendship." *New York Times*, August 28, 1994, Book Review Supplement, p. 7.

Weintraub, Daniel, and Bettina Boxall. "Ballot Fallout Expected from Wilson's Veto." *Los Angeles Times*, September 13, 1994, p. 3.

Wellington, Harry H. "Common Law Rules and Constitutional Double Standards: Some Notes on Adjudication." *Yale Law Journal*, vol. 83 (1973).

West, Robin. "Equality Theory, Marital Rape, and the Promise of the Fourteenth Amendment." *Florida Law Review*, vol. 42 (1990).

Weston, Kath. *Families We Choose: Lesbians, Gays, Kinship*. New York: Columbia University Press, 1991.

White, Edmund. *States of Desire: Travels in Gay America*. New York: Plume, 1991.

Whitehead, Harriet. "The Bow and the Burden Strap: A New Look at Institutionalized Homosexuality in Native North America." In *Sexual Meanings: The Cultural Construction of Gender and Sexuality*, edited by Sherry B. Ortner and Harriet Whitehead. New York: Cambridge University Press, 1981.

Williams, Bruce. "Homosexuality and Christianity: A Review Discussion." *The Thomist*, vol. 46 (1982).

Williams, Walter L. *The Spirit and the Flesh: Sexual Diversity in American Indian Culture*. Boston: Beacon Press, 1986.

Wilson, James D. "Gays Under Fire." *Newsweek*, September 14, 1992.

Wolfson, Evan. "Crossing the Threshold: Equal Marriage Rights for Lesbians and Gay Men and the Intra-Community Critique." *New York University Review of Law and Social Change*, vol. 21 (1994–1995).

Yourcenar, Marguerite. *Memoirs of Hadrian*. New York: Farrar, Straus, 1954.

ACKNOWLEDGMENTS

The Honorable Shellie Bowers of the District of Columbia Superior Court got me started on this book. Representing two gay men seeking District of Columbia recognition of same-sex marriages, I argued before Judge Bowers in opposition to the District's motion to dismiss our complaint. The judge was open about his reservations, and we engaged in a thoughtful two-hour conversation about gay marriage. In the course of this conversation Judge Bowers wondered, "What about the history of marriage? Where does all this fit in?" I did not have a satisfactory answer, and the judge asked the parties to submit separate memoranda on the history of marriage or same-sex marriage.

I spent the month of August 1991 holed up at the Library of Congress doing research for the memorandum requested by Judge Bowers. Critically useful primary source leads were provided by Professors William Leap and Geoffrey Burkhart, both anthropologists at American University, and by Father Alexei Michalenko, the chaplain at the Georgetown University Law Center, where I teach. What I found was amazing to me: source after source detailing same-sex unions and marriages in other cultures and other times, virtually none of them widely known today. I wrote the plaintiffs' "Memorandum on the History of Same-Sex Marriage" from these primary and secondary sources. My clients, Craig Dean and Patrick Gill, assembled letters from dozens of religious leaders who had given thought to the issue from various religious perspectives, and we filed those letters as an appendix to our memorandum.

289

Although Judge Bowers ruled against us as a matter of law, the historical and intellectual background of same-sex marriage had me hooked. Judge Richard Posner urged me to publish my research, and Donna Wilson gave me a forum for my historical essay when she and her colleagues on the *Virginia Law Review* organized a symposium on sexual orientation and the law. On the basis of my *Virginia Law Review* article, "A History of Same-Sex Marriage," Bruce Nichols suggested that I publish a book on this topic. Taken completely by surprise, I agreed. Dean Judith Areen of the Georgetown University Law Center provided me with a partial leave of absence, which made it possible for me to write the book expeditiously. Research leads from a semester sponsored by the Guggenheim Foundation were very useful as I wrote this book.

I have presented portions of this book to workshops or conferences at the Georgetown University Law Center (on two separate occasions), the Yale Law School, the New York University School of Law (on two separate occasions), the George Washington University National Law Center, the University of Pennsylvania Law School, Duke University School of Law, Quinnipiac College School of Law, the Fordham University School of Law, the University of Virginia School of Law, the Reading Group of the Gay and Lesbian Attorneys of Washington, D.C. (GAYLAW), and the District of Columbia Bar (on two separate occasions). I received helpful comments at each of these presentations and unusually helpful particularized comments at some point or another from Mark Agrast, Akhil Amar, Ian Ayres, Marc Arkin, Katharine Bartlett, Jennifer Brown, Naomi Cahn, Chandler Burr, Yair Chamudat, Paula Ettelbrick, Daniel Ernst, Owen Fiss, Paul Gewirtz, Jeanne Goldberg, Steven Goldberg, Andrea Grill, Rebecca Isaacs, Marcia Kuntz, Sylvia Law, Ira Lupu, William Nelson, Nancy Polikoff, Eric Posner, Richard Posner, Robert Raben, Milton Regan, David Richards, Mandy Rosenblum, Carol Rose, Paula Rubin, Joan Schaffner, Michael Seidman, Jonathan Siegel, Susan Silber, Gigi Sohn, Edward Stein, Thomas Stoddard, Mark Tushnet, Carlos Vazquez, Evan Wolfson, and Paul Wolfson. Glenn Edwards (Yale Law, Class of 1997) and Keith Franken (Georgetown Law, Class of 1997) provided timely and helpful research assistance.

I dedicate this book, in love, to Pedie.

INDEX